HANDBOOK OF

BASIC

TRIAL

EVIDENCE

A College Introduction

JOSEPH M. PELLICCIOTTI

 Wyndham Hall Press

HANDBOOK OF BASIC TRIAL EVIDENCE
A College Introduction

by

Joseph M. Pelicciotti

Library of Congress Catalog Card Number
91-050745

ISBN 1-55605-191-3

Printed in the United States of America

Wyndham Hall Press, Inc.
Bristol, IN 46507 USA

TO MY TWO CHILDREN,

Michael and
Anne Giulia

About the Author:

Joseph Pellicciotti is an Associate Professor, Assistant Dean of the School of Public & Environmental Affairs, and Director of the Division of Public & Environmental Affairs and Political Science, Indiana University Northwest, Gary, Indiana. He received his B.A. in Political Science from Alfred University (1972), Master of Public Administration degree from Syracuse University (1973), and Doctor of Jurisprudence degree, Cum Laude, from the Gonzaga University School of Law (1976). He has practiced law in both federal and state courts, and he is the author of numerous books and articles in professional journals.

TABLE OF CONTENTS

ii Table of Contents

PREFACE

This book is designed to meet the needs of those students in criminal justice, paralegal, legal studies, business law, and legal environment of business courses, who need a basic understanding of the courts and evidence processing. This work is not intended as a law school text.

This book focuses on the Federal Rules of Evidence. The federal rules regulate evidence processing in the federal courts, and they also serve as the model for the development of state evidence law. Of course, not all states follow the federal rules. Even those states that do rely heavily on federal rules precedent will vary their rules from the federal to some extent. Students should remember this as they study the rules described herein. This work also offers law generally applicable in both the civil and criminal courts. It is assumed that a general and balanced approach to the subject of Evidence is the best approach for teaching non-law students.

The book begins with an introductory discussion of the rationale for the existence of the courts and the trial process. There is also discussion in the Introduction of the historical development of the modern trial. Chapter One focuses on the pre-trial and jury trial process. Chapter Two considers the basic terms and concepts of evidence. The subsequent chapters consider the key subtopics in evidence law, including such matters as evidence relevancy (Chapter Three), witness competency (Chapter Four), witness examination (Chapter Five), opinion testimony (Chapter Six), the hearsay rule (Chapter Seven), exceptions to the hearsay rule (Chapter Eight), non-testimonial writings (Chapter Nine), exhibits and objections (Chapter Ten), the United States Constitution and evidence processing (Chapter Ten), evidence privileges (Chapter Eleven), and judicial notice of facts (Chapter Eleven). Additionally, five special focus segments are included at relevant points in the text. These focus segments go beyond the general discussion of the law of evidence. They raise in detail important legal issues and are useful in enhancing legal analysis and classroom discussion. The segments include:

Focus I: Peremtory Challenges and Racial Discrimination

> Chapter One, in considering the trial process, discusses the fact that peremptory challenges have been used freely to exclude prospective jurors from a case, even though no

good cause exists to do so. However, can such challenges be used to exclude an individual because of his or her race? The Supreme Court has most recently considered this issue in *Powers v. Ohio* (1991). Focus I presents that case.

Focus II: Children as Witnesses-the Confrontation Clause and Children Testifying Outside the Physical Presence of the Defendant

Chapter Four considers the issue of witness competency. In the chapter, there is a discussion of the special issue of children and their competency to testify. Another important issue involving children as witnesses is the constitutionality of statutes allowing children in child abuse cases to testify against a defendant outside of the defendant's physical presence. Do such laws violate the Confrontation Clause of the Sixth Amendment? The Supreme Court decided this issue in *Maryland v. Craig* (1990). Focus II presents that case.

Focus III: The Challenge in Applying Hearsay Exceptions-Focusing on the Rule 803(8) Public Records and Reports Exception

Chapters Seven and Eight wrestle with perhaps the most difficult subject in Evidence, the hearsay rule (which prohibits the use of hearsay at trial) and the rule's exceptions. One exception noted in Chapter Eight is the exception for public records and reports. What is the scope of that exception? Specifically, are the conclusions and opinions of public officials contained in official reports admissible? Focus III presents a case that provides the student with a view as to one court's interpretation in regard to this matter. Also, the case presented emphasizes the fact that escaping the prohibition in the hearsay rule (by finding an exception) does not, in itself, guarantee admissibility. Hearsay is but one basis for exclusion of evidence. Other bases can be used to exclude evidence even when the hearsay rule prohibition is successfully navigated by the proponent of the evidence.

Focus IV: Laying the Foundation for the Admission of Scientific Evidence-the Issue of DNA Evidence

What is the proper foundation for the admissibility of scientific evidence? New types of scientific evidence pose particular problems for the courts. One important new form of evidence is the results of DNA testing. Focus IV presents a case that deals directly with the issue of the foundation required for the admissibility of the results of DNA testing. Also, the same case, in discussing the DNA matter, reviews the admissibility of other forms of scientific evidence.

Focus V: The Attorney-Client Privilege and the Client's Desire to Testify Untruthfully

One of the great ethical dilemmas a defense attorney can face is the dilemma of knowing a client will testify untruthfully. Focus V reprints a journal article that discusses this dilemma and also offers a prescription for dealing with the difficult matter.

There are also appendices included in the book. They provide the student with the provisions of the Federal Rules of Evidence, key provisions of the United States Constitution, and a sample final examination.

I have taught Evidence to non-law students for many years. The material herein has been tested successfully in the classroom. I hope that this book will assist in de-mystifying court process. My goal in the classroom has always been to make the law clear. This has been my goal throughout the development of this book, as well.

Joseph M. Pellicciotti, J.D.
Assistant Dean, School of
Public & Environmental Affairs
and Division Director,
Division of Public &
Environmental Affairs
Indiana University Northwest

INTRODUCTION

The rules of evidence regulate the submission of evidence at trial. The modern trial process is reviewed in Chapter One. In Chapter Two, the definition of evidence, the development of the rules of evidence, and basic concepts of evidence are discussed. In Chapter Three and subsequent chapters, the particular rules of evidence, primarily in the form of the Federal Rules of Evidence, are presented. However, before this basic study begins, it is useful (1) to consider the purpose and rationale for courts and the modern trial in our society and (2) to place the modern jury trial in historical perspective.

The Purpose and Rationale for Courts and the Modern Trial

There are many ways by which disputes between individuals may be resolved. However, some ways are simply unacceptable in a civilized society. For example, the use of force by a disputant will likely not be tolerated. Acceptable methods for resolving disputes include an unsupervised agreement or settlement between the parties, mediation, and arbitration.

2 Introduction

Additionally, individuals may turn to society's formal institution for resolving disputes. That institution, of course, is the American court. The mechanism used in court for resolving disputes is the trial process.

To be an acceptable court mechanism for resolving disputes, the trial must attempt to do justice. A civilized society will tolerate no less. Therefore, the trial process must be so structured as to attempt to do justice. Such a structure is achieved by establishing trial procedures which are designed to provide fundamental fairness. The premise is that a fair trial process will more likely achieve a just result.

This is not to say that the modern trial always does justice. It does not. An innocent person may be convicted.[1] A guilty person may be found innocent and go free. In civil cases, where "justice" depends so much on individual perception, the plaintiff may win at trial and consider the judgment amount too small. The defendant may consider plaintiff's award too large or the judgment for the plaintiff an injustice in itself. Still, the trial is designed to provide fundamental fairness, and it thereby attempts to do justice. Its results can be supported by society.

In looking to the specific modern trial process outlined in Chapter One, the student should consider the steps shown in the light of the required attempt to do justice. Equal opportunities exist to argue and present evidence. Also, the student should consider the opportunities to rebut and cross-examine in the light of fundamental fairness. The process must occur before an unbiased and impartial judge and jury, and the trier of fact's decision must be based on the evidence presented at trial. Here, the rules of evidence exist to assist in bringing fairness to the trial.

The Modern Jury Trial in Historical Perspective

Sir William Blackstone was an extremely important eighteenth century legal writer. He served as the first Oxford University English law professor, and he is famous for his *Commentaries on the Law of England*, four books (volumes) of his lectures on the English law.[2] While the substance of the *Commentaries* may have been imperfect, the books were widely read and influenced legal development, particularly in the United States.[3]

In his fourth volume, *Of Public Wrongs*, Blackstone discussed the English criminal law. In doing so, he reviewed the basic trial methods in English history. A review of Blackstone's analysis of the early trial methods is useful to put our current jury trial system in historical perspective.

According to Blackstone, the oldest English trial method was the trial by ordeal.[4] There were two types: the fire-ordeal and the water-ordeal.

The fire-ordeal was available only to those of "higher rank." It consisted of either holding a red-hot iron in the hand or walking barefoot over red-hot ploughshares.[5] If the accused performed the ordeal without injury, he was innocent. However, guilt and punishment followed when injury happened.

The water-ordeal consisted of the accused either plunging his arm into boiling water or being thrown into a river or pond.[6] In the first situation, if the accused was not hurt by the boiling water, then he was innocent. In the second instance, if the individual floated, then he was guilty. He needed to sink to be acquitted.

In the trial by ordeal, God was the trier of fact intervening to do "justice." For the early English, there was no need for a judge or jury to determine the verdict. However, the Catholic Church frowned upon the practice and forbade priests to participate in such trials. In 1216, the Lateran Council in Rome formally prohibited such participation.[7] Also, according to Blackstone, the trial by ordeal was formally abolished by an Act of Parliament or order of the king in council.[8]

Another type of trial by ordeal, but noted separately by Blackstone in his *Commentaries*, was the trial by the "corsned, or morsel of execration."[9] This trial method involved the use of approximately an ounce of bread or cheese. The morsel was consecrated by clergy. God was asked to prevent the food from being swallowed by the accused, if he was guilty. As noted by Max Radin in his *Handbook of Anglo-American Legal History*, the guilty and God-fearing Englishman, believing in the affect of the consecration, might well choke.[10] To Blackstone in the eighteenth century, this method of trial and the other ordeal methods, were antiquated, having been principally used by the early, English Saxon ancestors.[11]

Blackstone discussed the "trial by battel" (sic), which involved individual combat and a similar appeal to God to intervene on the side of the innocent person.[12] This trial method was introduced into England by the Normans after their conquest of England in the eleventh century, and it was generally available only to Normans of high rank.[13]

Under this trial method, the accused would do battle with the victim (or in some cases champions would fight for the antagonists). The combat was entered into only after appropriate oaths and other religious invocations. If the accused was killed, then he was proven guilty. If he was so injured that he could no longer fight, then he was likewise proven guilty and hanged immediately. The trial by battle was used only rarely after 1500. It was finally abolished in England in 1819.[14]

In his *Commentaries*, Blackstone described trial by jury as "the grand bulwark" of every Englishman's liberties.[15] He went on to discuss its eighteenth century application. Still, how did the jury trial come to supersede the Heavenly adjudged trials previously noted?

The jury process in criminal matters involves the possible use of both the grand jury and the trial jury (i.e., the petit jury). The grand jury is a presenting jury; that is, it is used in the formal charging process. The prosecutor brings before it evidence of the criminal activity of an individual. If the grand jurors find sufficient evidence of liability, they return an indictment (a "True Bill"), the accusation. Thereupon, the defendant proceeds through the various court function steps, which may ultimately result in the actual trial of the matter before the trial (petit) jury.

The grand jury traces its origin to King Henry II's Assize of Clarendon in 1166.[16] It was already established then that no one could be tried, unless first accused by the voluntary presentment by individuals of specific charges.[17] The voluntary presentment was made compulsory by the Assize of Clarendon.[18] The modern grand jury's predecessor was in place.[19]

The ascendancy of the trial jury began as the ordeals fell into disfavor with the Church.[20] The presenting jury was looked to as the natural alternative to determine guilt or innocence.[21]

These early jurors did not render decisions by hearing evidence presented to them. Instead, these jurors would go forth to inquire of the facts or base their decision on their own knowledge.[22] This process continued until around 1450.[23] Also, the early jurors, as presenting jurors, could include those individuals who had initially accused the defendant of criminal conduct.[24] This fact made acquittal rather unlikely.[25] This problem, however, was dealt with in the middle of the fourteenth century, when it was decided that upon demand by the defendant the trial jury could not include any of the presenting jurors who had initially brought charges against the defendant.[26] Out of these beginnings the modern criminal jury trial developed, and out of the criminal jury trial developed the civil jury trial, as well.[27]

By 1700 it was firmly established that only sworn to, in court evidence could serve as evidence upon which to determine a verdict.[28]

As time went on, the law of evidence developed to protect the jury from being misled.[29]

The basic English trial practice was brought to America with colonization.[30] However, to the Americans of the eighteenth century, the jury trial represented an even more important institution. Colonial jurors often "stood up" to the British controlled judges in the pre-Revolutionary War period.[31] Therefore, the jury trial was seen as an instrument for liberty, and, after the Revolutionary War, was guaranteed with other essential liberties in the federal and state constitutions.[32]

NOTES

1. This is rare. However, consider the well-publicized Illinois case of Gary Dotson, who was convicted of rape in 1979. The woman who charged him with rape later recanted after Dotson served six years in prison. Even so, the trial judge did not accept the recantation. See A. M. Lipinski and J. Kass, "Rape Conviction Stands," CHICAGO TRIBUNE, April 12, 1985, at 1. Dotson was later released from prison on the order of the Governor of Illinois. He received a commutation to the time actually served.

2. See M. RABIN, HANDBOOK ON ANGLO-AMERICAN LEGAL HISTORY at 286 (1936).

3. Id. at 287.

4. 4 W. BLACKSTONE, COMMENTARIES *342.

5. Id.

6. Id. at 343.

7. M. RABIN, supra at 36.

8. 4 W. BLACKSTONE, supra at 345 (Henry III's reign).

9. Id.

10. M. RABIN, supra at 37.

11. 4 W. BLACKSTONE, supra at 346.

12. Id.

13. M. RABIN, supra at 193.

14. M. RABIN, supra at 226-227. This formal abolition by Act of Parliament came after a celebrated case in which a defendant escaped punishment for a capital crime by demanding trial by battle. His antagonist, however, refused to fight and the charges were dismissed. *Ashford v. Thornton*, 1 B. & Ald. 405.

15. 4 W. BLACKSTONE, supra at 349.

16. F. KEMPIN, HISTORICAL INTRODUCTION TO ANGLO-AMERICAN LAW IN A NUTSHELL 51 (1973).

17. Id.

18. Id.

19. Id.

20. Id. at 55.

21. Id.

22. Id. at 56.

23. Id. at 57.

24. Id.

25. Id.

26. Id.

27. Id. at 59. The use of the jury in civil cases developed during the fourteenth and fifteenth centuries.

28. M. RABIN, supra at 215.

29. Id. at 216.

30. That is not to say that all of English law became colonial law, or that all colonial law was the same. See the excellent, one volume work L.M. FRIEDMAN, A HISTORY OF AMERICAN LAW (1973).

31. J. FRANK, COURTS ON TRIAL 109 (1950).

32. Id.

BIBLIOGRAPHICAL NOTE
ON ANGLO-AMERICAN LAW

Those students interested in reading further as to the history of Anglo-American law will find the sources cited in this bibliographical note useful. These materials should be considered along with those cited in the footnotes to this handbook.

Perhaps the most famous work on early English law is the two-volume F. POLLACK & F. MAITLAND, THE HISTORY OF ENGLISH LAW (2d ed. 1898). Another view of early English law (in this case from the Norman invasion in 1066 to the thirteenth century) is found in G.B. ADAMS, COUNCIL AND COURTS IN ANGLO-NORMAN ENGLAND (1965). Also, the student should see G.W. KEETON, THE NORMAN CONQUEST AND THE COMMON LAW (1966). Essays on sixteenth century English law will be found in TUDOR MEN AND INSTITUTIONS (A.J. Slavin, ed. 1972). Additionally, the student may wish to consider A.R. HOGUE, ORIGINS OF THE COMMON LAW (1974) and O.W. HOLMES' classic work THE COMMON LAW (1881).

Those students interested in travelling intellectually beyond the Anglo-American sphere and further back in time should consider reading R.A. WORMSER, THE STORY OF THE LAW (1962).

As to American colonial law, the student should consider G.L. HASKIN, LAW AND AUTHORITY IN EARLY MASSACHUSETTS (1960) and ESSAYS IN HISTORY OF EARLY AMERICAN LAW (D.H. FLAHERTY, ed. 1969). This latter work contains a particularly interesting essay by Julius S. Waterman titled "Thomas Jefferson and Blackstone's Commentaries" (a reprint of a 1933 ILLINOIS LAW REVIEW article). For a personal look at colonial law, the student should consider the three-volume LEGAL PAPERS OF JOHN ADAMS (L.K. Wroth & H.B. Zobel, eds. 1965).

As to post-colonial American law, in general, the student will profit from M.J. HORWITZ, THE TRANSFORMATION OF AMERICAN LAW, 1780-1860 (1977) and J.W. HURST, THE GROWTH OF AMERICAN LAW: THE LAW MAKERS (1950).

A very useful process for the student to use in learning more of the history of law and about trial practice and evidence law and procedure, as well, is to read one or more of the many books that exist on particular trials. The following represents but a brief sample: IN RE ALGER HISS (Edith Tiger, ed. 1979) (a detailed record of pleadings and exhibits filed in Hiss' writ of coram nobis); R.H. FROST, THE MOONEY CASE (1968) (a look at the trial of radicals arising out of a 1916 bombing

incident); R. RADOSH & J. MILTON, THE ROSENBERG
FILE (1983) (a new look at the famous treason
trial of Ethel and Julius Rosenberg); R.S.
FEURLICHT, JUSTICE CRUCIFIED (1977) (a look at
the 1920s story of the Sacco and Vanzetti
trial); J. DREYFUSS & C. LAURENCE III, THE BAKKE
CASE (1979) (a detailed look at the famous
"reverse discrimination" case); L. JAWORSKI, THE
RIGHT AND THE POWER (1976) (an extremely good
book on the Watergate prosecutions); A. LEWIS,
GIDEON'S TRUMPET (1964) (the famous work
concerning criminal procedure and the right to
an attorney); R.A. SMOLLA, JERRY FALWELL V.
LARRY FLYNT (1990) (a consideration of this
important First Amendment case); B.H. CRAIG,
CHADA (1988) (a detailed examination of an
immigration case that led to a further
delineation of the concept of separation of
powers); and SIX TRIALS (R.S. Brumbaugh, ed.
1969) (one of the trials reviewed is the famous
"monkey trial" of John T. Scopes).

Some complete trial records have been
published. The student interested in such
publications may wish to review NEGRO
UNIVERSITIES PRESS' reprint of the 1852 REPORT
OF THE TRIAL OF CASTNER HANWAY (a treason trial
for refusing to follow the 1850 Fugitive Slave
Law) and ARNCO PRESS' reprint of AN ACCOUNT OF
THE PROCEEDINGS IN THE TRIAL OF SUSAN B. ANTHONY
(a trial for illegally voting in the 1872
Presidential election).

14 Bibliographical Note

For a general introduction to American law, the student should read L.M. Friedman, AMERICAN LAW (1984). An excellent introduction to the American legal system from the political perspective is found in H. JACOB, LAW AND POLITICS IN THE UNITED STATES (1986). For an introduction to criminal law from the sociological perspective, the student should review J. INVERARITY, P. LAUDERDALE & B.C. FELD, LAW AND SOCIETY (1983).

Chapter One

THE TRIAL PROCESS

An Overview of the Trial Process

To understand basic trial evidence, the student must first understand the trial process within which the rules of trial evidence are applied. The trial process refers to the sequence of activities which make up the trial of a case. The sequence of activities is much the same in the criminal trial and the civil trial.[1] The typical chronology of trial activities is as follows:

(1) JURY SELECTION;

(2) PRELIMINARY JURY INSTRUCTIONS;

(3) OPENING STATEMENTS;

(4) PRESENTATION OF PLAINTIFF'S (CIVIL) OR STATE'S (CRIMINAL) CASE;

(5) MOTION FOR NON-SUIT/DIRECTED VERDICT;

(7) PRESENTATION OF DEFENDANT'S CASE;

(8)   PLAINTIFF'S (CIVIL) OR STATE'S (CRIMINAL) REBUTTAL (AND POSSIBLE REJOINDER BY THE DEFENDANT);

(9)   MOTION FOR DIRECTED VERDICT;

(10) CLOSING STATEMENTS;

(11) FINAL JURY INSTRUCTIONS;

(12) DELIBERATION;

(13) RETURN OF VERDICT;

(14) JUDGMENT (CIVIL).

Each of these activities will be discussed later in this chapter. However, as background to this discussion, it is important to first consider the concepts of parties to the trial and the trier of fact and to look to both criminal and civil pretrial procedure.

Parties to the Trial

In the typical civil case, the plaintiff is the individual who is suing the defendant, seeking a judgment from the court against the defendant upon any number of claims for relief. Upon being sued, the defendant has the opportunity to assert claims that he or she may have against the plaintiff. The filing of such a claim is called a counterclaim.

Example.

> Plaintiff A brings suit against defendant B for faulty workmanship on A's truck. A has not paid B for B's work on the truck. B will likely file a counterclaim against A, claiming non-payment and seeking a judgment for the amount owed to B. In such a case, B is commonly referred to as the defendant-counterplaintiff, and A is commonly referred to as the plaintiff-counterdefendant.

While the application of the plaintiff and defendant terminology holds true for most civil cases, there are some cases which apply different terminology. For example, in the dissolution (divorce) cases in many states the terms petitioner (rather than plaintiff) and respondent (rather than defendant) are used.

In the criminal case, prosecution is maintained by the state against the accused, the defendant. The defendant's trial process activities remain basically the same as in the civil case, and the state's role in the criminal case is much the same as the plaintiff's in the civil matter.

The Trier of Fact

The factual matters at a trial may be determined by either a jury or a judge. If a jury trial is held, then the jury is the "trier of fact." If a jury trial is not held, then the judge (in the "bench trial") is the "trier of fact."

Regardless of whether a jury or the judge is the trier of fact, much of the sequence of activities in the trial is the same. However, in a bench trial, there is, of course, no need for a selection of jury, jury instructions, and the jury's return of the verdict.

The Pretrial Process

Before considering jury selection procedure and the other trial process activities, the student should remember that a number of important court activities take place prior to trial. These pretrial activities may involve evidence submission. Therefore, the student should have a basic understanding of the pretrial process.

Basic Criminal Court Pretrial Activities

There are seven major criminal court pretrial activities:

(1) The initial appearance of the defendant;

(2) The defendant's preliminary hearing;

(3) The state's formal charging process;

(4) The arraignment of the defendant;

(5) The parties' discovery;

(6) Motion hearings; and

(7) The pretrial conference.

Defendant's Initial
Appearance and Preliminary Hearing

Common practice requires that the defendant be brought before the court for his or her initial appearance without unnecessary delay. At the initial appearance, the defendant is notified formally of the complaint against him or her, bail may be set, and the defendant is informed of his or her rights (e.g., the right to counsel). The defendant is also usually informed of the right to preliminary hearing.[2]

The preliminary hearing is an initial examination of evidence to determine if probable cause exists to hold the defendant over to answer to the allegations. The government bears the burden of establishing the existence of probable cause. The defendant may offer evidence and cross-examine the prosecutor's witnesses. While the preliminary hearing may be waived by the defendant, defense attorneys often advise their clients not to do so, as the hearing offers easy, initial discovery by the defendant of at least a part of the evidence in the hands of the prosecutor against the defendant. If cause is not shown "to believe that an offense has been committed or that the defendant committed it," the judge will dismiss the complaint against the defendant.[3]

The State's Formal Charging
Process and the Resulting Arraignment

The state's formal charging process involves the use of either the grand jury indictment procedure or the information.

The grand jury tradition has been noted in the Introduction. The procedure is a closed one, where the prosecutor presents evidence of probable cause to the grand jurors. The frequency of use of the grand jury to charge an individual varies from state to state, prosecutor to prosecutor, and with the crime involved. On the federal level, the grand jury indictment procedure must be used where the crime involved may be punished by death or involves an offense punishable by imprisonment for a term exceeding one year or at hard labor.[4]

The information is a formal charge filed directly by the prosecutor under oath and showing probable cause. It is based upon information submitted to the prosecutor by citizens and/or law enforcement personnel. This "by-passing" of the grand jury indictment process, where allowed by law, provides for a faster, less-costly charging process.

The arraignment follows the formal charge. The defendant is required to appear in open court. The indictment or information is usually read to the defendant (unless reading is waived). The defendant will then be called upon to enter a plea of guilty, not guilty, or, in some jurisdictions, nolo contendere. Nolo contendere is a "no contest" plea which is the practical equivalent of a guilty plea.[5] A plea of guilty or nolo contendere will be accepted by the court only upon the judge's determination of defendant's voluntary presentation of same.[6] Other commonly found arraignment activities include the appointment of counsel for indigent persons and the presentation of plea agreements.

Criminal Court Discovery

Discovery is the process by which one party learns of the other party's evidence before it is introduced at trial. Discovery may be either informal or formal. Informal discovery is non-court sanctioned discovery; that is, it is not formally required by law.

Example.

Defense attorney meets prosecutor in the courthouse, and she is told by the prosecutor of a particular testimony or other evidence unknown to the defense. Also, the same defense attorney takes part in the preliminary hearing and is informed through the prosecutor's evidence presented of key aspects of the state's case.

Formal or court sanctioned discovery is generally more developed in civil court (see below). However, its availability in criminal court, particularly to the defendant, has increased in recent years. Availability varies from state to state. On the federal level, formal discovery, from a relative point of view, is liberally available. Rule 16 of the Federal Rules of Criminal Procedure grants the defendant a general right to discover statements of the defendant in the government's possession, a copy of the defendant's prior criminal record, documents and tangible objects in the government's possession and material to defendant's case, and tests and reports concerning physical and mental examinations and scientific tests or experiments in the government's possession and material to defendant's case.[7] The rule also provides to the government some corresponding discovery. If the defendant has requested the discovery of documents, tangible objects and/or reports of examinations and tests, then the government may discover similar material from the defendant, to the extent that the material sought is material which the defendant intends to introduce as evidence at trial.[8]

Formal discovery is regulated by the court, and the judge may order a party to allow discovery where it is required, and the party has failed to make the discoverable material available.[9]

Motion Hearings and the Pretrial Conference

Numerous pretrial motions may be filed and heard by the judge as the parties proceed toward trial. Hearings may be held on claimed defects in the institution of prosecution, defects in the indictment or information, requests for severance of charges or defendants, requests for discovery, requests for reduction of bail, requests for change of judge, requests for change of venue from the county, among other matters.

One common motion is the motion to suppress evidence. In the Motion to Suppress, the defendant attacks the admissibility at trial of certain evidence in the state's possession. The motion is based on the exclusionary rule (discussed in Chapter 10). The exclusionary rule may exclude at trial evidence obtained by the government in violation of the defendant's constitutional rights. At the motion hearing, the prosecutor presents evidence of the validity of the government's actions. The defendant attacks the validity; the judge then decides admissibility.

The pretrial conference is a conference among the judge and the parties' attorneys. The general purpose of the conference is "to consider such matters as will promote a fair and expeditious trial."[10] The use of the conference is becoming more common in criminal cases. The pretrial conference is well established in civil litigation (discussed below).

A variety of matters may be considered at the conference. Common issues include trial date, probable length of trial, marking of documents and other exhibits, exploration of the particular judge's trial procedures, and entering of stipulations. Stipulations are agreements between the parties as to certain facts. The facts are then admitted as being true for purposes of the trial. The primary advantage of the stipulation is that it saves trial time in establishing facts as true without the necessity of formal proof. At the close of the conference, the court prepares and files a memorandum concerning the matters discovered and agreed upon in conference.

Basic Civil Court Pretrial Activities

There are six major civil court pretrial activities:

(1) The commencement of the action;

(2) Service of process;

(3) The responsive pleading;

(4) The parties' discovery;

(5) Motion hearings; and

(6) The pretrial conference.

Plaintiff's Commencement of the Action and Service of Process

The suit against the defendant begins when the plaintiff files a complaint with the court. The complaint is a writing which presents plaintiff's allegations against the defendant and asserts the plaintiff's right to recovery. In most jurisdictions, the complaint may be drawn in a simple manner. It must reasonably inform the defendant of the plaintiff's claim, so that the defendant has notice and can frame a responsive pleading.

Example.

```
ST. OF IND.)       LAKE SUP. COURT
           ) SS:  ROOM TWO
CO. OF LAKE)       GARY, IND.


Ann Smith,      )
  Plaintiff     )
       v.       )   Cause No._____
John Doe,       )
  Defendant     )
```

Complaint

Comes now the plaintiff, by her attorney, and for cause of action against the defendant states:

(1) On or about October 1, 1989, the defendant was driving his automobile in a public street called Elmwood Drive, Munster, Lake County, Indiana.

(2) On said date and at said place, the defendant negligently drove his automobile against plaintiff who was then crossing said street.

(3) As a result, plaintiff was injured, suffered a loss of wages, suffered great pain and mental anguish, and incurred medical and hospital costs in the sum of two thousand dollars.

WHEREFORE, plaintiff demands judgment against defendant in the sum of ten thousand dollars, for costs and all other proper relief.

Signed:_____

Attorney for Plaintiff

After the complaint is filed with the court, a copy (along with a summons) is served on the defendant. Service of process, once effected, provides the court with jurisdiction over the defendant. Service of process is effected in a variety of ways.[11] A traditional way of service is by the sheriff delivering a copy of the summons and complaint to the defendant personally at his home. A common, modern form of service is by certified mail, return receipt requested.

The Responsive Pleading

In most civil actions, the defendant is required to file with the court a pleading in response to the plaintiff's complaint. This pleading is called an answer. The failure to file an answer within the time permitted by a jurisdiction may result in a judgment being entered against the defendant by default.

The answer provides the defendant's good faith response to the plaintiff's allegations.

Example.

The defendant's response to the plaintiff's complaint set out in the preceding example may take the following form:

```
ST. OF IND.)        LAKE SUP. COURT
           ) SS: ROOM TWO
CO. OF LAKE)        GARY, IND.

Ann Smith,     )
   Plaintiff  )
        v.    )   Cause No._____
John Doe,      )
   Defendant  )
```

Answer

Comes now the defendant, by his attorney, and in answer to the plaintiff's complaint states:

(1) Defendant admits the allegations contained in paragraph 1 of the complaint.

(2) Defendant denies the allegations contained in paragraph 2 of the complaint.

(3) Defendant denies the allegations contained in paragraph 3 of the complaint.

WHEREFORE, defendant prays that the plaintiff take nothing by way of her

complaint, for costs and all other proper
relief.

Signed:_____

Attorney for Defendant

The answer may also include a
counterclaim, a cross-claim against a co-
defendant, and a third-party claim against a
non-party who may be liable to the defendant for
all or a portion of the plaintiff's claim
against the defendant. Upon the filing of the
third-party complaint and service of process,
the third party becomes a third-party
defendant.[12] The complaint will also include
the defendant's "affirmative defenses."
Examples of such defenses are included in the
Federal Rules of Civil Procedure: "accord and
satisfaction, arbitration and award, assumption
of risk, contributory negligence, discharge in
bankruptcy, duress, estoppel, failure of
consideration, fraud, illegality, injury by
fellow servant, laches, license, payment,
release, res judicata, statute of frauds,
statute of limitations, waiver, and any other
matter constituting an avoidance or affirmative
defense."[13]

Example.

The statute of limitations in State
X for an automobile accident tort

suit is two years from the date of the accident. The suit must be commenced against the defendant within the two year period of time. If suit is commenced after the statute of limitations period has run, then the right to suit is lost. The defendant will raise the issue of the running of the statute of limitations as an affirmative defense.

Some defenses may be raised by motion prior to the filing of the answer: "(1) lack of jurisdiction over the subject matter, (2) lack of jurisdiction over the person, (3) improper venue, (4) insufficiency of process, (5) failure to state a claim upon which relief can be granted, (6) failure to join a party under Rule 19."[14]

Once the answer has been filed, the issues are joined, and the parties proceed toward trial.

The Parties' Discovery

Discovery is well developed in civil court. Rule 26 of the Federal Rules of Civil Procedure provides for a broad scope of discovery in federal civil proceedings:

Parties may obtain discovery regarding any matter, not privileged, which is relevant to the subject matter involved in the pending action, whether it relates to the claim or defense of the party seeking discovery or to the claim or defense of any other party, including the existence, description, nature, custody, condition and location of any books, documents, or other tangible things and the identity and location of persons having knowledge of any discoverable matter. It is not a ground for objection that the information sought will be inadmissible at the trial if the information sought appears reasonably calculated to lead to the discovery of admissible evidence.[15]

There are six key forms of discovery: (1) depositions, (2) interrogatories to parties, (3) production of documents and other things, (4) entry upon land for inspection and other purposes, (5) examinations of persons, and (6) requests for admission.

Depositions represent a form of discovery that is often used. The deposition process is an out-of-court, trial-like process where a witness is placed under oath and questioned by all parties' attorneys.[16] The witness' testimony is normally stenographically taken.[17] The deposition is used at trial to impeach a non-party witness, or it may be used for any purpose against a witness who is also a party or any unavailable witness.[18]

Interrogatories are written questions from one party to another party. The party receiving the interrogatories must answer each question in writing under oath, unless it is objected to. If a particular question is objected to, then the reasons for the objection must be set forth. A party will often serve a Request for Production in conjunction with a Request for Interrogatories. This is a request from one party to another to produce for inspection and copying designated documents or tangible items in the party's possession.

A jurisdiction's discovery law may also permit the entry upon designated land in another party's possession "for the purpose of inspection and measuring, surveying, photographing, testing or sampling the property or any designated object or operation thereon."[19] The ability to examine may also extend to the examination of persons. Under federal law, if the mental or physical condition of a party, or of someone in the custody of a party, is in issue, then the court may order the party to submit to examination or produce for examination the person in his or her custody.[20]

Requests for admission, the final key form of discovery, represent a method of narrowing the number of facts that need be established at trial. A party may serve upon another party a written request for the admission of the truth of designated facts, including the genuineness of documents. The party upon whom the request is served must in good faith deny the matter, set forth the reasons why he or she cannot admit or deny the matter, or object to the answer within a designated period of time (e.g., within 30 days after service). If the required response is not made within the designated period of time, the fact(s) is(are) deemed admitted.[21]

As with criminal court discovery, the judge regulates the discovery process. The judge may order a party to allow discovery where it is required and the party has failed to make the discoverable material available.[22]

Motion Hearings and the Civil Court
Pretrial Conference

As with the criminal court process, numerous pretrial motions may be filed and heard by the judge as the parties proceed toward trial. Hearings may be held on claimed lack of court jurisdiction, alleged failure to state a claim in the complaint, requests for leave to file amended complaint, requests for protective orders barring certain discovery, requests to complete discovery, among other matters.

One important motion is the Motion for Summary Judgment. In the Motion for Summary Judgment, either party may request a judgment in the party's favor, without trial, based upon the showing that "there is no genuine issue as to any material fact (in the case) and that the moving party is entitled to judgment as a matter of law."[23] The purpose of the summary judgment is to quickly dispose of those cases where there are no real issues to justify trial. In establishing the absence of issues, the moving party presents evidence in the form of affidavits and the discovery on file with the court (e.g., depositions). The opposing party may resist summary judgment with like forms of evidence showing a genuine issue for trial.

Example.

> The plaintiff sues the employer of the person who struck her with his automobile while she was crossing Elmwood Drive. The plaintiff alleges in her suit that the defendant employer is liable to her for her damages because at the time of the accident the driver was acting within the scope of his employment with the defendant. The defendant moves for summary judgment and

establishes that the driver was solely on personal business at the time of the accident. The judge finds that there is no genuine issue in this regard and that the defendant, under the state's law, is not responsible for the driver's negligence. Since the defendant is entitled to judgment as a matter of law, summary judgment is entered by the court.

As a practical point, a summary judgment is not given unless it is very clear that no genuine issue exists. In doubtful situations, the courts tend to deny summary judgment and, therefore, give the parties their "day in court" at trial.

As noted previously, the pretrial conference is well established in civil litigation. A variety of matters may be considered by the attorneys and the judge at the conference, including those common issues identified above in the discussion of the criminal court pretrial conference. Additionally, the pretrial conference may be used to encourage settlements in civil court. Judges differ greatly in their attitude as to the extent to which the conference should be used to encourage settlement. However, while the judge may or may not encourage settlement during the conference, it is rare for the issue of settlement to not at least be raised.

If there is no settlement, then the parties move toward trial. In the jury trial, the first formal trial activity is the selection of the jurors.

Jury Selection

Prospective jurors are summoned to the court for jury duty. The panel of prospective jurors is usually selected at random from the community. A typical source for selection is the list of registered voters.

The actual jury is selected through the process of the voir dire examination. This is the process by which the prospective jurors are questioned to determine if they are fit and proper people to sit in judgment in the particular case.

Typically, the parties' attorneys conduct the examination of the prospective jurors, although in some courts (a growing number) the judge may conduct the examination (usually allowing some supplemental inquiry from the parties' attorneys). The basic purpose of the voir dire is to insure an impartial jury.

After the examination of a prospective juror, the attorney for a party may object to the prospective juror by use of a challenge for cause or a peremptory challenge.

Challenges for cause are unlimited in number and are granted where good cause is shown why a particular juror should not serve.

Example.

> Juror #1 is a friend of the defendant, a friend of the defendant's attorney, or a relative of the defendant. The Plaintiff will challenge Juror #1 for cause (i.e., bias toward the defendant).

The number of available peremptory challenges is limited. For example, in federal criminal court, if the offense charged is punishable by death, each party is entitled to 12 peremptory challenges; if the offense charged is a non-capital felony, each party is entitled to 5 peremptory challenges.[24] It is not necessary to establish cause for the peremptory challenge to be used to exclude a prospective juror. They are applied freely within their limited numbers and in line with the particular attorney's philosophy regarding jury panels in the particular case. However, while they are generally applied freely, recent case law has imposed some limits on their use (see Focus I discussion concerning the use of peremptory challenges and racial discrimination).

The examination and challenge process continues until ultimately a jury of sufficient number (e.g., a twelve person jury) is selected. A limited number of alternate jurors may also be selected in addition to the regular jury members. Alternate jurors take the place of regular jurors who become unable or disqualified to function during the trial.

The regular and alternate jurors are sworn. Thereafter, the judge presents to the jury preliminary instructions "as to the issues for trial, the burden of proof, the credibility of witnesses, and the manner of weighing the testimony to be received."[25] These preliminary instructions are given to the jury after the parties' attorneys have had the opportunity to examine and object to them. The parties' attorneys may also be allowed to submit to the judge proposed preliminary instructions for the judge to consider for inclusion as preliminary instructions to the jury. The trial process then proceeds to the next activity, the opening statements.

Opening Statements

Opening statements represent the parties' introduction to the case.[26] In their opening statements, the parties' attorneys set out the issues of the case and what they intend to prove. The idea is to establish a general overview of the case so that the trier of fact will be in a better position to understand the evidence.

The party with the initial burden in the case goes first. The issue of burden is discussed later in this chapter. However, in terms of the parties, this means that, in the civil case, the plaintiff's attorney presents his or her opening statement first, and, in the criminal case, the state presents its opening statement first. Following the opening statements of both parties, the trial process proceeds to the presentation of the plaintiff's case (in the civil trial) or the state's case (in the criminal trial).

Presentation of
Plaintiff's/State's Case

The plaintiff or state (in the criminal trial) presents that evidence which will establish the essential allegations of the case. The plaintiff's or state's witnesses are called and exhibits are admitted into evidence.

The testimony of witnesses is secured by voluntary attendance or by use of a subpoena. A subpoena is a written document evidencing a command by the court to the witness to appear and give testimony. Additionally, a subpoena ducus tecum is available to subpoena the production of documents at trial. If a person subpoenaed fails to comply, then he or she may be deemed in contempt of the court and can be punished by the court for such contempt.

The process of presenting evidence continues until the plaintiff or state "rests." This means that the party has presented all available and proper evidence to establish the allegations of the case against the defendant. If there is a question whether the allegations are supported by sufficient evidence, the defendant's attorney will likely move for a directed verdict.

Motion for Directed Verdict/Non-Suit Verdict

A motion for a directed verdict (also called a motion for a non-suit) is often made by defendant's attorney at the end of the plaintiff's or state's presentation of case. Since the plaintiff or state must make out a prima facie case in its presentation of case, if it fails to do so, there is no need to proceed with the trial.

A prima facie case is a case which "will suffice until contradicted and overcome by other evidence."[27] If the evidence is sufficiently strong so as to require rebuttal by the defendant, then the prima facie case is met. In ruling on the defendant's motion, the judge will consider the evidence in a light most favorable to the plaintiff or state. If the defendant's motion is granted, the defendant wins. However, if, as is more likely, the defendant's motion is denied, the trial proceeds to the presentation of defendant's case.

Presentation of Defendant's Case

The defendant presents his or her case in the same manner as the plaintiff and state. Witnesses for the defendant are called and exhibits are admitted into evidence. The witness subpoena and the subpoena ducus tecum are also available to the defendant.

In both the presentation of the plaintiff's or state's case and the defendant's case, a party's witness is questioned by direct examination. Thereafter, the other party's attorney may question the adverse witness by means of cross-examination. The processes for both direct and cross-examination are discussed in Chapter Five.

Redirect examination is available of a party's own witness where the opposing party's attorney brought forth new matters in cross-examination. In the court's discretion, re-cross may also be held.

During the direct examination, cross-examination, redirect examination, and re-cross examination (where held), objections are made to questions asked and exhibits presented. The basic rules of evidence dealing with such objections are discussed in subsequent chapters to the book.

When the defendant has "rested" his or her defense, the trial process proceeds to the rebuttal and motion for directed verdict.

Rebuttal and
Motion for Directed Verdict

If the plaintiff or state, as the case may be, elects, the party may proceed to introduce rebuttal evidence to the defendant's evidence. The purpose of rebuttal is to give to the plaintiff and state the opportunity to refute defendant's evidence. In some cases, after rebuttal, the defendant may introduce evidence to refute the rebuttal evidence. This process is called rejoinder.

Upon the completion of the rebuttal, either party may make a motion to the court for a directed verdict. For the motion to be granted, the evidence must be so clear that a reasonable person could not differ as to the result. In considering the motion, the judge should consider the evidence in a light most favorable to the party against whom the motion is made. If the motion is granted, the moving party prevails. If this motion is denied, the case goes to the trier of fact for decision.

Closing Statements

Before the case "goes to the jury," each party may summarize the case with a closing statement (also called closing argument). As with the opening statement, the plaintiff or state usually goes first. On some occasions, a rebuttal to the defendant's closing statement is permitted. The trial process then proceeds to final jury instructions.

Final Jury Instructions

After the closing statements, the judge instructs the jury as to the law in regard to the issues presented by the evidence. Each party is given an opportunity to request that particular instructions be given to the jury. The parties may also object to the giving of certain instructions. An example of an offered jury instruction is found below:

Example.

JURY INSTRUCTION GIVEN AT TRIAL
AND APPROVED BY THE
SUPREME COURT OF INDIANA IN:

Reighard v. State,
457 N.E.2d 557 (Ind. 1984:

COURT'S FINAL INSTRUCTION
NO. 31

"In the course of the trial there has been introduced the testimony of several witnesses, some of whom are referred to as expert witnesses, and some of whom are referred to as lay witnesses. You are instructed that an expert witness is one who is presumed to have special qualifications in his profession or vocation by reason of education, training and experience. You are to weigh the testimony of an expert witness in the same manner as you do the testimony of any other witness, taking into consideration the probability of the truth of which he speaks, together with the facts from which he draws his conclusion. You as jurors are not bound by definitions or conclusions as to what experts state is mental disease or defect. Mental disease or mental defect includes any abnormal condition of the mind which substantially impairs behavior controls. Experts have testified as to their findings and conclusions as to the mental condition of the defendant. You should consider the expert testimony in light of all other testimony presented concerning the development, adaption and functioning of the defendant's mental and emotional processes and behavior controls.

"Generally, a lay witness may not express an opinion; however, any person who had the opportunity to observe the defendant is permitted to express an opinion as to sanity. In determining the value of such opinion, you should consider the opportunity that such witness had to observe the facts and his knowledge of an experience with the defendant.

"The jury has the right to accept or reject any or all of the testimony of witnesses, either expert or lay witnesses on the question of insanity and mental illness. You will apply the general rules for determining the credibility of witnesses. You are not required to necessarily accept the ultimate conclusions of experts or lay witnesses as these opinions may be used by you to aid you in your deliberations. You, the jury, must determine for yourselves from

> all testimony, lay and expert, whether the nature and degree of any disability are sufficient to establish a mental disease, a mental defect or a mental illness."

The judge reads the instructions accepted by him or her to the jury. Lengthy instructions, such as the one in the above example, are not unusual. It is often a fair question as to whether the jurors fully comprehend the instructions given. Would you fully understand the law presented in the example if read to you (along with several other similar instructions on different points of law)? On the other hand, a lack of precision in instructions may fail to adequately inform the jurors of necessary law.

Deliberation, Return of Verdict and Judgment

After the reading by the judge of the jury instructions, the jury retires to deliberate. The deliberations are held in secret. The jury ultimately decides the facts, reaching an unanimous verdict.

Example.

> "We, the Jury, find for the Defendant, John Doe, and against the

Plaintiff, Jane Smith, on Plaintiff's Complaint.

We further find for the Counter-Plaintiff, John Doe, and against the Counter-Defendant, Jane Smith, on Defendant's Counterclaim, and assess said Counter-Plaintiff's damage in the sum of $1,000.

Date: January 15, 1989

> Thomas Roe
> Foreman"

After the announcement by the jury of its verdict in a civil case, the judge prepares and signs a judgment conforming to the verdict, and the judgment is entered of record. In a criminal case, if the defendant is found guilty, a sentencing hearing is set by the court. At this point, although the parties, parties' attorneys and the judge may engage in numerous post-trial activities, the trial process activities end.

Burden of Proof

One additional concept that should be discussed at this point is the concept of burden of proof. Burden of proof is defined technically as the "duty of affirmatively proving a fact or facts in dispute on an issue

raised between the parties in a cause."[28] It
should not be confused with the concept of prima
facie case, discussed above. One may well
establish a prima facie case, but not carry his
or her burden of proof to ultimately prevail in
the trial.

While a variety of subtleties surround the
concept of burden of proof, the basic student
concern must be with understanding the
plaintiff's burden of proof in the civil case
and the state's burden of proof in the criminal
case.

In the civil case, the plaintiff, in most
instances,[29] must establish his or her claim by
a preponderance of the evidence. Preponderance
of the evidence has been defined as the
"(g)reater weight of evidence, or evidence which
is more credible and convincing to the mind."[30]
This does not necessarily mean that the
plaintiff must have the greater number of
witnesses or exhibits. The plaintiff's three
brothers and father testifying on his behalf may
not be as convincing to the jury as one neutral,
eyewitness' testimony for the defendant.

In the criminal case, the defendant is not
required to prove his innocence. The state,
through the prosecutor, must prove the
defendant's guilt beyond a reasonable doubt.
Proof beyond a reasonable doubt exists when the
trier of fact is "fully satisfied, entirely

convinced, satisfied to a moral certainty" of the guilt of the defendant.[31] Every essential element of the offense charged must be established beyond a reasonable doubt. Obviously, the burden of proof on the state in the criminal case is higher than that of the plaintiff in the civil case.

Example.

> Defendant D is charged with the crime of battery, for striking V in the face with his fist. In addition to the state prosecuting D for the crime of battery, V sues D in civil court for damages for the battery (also a civil wrong). It is possible for V, the plaintiff, to prevail against D in civil court (where V's burden of proof is the preponderance of the evidence); and yet, D may prevail against the state in criminal court (where the prosecutor's burden of proof is beyond a reasonable doubt).

NOTES

1. That is not to say that there are no differences between civil court and criminal court trial procedure; there are, e.g., the number of required jurors may vary. However, the basics are the same. There are, of course,

major differences in the processing of civil cases and criminal cases outside of the trial procedure itself.

2. See FED. R. CRIM. P. 5.

3. FED. R. CRIM. P. 5.1. The dismissal and discharge of the defendant does not prevent the government from instituting later prosecution for the same offense. Id.

4. FED. R. CRIM. P. 7. This requirement is mandated by the grand jury clause of the Fifth Amendment to the U.S. Constitution. See Appendix B.

5. See FED. R. CRIM. P. 10. The nolo contendere plea is available in federal court only "with the consent of the court." Id.

6. Id.

7. FED. R. CRIM. P. 16(a).

8. FED. R. CRIM. P. 16(b).

9. See FED. R. CRIM. P. 16(d).

10. FED. R. CRIM. P. 17.1.

11. See FED. R. CIV. P. 4.

12. See FED. R. CIV. P. 14.

13. FED. R. CIV. P. 8(c).

14.   FED. R. CIV. P. 12(b).

15.   See FED. R. CIV. P. 26(b)(1).

16.   The witness for a deposition may be a party or a non-party. The attendance of witnesses may be compelled by subpoena. The subpoena process is discussed later in this chapter. Direct examination and cross-examination are permitted at the deposition.

17.   Depositions upon written questions may be permitted. See FED. R. CIV. P. 31. Also, a non-stenographic form of deposition (e.g., a videotaped deposition) or a deposition by telephone may be used where the parties stipulate to such use. FED. R. CIV. P. 30.

18.   See FED. R. CIV. P. 32.

19.   FED. R. CIV. P. 34.

20.   FED. R. CIV. P. 35.

21.   See FED. R. CIV. P. 36.

22.   A number of forms of court discovery sanctions exist. See FED. R. CIV. P. 37.

23.   FED. R. CIV. P. 56(c).

24.   FED. R. CRIM. P. 24(b)(1). In the typical federal civil case, each party is

entitled to 3 peremptory challenges. 28 U.S.C. Sec. 1870.

25. Indiana Rules of Procedure, Trial Rule 51(A).

26. See Id. at Trial Rule 43(G).

27. BLACK'S LAW DICTIONARY 1353 (4th ed. 1968). Note: A law dictionary is an extremely useful tool for the student studying law. BLACK'S LAW DICTIONARY is one of the best. It is published by the West Publishing Co., St. Paul, Minn.

28. Id. at 246.

29. Preponderance of the evidence is the typical quantum of evidence in most civil cases, but not all, e.g.,a "clear and convincing" standard is used in some states for a limited number of civil matters. See, e.g., *Traveler's Indemnity Co. v. Armstrong*, 442 N.E.2d 349 (Ind. 1982), where the Indiana court required a "clear and convincing" standard to establish punitive damages in a tortious breach of contract case.

30. BLACK'S LAW DICTIONARY, supra at 1344.

31. Id. at 204.

REVIEW AND DISCUSSION QUESTIONS

1. What is the purpose of the preliminary hearing in criminal court?

2. The Information allows for the "by-passing" of the grand jury indictment process. A faster, less-costly charging process results. However, even where the Information is available to the prosecutor by law, are there any instances where a prosecutor might choose to use the grand jury indictment process?

3. Distinguish informal discovery from formal discovery.

4. What may a defendant include in his or her civil court answer?

5. Describe the voir dire examination process. What is the difference in use of the challenge for cause and peremptory challenge?

6. What is the purpose of the plaintiff's and state's presentation of case?

7. Distinguish the witness subpoena from the subpoena ducus tecum.

8. A motion for a directed verdict is often made by defendant's attorney at the end of the plaintiff's or state's presentation of

case. What is the basis for such a motion? What is the basis for the motion for directed verdict at the end of the defendant's presentation of case?

9. In a jury trial, what occurs after the parties present their closing statements?

10. Distinguish between the following typical quantum of evidence: preponderance of the evidence and guilt beyond a reasonable doubt.

11. Review the sequence of activities which make up the trial of a case. Interview a judge, prosecutor, or lawyer in your jurisdiction. Is it possible to "streamline" the trial process? Is this desirable? How might this be done? How is this being done in the courts in your area? Do lengthy jury instructions pose a serious comprehension problem for jurors? Are such instructions really necessary?

PEREMPTORY CHALLENGES

Issue: Peremptory challenges have been used freely to exclude prospective jurors, even though no good cause exists to do so. However, can such challenges be used to exclude an individual because of his or her race? The Supreme Court has most recently considered this issue in *Powers v. Ohio*.

Powers v. Ohio

499 U.S. - ,
113 L Ed.2d 411, 111 S.Ct. - (1991)

Justice Kennedy delivered the opinion of the Court.

Jury service is an exercise of responsible citizenship by all members of the community, including those who otherwise might not have the opportunity to contribute to our civic life. Congress recognized this over a century ago in the Civil Rights Act of 1975, which made it a criminal offense to exclude persons from jury service on account of their race. .... In a trilogy of cases decided soon after enactment of this prohibition, our Court confirmed the validity of the statute, as well as the broader constitutional imperative of race neutrality in jury selection. .... In the many times we have confronted the issue since those cases, we have not questioned the premise that racial discrimination in the qualification or selection of jurors offends the dignity of persons and the integrity of the courts. Despite the clarity of these commands to eliminate the taint of racial discrimination in the administration of justice, allegations of bias in the jury selection process persist. In this case, petitioner alleges racial discrimination in the prosecution's use of peremptory challenges. Invoking the Equal Protection Clause and federal statutory law, and relying upon well established principles of standing, we hold that a criminal defendant may object to race biased exclusions of jurors effected through peremptory challenges whether or not the defendant and the excluded juror share the same race.

Petitioner Larry Joe Powers, a white man, was indicted in Franklin County, Ohio on two counts of aggravated murder and one count of attempted aggravated murder. Each count also included a separate allegation that petitioner had a firearm while committing the offense. Powers pleaded not guilty and invoked his right to a jury trial.

In the jury selection process, Powers objected when the prosecutor exercised his first peremptory challenge to remove a black venireperson. Powers requested the trial court to compel the prosecutor to explain on the record his reasons for excluding a black person. The trial court denied the request and excused the juror. The state proceeded to use nine more peremptory challenges, six of which removed black venirepersons from the jury. Each time the prosecution challenged a black prospective juror, Powers renewed his objections, citing our decision in Batson v. Kentucky, 476 U.S. 79, 90 L. Ed.2d 69, 106 S.Ct. 1762 (1986). His objections were overruled. The record does not indicate that race was somehow implicated in the crime or if any of the nine jurors the petitioner excluded by peremptory challenges were black persons.

The impaneled jury convicted Powers ..., and the trial court sentenced him to a term of imprisonment of 53 years to life. Powers appealed his conviction to the Ohio Court of Appeals, contending that the prosecutor's discriminatory use of peremptories violated the Sixth Amendment's guarantee of a fair cross section in his petit jury, the Fourteenth Amendment's Equal Protection Clause, and Article I, Sec. 10 and 16, of the Ohio Constitution. Powers contended that his own race was irrelevant to the right to object to the prosecutor's peremptory challenges. The Court of Appeals affirmed the conviction, and the

Supreme Court of Ohio dismissed Powers' appeal on the ground that it presented no substantial constitutional question.

Petitioner sought review before us, renewing his Sixth Amendment fair cross section and Fourteenth Amendment equal protection claims. While the petition for certiorari was pending, we decided Holland v Illinois, 493 US - , 107 L Ed 2d 905, 110 S Ct 803 (1990). In Holland it was alleged the prosecution had used its peremptory challenges to exclude from the jury members of a race other than the defendant's. We held the Sixth Amendment did not restrict the exclusion of a racial group at the peremptory challenge stage. Five members of the Court there said a defendant might be able to make the objection on equal protection grounds. See id, at -, 107 L Ed 2d 905, 110 S Ct 803 (Kennedy, J., concurring); id., at -, 107 L Ed 2d 905, 110 S Ct 803 (Marshall, J. dissenting, joined by Brennan and Blackmun, J.); id., at -, 107 L Ed 2d 905, 110 S Ct 803 Stevens, J. dissenting). After our decision in Holland, we granted Powers' petition for certiorari limited to the question whether, based on the Equal Protection Clause, a white defendant may object to the prosecution's peremptory challenges of black venirepersons. 493 US -, 107 L Ed 2d 1017, 110 S Ct 110 (1990). We now reverse and remand.

For over a century, this Country has been unyielding in its position that a defendant is denied equal protection of the laws when tried before a jury from which members of his or her race have been excluded by the State's purposeful conduct. "The Equal Protection Clause guarantees the defendant that the State will not exclude members of his race from the jury venire on account of race, Strauder, 100 US, at 305, or on the false assumption that members of his race as a group are not qualified to serve as jurors, see Norris v Alabama, 294 US 587, 599 (1935); Neal v Delaware, 103 US 370, 397 (1881)." Batson, supra, at 86, 90 L Ed 2d 69, 106 S Ct 1712. Although a defendant has no right to a "petit jury composed in whole or in part of persons of [the defendant's] own race," Strauder, 100 US at 305, 25 L Ed 664, he or she does have the right to be tried by a jury whose members are selected by nondiscriminatory criteria.

We confronted the use of peremptory challenges as a device to exclude jurors because of their race for the first time in Swain v Alabama, 380 US 202, 13 L Ed 2d 759, 85 S Ct 824 (1965). Swain involved a challenge to the so-called struck jury system, a procedure designed to allow both the prosecution and the defense a maximum number of peremptory challenges. The venire in noncapital cases started with about 35 potential jurors, from which the defense and the prosecution alternated with strikes until a petit panel of 12 jurors remained. The defendant in Swain, who was himself black, alleged that the prosecutor had used the struck jury system and its numerous peremptory challenges for the purpose of excluding black persons from his petit jury. In finding that no constitutional harm was alleged, the Court in Swain sought to reconcile the command of racial neutrality in jury selection with the utility, and the tradition, of peremptory challenges. The Court declined to permit an equal protection claim premised on a pattern of jury strikes in a particular case, but acknowledged that proof of systematic exclusion of black persons through the use of peremptories over a period of time might establish an equal protection violation. Id., at 222-228, 13 L Ed 2d 759, 85 S Ct 824.

We returned to the problem of a prosecutor's discriminatory use of peremptory challenges in Batson v Kentucky. There, we considered a situation similar to the one before us today, but with one exception: Batson, the defendant who complained that black persons were being excluded from his petit jury, was himself black. During the voir dire examination of the venire for Batson's trial, the prosecutor used his peremptory challenges to strike all four black persons on the venire, resulting in a petit jury composed only of white persons. Batson's counsel moved without success to discharge the jury before it was impaneled on the ground that the prosecutor's removal of black venirepersons violated his rights under the Sixth and Fourteenth Amendments. Relying upon the Equal Protection Clause alone, we overruled Swain to the extent it foreclosed objections to the discriminatory use of peremptories in the course of a specific trial. 476 US, at 90-93, 90 L Ed 2d 69, 106 S Ct 1712. In Batson we held that a defendant can raise an equal protection challenge to the use of peremptories at his own trial by showing that the prosecutor used them for the purpose of excluding members of the defendant's race. Id., at 96, 90 L Ed 2d 69, 106 S Ct 1712.

The State contends that our holding in the case now before us must be limited to the circumstances prevailing in Batson and that in equal protection analysis the race of the objecting defendant constitutes a relevant precondition for a Batson challenge. Because Powers is white, the State argues he cannot object to the exclusion of black prospective jurors. This limitation on a defendant's right to object conforms neither with our accepted rules of standing to raise a constitutional claim nor with the substantive guarantees of the Equal Protection Clause and the policies underlying federal statutory law.

In Batson, we spoke of the harm caused when a defendant is tried by a tribunal from which members of his own race have been excluded. But we did not limit our discussion in Batson to that one aspect of the harm caused by the violation. Batson "was designed 'to serve multiple ends,'" only one of which was to protect individual defendants from discrimination in the selection of jurors. Allen v Hardy, 478 US 255, 259, 92 L Ed 2d 199, 106 S Ct 2878 (1986)(per curiam)(quoting Brown v Louisiana, 447 US 323, 329, 65 L Ed 2d 159, 100 S Ct 2214 (1980)). Batson recognized that a prosecutor's discriminatory use of peremptory challenges harms the excluded jurors and the community at large. 476 US, at 87, 90 L Ed 2d 69, 106 S Ct 1712.

The opportunity for ordinary citizens to participate in the administration of justice has long been recognized as one of the principal justifications for retaining the jury system. See Duncan v Louisiana, 391 US 145, 147-158, 20 L Ed 2d 491, 88 S Ct 1444 (1968). In Balzac v Puerto Rico, 258 US 298, 66 L Ed 627, 42 S Ct 343 (1922), Chief Justice Taft wrote for the Court:

> "The jury system postulates a conscious duty of participation in the machinery of justice....One of its greatest benefits is in the security it gives the people that they, as jurors actual or possible, being part of the judicial system of

the country can prevent its arbitrary use or abuse." Id., at 310, 66 L Ed 627, 42 S Ct 343.

And, over 150 years ago, Alexis DeTocqueville remarked:

"[T]he institution of the jury raises the people itself, or at least a class of citizens, to the bench of judicial authority [and] invests the people, or that class of citizens, with the direction of society.

"...The jury...invests each citizen with a kind of magistracy; it makes them all feel the duties which they are bound to discharge towards society; and the part which they take in the Government. By obliging men to turn their attention to affairs which are not exclusively their own, it rubs off that individual egotism which is the rust of society.

"I do not know whether the jury is useful to those who are in litigation; but I am certain it is highly beneficial to those who decide the litigation; and I look upon it as one of the most efficacious means for the education of the people which society can employ." 1 Democracy in American 334-337 (Schocken 1st ed 1961).

Jury service preserves the democratic element of the law, as it guards the rights of the parties and insures continued acceptance of the laws by all people. See Green v United States, 356 US 165, 215, 2 L Ed 2d 672, 78 S Ct 632 (1958) (Black, J., dissenting). It 'affords ordinary citizens a valuable opportunity to participate in a process of government, an experience fostering, one hopes, a respect for law." Duncan, supra, at 187, 20 L Ed 2d 491, 88 S Ct 1444 (Harlan, J., dissenting). Indeed, with the exception of voting, for most citizens the honor and privilege of jury duty is their most significant opportunity to participate in the democratic process.

While States may prescribe relevant qualifications for their jurors, see Carter v Jury Comm'n of Green County, 396 US 320, 332, 24 L Ed 549, 90 S Ct 518 (1970), a member of the community may not be excluded from jury service on account of his or her race. .... "Whether jury service be deemed a right, a privilege, or a duty, the State may no more extend it to some of its citizens and deny it to others on racial grounds than it may invidiously discriminate in the offering and withholding of the elective franchise." Carter, supra, at 330, 24 L Ed 2d

549, 90 S Ct 518. Over a century ago, we recognized that:

> "The very fact that [members of a particular race] are singled out and expressly denied... all right to participate in the administration of the law, as jurors, because of their color, though they are citizens, and may be in other respects fully qualified, is practically a brand upon them, affixed by the law, an assertion of their inferiority, and a stimulant to that race prejudice which is an impediment to securing to individuals of the race that equal justice which the law aims to secure to all others." Strauder, supra, at 308, 25 L Ed 664.

Discrimination in the jury selection process is the subject of a federal criminal prohibition, and has been since Congress enacted the Civil Rights Act of 1875. The prohibition has been codified at 18 USC Sec. 243, which provides:

> "No citizen possessing all other qualifications which are or may be prescribed by law shall be disqualified for service as grand or petit juror in any court of the

United States, or of any State on account of race, color, or previous condition of servitude; and whoever, being an officer or other person charged with any duty in the selection or summoning of jurors, excludes or fails to summon any citizen for such cause, shall be fined not more than $5,000."

In Peters v Kiff, 407 US 493, 33 L Ed 2d 83, 92 S Ct 2163 (1972), Justice White spoke of "the strong statutory policy of Sec. 243, which reflects the central concern of the Fourteenth Amendment." Id., at 507, 33 L Ed 2d 83, 92 S Ct 2163 (concurring in judgment). The Court permitted a white defendant to challenge the systematic exclusion of black persons from grand and petit juries. While Peters did not produce a single majority opinion, six of the Justices agreed that racial discrimination in the jury selection process cannot be tolerated and that the race of the defendant has no relevance to his or her standing to raise the claim. See id., at 504-505, 33 L Ed 2d 83, 92 S Ct 2163 (White, J., concurring in judgment).

Racial discrimination in the selection of jurors in the context of an individual trial violates these same prohibitions. A State "may not draw up its jury lists pursuant to neutral procedures but then resort to discrimination at 'other stages in the selection process.'"

Batson, supra, at 88 (1953). We so held in Batson, and reaffirmed that holding in Holland. See 493 US, at -, 107 L Ed 2d 905, 110 S Ct 803. In Holland, the Court held that a defendant could not rely on the Sixth Amendment to object to the exclusion of members of any distinctive group at the peremptory challenge stage. We noted that the peremptory challenge procedure has acceptance in our legal tradition. See id., at -, 107 L Ed 2d 905, 110 S Ct 803. On this reasoning we declined to permit an objection to the peremptory challenge of a juror on racial grounds as a Sixth Amendment matter. As the Holland Court made explicit, however, racial exclusion of prospective jurors violates the overriding command of the Equal Protection Clause, and "racebased exclusion is no more permissible at the individual petit jury state than at the venire stage." Id., at -, 107 L Ed 2d 905, 110 S Ct 803.

We hold that the Equal Protection Clause prohibits a prosecutor from using the State's peremptory challenges to exclude otherwise qualified and unbiased persons from the petit jury solely by reason of their race, a practice that forecloses a significant opportunity to participate in civic life. An individual juror does not have a right to set on any particular petit jury, but he or she does possess the right not to be excluded from one on account of race.

It is suggested that no particular stigma or dishonor results if a prosecutor uses the raw fact of skin color to determine the objectivity or qualifications of a juror. We do not believe a victim of the classification would endorse this view; the assumption that no stigma or dishonor attaches contravenes accepted equal protection principles. Race cannot be a proxy for determining juror bias or competence. "A person's race simply 'is unrelated to his fitness as a juror.'" Batson, supra, at 87 (quoting Thiel V Southern Pacific Co., supra, at 227, (Frankfurter, J., dissenting)). We may not accept as a defense to racial discrimination the very stereotype the law condemns.

We reject as well the view that race-based peremptory challenges survive equal protection scrutiny because members of all races are subject to like treatment, which is to say that white jurors are subject to the same risk of peremptory challenges based on race as are all other jurors. The suggestion that racial classifications may survive when visited upon all persons is no more authoritative today than the case which advanced the theorem, Plessy v Ferguson, 163 US 537 (1896). This idea has no place in our modern equal protection jurisprudence. It is axiomatic that racial classifications do not become legitimate on the assumption that all persons suffer them in equal degree. Loving v Virginia, 388 US 17 (1967).

We must consider whether a criminal defendant has standing to raise the equal protection rights of a juror excluded from service in violation of these principles. In the ordinary course, a litigant must assert his or her own legal rights and interests, and cannot rest a claim to relief premised on the legal rights or interests of third parties. United States Dept. of Labor v Triplett, 494 US -, 108 L Ed 2d 701, 110 S Ct 1428 (1990); Singleton v Wulff, 428 US 106 (1967). This fundamental restriction on our authority admits of certain, limited exceptions. We have recognized the right of litigants to bring actions on behalf of third parties, provided three important criteria are satisfied: the litigant must have suffered an "injury-in-fact," thus giving him or her a "sufficiently concrete interest" in the outcome of the issue in dispute, Singleton, supra, at 112; the litigant must have a close relation to the third party, id., at 113-114; and there must exist some hindrance to the third party's ability to protect his or her own interests. Id., at 115-116. See Also Craig v Boren, 429 US 190 (1976). These criteria have been satisfied in cases where we have permitted criminal defendants to challenge their convictions by raising the rights of third parties. See, e.g., Eisenstadt v Baird, 405 US 438 (1976); Griswold v Connecticut, 381 US 479 (1965); see also McGowan v Maryland, 366 US 420 (1961). By similar reasoning, we have permitted litigants to raise third-party rights in order to prevent possible future prosecution. See, e.g., Doe v Bolton, 410 US 179 (1973).

The discriminatory use of peremptory challenges by the prosecution causes a criminal defendant cognizable injury, and the defendant has a concrete interest in challenging the practice. See Allen v Hardy, 478 US, at 259, 92 L Ed 2d 199, 106 S Ct 2878 (recognizing a defendant's interest in "neutral jury selection procedures"). This is not because the individual jurors dismissed by the prosecution may have been predisposed to favor the defendant; if that were true, the jurors might have been excused for cause. Rather, it is because racial discrimination in the selection of jurors "casts doubt on the integrity of the judicial process," Rose v Mitchell, 443 US 545, 556 (1979), and places the fairness of a criminal proceeding in doubt.

The jury acts as a vital check against wrongful exercise of power by the State and its prosecutors. Batson, supra, at 86. The intrusion of racial discrimination into the jury selection process damages both the fact and the perception of this guarantee. "Jury selection is the primary means by which a court may enforce a defendant's right to be tried by a jury free from ethnic, racial, or political prejudice, Rosales-Lopez v United States, 451

US 182, 188 (1981); Ham v South Carolina, 409 US 524 (1973); Dennis v United States, 339 US 162 (1950), or predisposition about the defendant's culpability, Irvin v Dowd, 366 US 717 (1961)." Gomez v United States, 490 US 858, 873, 104 L Ed 2d 923, 109 S Ct 2237 (1989). Active discrimination by a prosecutor during this process condones violations of the United States Constitution within the very institution entrusted with its enforcement, and so invites cynicism respecting the jury's neutrality and its obligation to adhere to the law. The cynicism may be aggravated if race is implicated in the trial, either in a direct way as with an alleged racial motivation of the defendant or a victim, or in some more subtle manner as by casting doubt upon the credibility or dignity of a witness, or even upon the standing or due regard of an attorney who appears in the cause.

Unlike the instances where a defendant seeks to object to the introduction of evidence obtained illegally from a third party, see, e.g., United States v Payner, 447 US 727, 65 L Ed 2d 468, 100 S Ct 2439 (1980), here petitioner alleges that the primary constitutional violation occurred during the trial itself. A prosecutor's wrongful exclusion of a juror by a race-based peremptory challenge is a constitutional violation committed in open court at the outset of the proceedings. The overt wrong, often apparent to the entire jury panel, casts doubt over the obligation of the parties, the jury and indeed the court to adhere to the law throughout the trial of the cause. The voir dire phase of the trial represents the "jurors' first introduction to the substantive factual and legal issues in a case." Gomez, supra, at 874. The influence of the voir dire process may persist through the whole course of the trial proceedings. Ibid. If the defendant has no right to object to the prosecutor's improper exclusion of jurors, and if the trial court has no duty to make a prompt inquiry when the defendant shows, by adequate grounds, a likelihood of impropriety in the exercise of a challenge, there arise legitimate doubts that the jury has been chosen by proper means. The composition of the trier of fact itself is called in question, and the irregularity may pervade all the proceedings that follow.

The purpose of the jury system is to impress upon the criminal defendant and the community as a whole that a verdict of conviction or acquittal is given in accordance with the law by persons who are fair. The verdict will not be accepted or understood in these terms if the jury is chosen by unlawful means at the outset. Upon these considerations, we find that a criminal defendant suffers a real injury when the prosecutor excludes jurors at his or her own trial on account of race.

We noted in Singleton that in certain circumstances "the relationship between the litigant and the third party may be such that the former is fully, or very nearly, as effective a proponent of the right as the latter." 428 US, at 115. Here, the relation between petitioner and the excluded jurors is as close as, if not closer than, those we have recognized to convey third-party standing in our prior cases. See, e.g., Griswold v Connecticut, supra (Planned Parenthood official and a licensed physician can raise the constitutional rights of contraceptive users with whom they had professional relationships); Crain, supra (licensed beer vendor has standing to raise the equal protection claim of a male customer challenging a statutory scheme prohibiting the sale of beer to males under the age of 21 and to females under the age of 18); Triplett, supra (attorney may challenge an attorney's fees restriction by asserting the due process rights of the client). Voir dire permits a party to establish a relation, if not a bond of trust, with the jurors. This relation continues throughout the entire trial and may in some cases extend to the sentencing as well.

Both the excluded juror and the criminal defendant have a common interest in eliminating racial discrimination from the courtroom. A venireperson excluded from jury service because of race suffers a profound personal humiliation heightened by its public character. The rejected juror may lose confidence in the court and its verdicts, as may the defendant if his or her objections cannot be heard. This congruence of interests makes it necessary and appropriate for the defendant to raise the rights of the juror. And, there can be no doubt that petitioner will be a motivated, effective advocate for the excluded venirepersons' rights. Petitioner has much at stake in proving that his jury was improperly constituted due to an equal protection violation, for we have recognized that discrimination in the jury selection process may lead to the reversal of a conviction. See Batson, supra, at 100; Vasquez v Hillery, 474 US 254, 264, 88 L Ed 2d 598, 106 S Ct 617 (1986); Rose v Mitchell, supra, at 551; Cassell v Texas, 339 US 282, 94 L Ed 839, 70 S Ct 629 (1949). Thus, "'there seems little loss in terms of effective advocacy from allowing [the assertion of this claim] by' the present jus tertii champion." Craig, supra, at 194 (quoting Singleton, supra, at 118).

The final inquiry in our third-party standing analysis involves the likelihood and ability of the third parties, the excluded venirepersons, to assert their own rights. See Singleton, supra, at 115-116. We have held that individual jurors subjected to racial exclusion have the legal right to bring suit on their own behalf. Carter, 396 US, at 329-330. As a practical matter, however, these challenges are rare. See Alschuler, The Supreme Court and the Jury: Voir Dire, Peremptory Challenges, and the Review of Jury Verdicts, 56 U Chi L Rev 153, 193-195 (1989). Indeed, it took nearly a century after the Fourteenth Amendment and the Civil Rights Act of 1875 came into being for the first such case to reach this Court. See Carter, supra, at 320.

The barriers to a suit by an excluded juror are daunting. Potential jurors are not parties to the jury selection process and have no opportunity to be heard at the time of their exclusion. Nor can excluded jurors easily obtain declaratory or injunctive relief when discrimination occurs through an individual prosecutor's exercise of peremptory challenges. Unlike a challenge to systematic practices of the jury clerk and commissioners such as we considered in Carter, it would be difficult for an individual juror to show a likelihood that discrimination against him at the voir dire stage will recur. See Los Angeles v Lyons, 461 US 95, 105-110, 75 L Ed 2d 675, 103 S Ct 1660 (1983). And, there exist considerable practical barriers to suit by the excluded juror because of the small financial stake involved and the economic burdens of litigation. See Vasquez, supra, at 262, n 5; Rose v Mitchell, supra, at 558. The reality is that a juror dismissed because of race probably will leave the courtroom possessing little incentive to set in motion the arduous process needed to vindicate his own rights. See Barrows v Jackson, 346 US 249, 257, 97 L Ed 1586, 73 S Ct 1031 (1953).

We conclude that a defendant in a criminal case can raise the third-party equal protection claims of jurors excluded by the prosecution because of their race. In so doing, we once again decline "to reverse a course of decisions of long standing directed against racial discrimination in the administration of justice." Cassell v Texas, 339 US 282, 290. 94 L Ed 839, 70 S Ct 629 (1950) (Frankfurter, J., concurring in judgment). To bar petitioner's claim because his race differs from that of the excluded jurors would be to condone the arbitrary exclusion of citizens from the duty, honor, and privilege of jury service. In Holland and Batson, we spoke of the significant role peremptory challenges play in our trial procedures, but we noted also that the utility of the peremptory challenge system must be accommodated to the command of racial neutrality. Holland, supra, at -, 107 L Ed 2d 905, 110 S Ct 803; Batson, supra, at 98-99.

The Fourteenth Amendment's mandate that race discrimination be eliminated from all official acts and proceedings of the State is most compelling in the judicial system. Rose v Mitchell, supra, at 555. We have held, for example, that prosecutorial discretion cannot be exercised on the basis of race, Wayte v United States, 470 US 598, 608, 84 L Ed 2d 547, 105 S Ct 1524 (1985), and that, where racial bias is likely to influence a jury, an inquiry must be made into such bias. Ristaino v Ross, 424 US 589, 596, 47 L Ed 2d 258, 96 S Ct 1017 (1976); see also Turner v Murray, 476 US 28, 90 L Ed 2d 27, 106 S Ct 1683 (1986). The statutory prohibition on discrimination in the selection of jurors, 18 USC SS 243, enacted pursuant to the Fourteenth Amendment's Enabling Clause, makes race neutrality in jury selection a visible, and inevitable, measure of the judicial system's own commitment to the commands of the Constitution. The courts are under an affirmative duty to enforce the strong statutory and constitutional policies embodied in that prohibition. See Peters v Kiff, 407 US, at 507, 33 L Ed 2d 83, 92 S Ct 2163 (White, J., concurring in judgment)....

The emphasis in Batson on racial identity between the defendant and the excused prospective juror is not inconsistent with our holding today that race is irrelevant to a defendant's standing to object to the discriminatory use of peremptory challenges. Racial identity between the defendant and the excused person might in some cases be the explanation for the prosecution's adoption of the forbidden stereotype, and if the alleged race bias takes this form, it may provide one of the easier cases to establish both a prima facie case and a conclusive showing that wrongful discrimination has occurred. But to say that the race of the defendant may be relevant to discerning bias in some cases does not mean that it will be a factor in others, for race prejudice stems from various causes and may manifest itself in different forms.

It remains for the trial courts to develop rules, without unnecessary disruption of the jury selection process, to permit legitimate and wellfounded objections to the use of peremptory challenges as a mask for race prejudice. In this case, the State concedes that, if we find the petitioner has standing to object to the prosecution's use of the peremptory challenges, the case should be remanded. We find that petitioner does have standing. The judgment is reversed, and the case is remanded for further proceedings not inconsistent with our opinion.

It is so ordered.

Chapter Two

TERMS AND CONCEPTS OF EVIDENCE

The Definition of Evidence

Evidence is a broad term. It is broader than the concept of admissible evidence. Evidence includes all material in any form submitted at trial to establish a matter of fact in the case (regardless of whether the evidence is ultimately admitted or not).[1]

Example.

> If one of the factual concerns in a case is whether the defendant signed a document, then placing a handwriting expert on the stand to testify as to her opinion that the defendant did sign the document is evidence, since the testimony is submitted to establish that matter of fact.

The Rules of Evidence

While evidence includes all material in any form submitted at trial to establish a matter of fact, the rules of evidence are the rules which <u>regulate</u> such submissions.

Example.

> Before the handwriting expert can testify as to her opinion that the defendant did sign the document in question, it must be shown that the witness is truly an expert witness. This is done by establishing to the satisfaction of the court the qualifications of the expert on the record. The rule that the qualifications which entitle the expert to present her opinion must be set forth on the record is a rule of evidence-a rule which regulates the submission of the evidence.

The Development of the Rules of Evidence

In considering the development of the rules of evidence, the student must first recognize that the rules of evidence, like all law, have gone through and will continue to go through change. For example, at one time a person who had a financial interest in the outcome of a case was disqualified as a witness (e.g., the party to a civil action or the party's business partner). Today, the person is not incompetent to testify, but the judge or jury can consider the interest of the party in determining what weight and credibility to give to the testimony (see Chapter Four for a discussion of modern witness competency law).

The rules of evidence evolved with the jury trial. As first stated in the Introduction, the jury process developed over time from a process in which jurors went forth to inquire of the facts, or based their decisions on their own knowledge, to the opposite system of having sworn to, in court evidence presented and requiring that determinations be made solely upon such evidence. With this system, it was necessary to develop rules of evidence to help protect untrained jurors from being misled.

Rules regulating various forms of evidence began to develop in the seventeenth and eighteenth centuries.[2] This regulation became more intense in the 1800s.[3]

Professor Blackstone, in his eighteenth century *Commentaries*, sets forth numerous examples of such rules of evidence. One example is the "dying declaration" exception to the hearsay rule. The hearsay rule is a classic example of a rule of evidence that developed to help protect untrained jurors from being misled. Simply (more precisely defined in Chapter Seven), hearsay is an out-of-court statement offered at trial to prove a matter of fact. The hearsay rule prohibits such evidence from being admissible because such evidence tends to lack trustworthiness. However, numerous exceptions to this rule of inadmissibility of hearsay developed, since some hearsay is more reliable than other forms. One traditional exception is the "dying declaration," a hearsay statement made by one in fear of immediately impending death.

Example.

> X, the witness in the murder trial, takes the stand and testifies: "I held Z (the victim) in my arms until he died; just before he died Z exclaimed to me, 'Y (the defendant) knifed me!'."

The exception was described by Blackstone in the following manner:

> [D]ying declarations form a species of evidence admissible only in a single instance of homicide; where the death of the deceased is the subject of the charge, and the circumstances of the death are the subject of the dying declarations made in extremity when the party is at the point of death, and when every hope of this world is gone, when every motive to falsehood is

silenced, and the mind is induced by the most powerful considerations to speak the truth, have, although made in the absence of the accused, the weight of testimony given on oath in the presence of the accused. It is essential to the admissibility of these declarations, first, that at the time they were made the declarant should have been in actual danger of death; secondly, that he should have had a full apprehension of this danger; and lastly, that death should have ensued.[4]

The student can find the description of the current federal rule for the dying declaration hearsay exception in the Chapter Eight Rule 804(b)(2) commentary.

In fashioning the rules of evidence, the judges, and, at times, the legislators, as well, worked to develop, as Professor John Henry Wigmore wrote, "a network of rules, like a sieve, which allowed only the rational and safe and valued tidbits to get through to the jury."[5]

Until recent years, the rules of evidence in the United States were not brought together, or codified, in statutes. They generally existed independently in the form of judicial decisions in cases (case precedent), judicial mandates, and, to some extent, separate statutory enactments. However, lately, the federal government and a number of states have moved to codify their rules of evidence. The Evidence Code of the State of California was adopted in 1965.[6] In 1975 the most important codification occurred with the promulgation of the Federal Rules of Evidence.[7]

The Federal Rules of Evidence

The Federal Rules of Evidence are actually the product of Congress' review and modification of the uniform rules of evidence first approved by the United States Supreme Court in 1972.[8]

The Federal Rules of Evidence govern the proceedings in federal courts. They are not applicable to the states. However, since their adoption by Congress, these rules have been influential, and they have served as the model for a number of states in the states' codification efforts. In those states which have patterned their evidence law after the federal rules, it is commonplace for these states' courts to look to federal case decisions for interpretation guidance. Still, the student is cautioned to remember that not all states have accepted the federal rules model, and even those that have accepted the rules have made at least minor changes in them.

While the Federal Rules of Evidence generally have a "liberal" thrust, they do not depart in a very serious way from the rules of evidence that had already developed in this country at the time of their enactment. Much of the basic law as was collected, analyzed, and set out in the great legal treatises on evidence is continued, with some modifications and departures, in the federal rules.[9]

The text of the Federal Rules of Evidence is included in the Appendix A. Additionally, some of the less lengthy federal rules are set forth throughout the book where relevant to serve as examples of law. Reference to the Appendix is made for longer rules when they are discussed, so as not to distract from the narrative.

Types of Evidence

The two basic types of evidence are direct evidence and circumstantial evidence.

Direct Evidence

Direct evidence has been defined as "that means of proof which tends to show the existence of a fact in question, without the intervention of the proof of any other fact...."[10] When direct evidence is submitted, the jury or judge is called upon to merely decide if the evidence is to be believed. It is not necessary for the jury or judge to make inferences or draw conclusions.

Example.

> X is a witness in a murder trial. X takes the stand and testifies: "I saw Y (the defendant) pick up an ax from the garage floor and swing it at Z (the victim), chopping off Z's head with one swing." The jury or judge must decide one thing; that is whether or not X is to be believed. If the trier of fact believes X, then the matter of fact has been established.

Circumstantial Evidence

Direct evidence must be contrasted with circumstantial evidence. Circumstantial evidence is indirect evidence of the existence of the matter of fact. As to circumstantial evidence, inferences or conclusions must be drawn.

Example.

> X, the witness in the murder trial, takes the stand and testifies: "I was standing outside Y's (the defendant's) garage. I heard a scream, and I entered the garage. I saw Z (the victim) lying on the floor, Z's head severed from the rest of the bloody body, and Y was

standing over Z's body, holding a
bloody ax." Here, the jury or judge
must decide two things. First, the
trier of fact must decide if it is
to believe X. If the jury or judge
decides that it believes X, then it
must draw the inference or
conclusion that, because Y stood
over the decapitated body of Z with
a bloody ax in his hand, he was the
one who killed Z.

Testimonial Evidence and Non-Testimonial Evidence

Testimonial evidence is evidence founded
upon a witness' testimony in court. The above
examples of direct evidence and circumstantial
evidence are presented in the form of
testimonial evidence.

In addition to testimonial evidence, there
is non-testimonial evidence. Non-testimonial
evidence is presented in the form of physical
objects as exhibits. Non-testimonial evidence
is generally subdivided into two categories: (1)
real evidence and (2) demonstrative evidence.

Real Evidence

Real evidence involves the submission of
some physical object which was a direct part of
the situation or incident in question.

Example.

> Y's ax (in the above example) is the murder weapon. Its submission at trial is the submission of real evidence.

Demonstrative Evidence

Demonstrative evidence is to be distinguished from real evidence in that, unlike real evidence, it does not have independent probative value. It merely serves as a visual or audiovisual aid to the jury or judge. It is designed to assist the trier of fact in understanding the testimony of a witness.

Example.

> A diagram of Y's garage (in the above example) would be a diagram of the crime scene. The submission of the diagram at trial is a submission of demonstrative evidence.

Other examples of demonstrative evidence include x-rays, models, charts, maps, diagrams of accident scenes. There are many possibilities. The use of computer graphics and computer simulations is bringing computer applications into the field of demonstrative evidence.[11] Of course, lawyers will seek to use whatever evidence they can to aid in the presentation of a witness' testimony.

Judicial Notice

Certain factual matters may be established at trial without the submission of actual proof. This process of taking "judicial notice" of facts by the judge is limited to facts of general knowledge in the community. Judicial notice is considered in detail in Chapter 11.

Example.

It is unlikely that a party would be required to prove that the sun rises in the east and sets in the west.

The Question of Admissibility

Evidence includes all material in any form submitted at trial to establish a matter of fact in the case. Since the term is broader than the concept of admissible evidence, evidence may ultimately be admitted or excluded from reaching the jury. The trier of fact is allowed to consider only that evidence which is admissible.

What is admitted into evidence depends upon the application of the rules of evidence. The question of whether evidence will be admitted into trial is the chief concern of the subsequent chapters to this book.

NOTES

1. See BLACK'S LAW DICTIONARY 656 (4th ed. 1968).

2. J. H. WIGMORE, A STUDENT'S TEXTBOOK OF THE LAW OF EVIDENCE 1ff. (1935), reprinted in H. J. GERMAN & W. R. GREINER, THE NATURE AND FUNCTION OF LAW 323 (3d ed. 1972).

3. Id.

4. 4 W. BLACKSTONE, COMMENTARIES *359.

5. J. H. WIGMORE, supra.

6. See Stats. 1965, c.299, as amended.

7. P.L. 93-595. The Federal Rules of Evidence were enacted by Congress on January 2, 1975. A small number of amendments have been adopted by Congress over the past decade. Appendix A presents the federal rules, as amended through January 1, 1991. The federal rules can be found in Title 28 of the United State Code. The amendment process for the federal rules is discussed at the end of Appendix A.

8. For the Supreme Court approved draft, see 56 F.R.D. 183 (1972).

9. A number of great legal treatises on evidence exist. One of the most influential is

WIGMORE, EVIDENCE (3d ed. 1940). Volumes of Professor Wigmore's work have been revised in recent years by legal scholars. McCORMICK, EVIDENCE (2d ed. 1972) is a great single volume treatise. This treatise has been updated, as well, to cover the Federal Rules of Evidence. The third edition (edited by E. W. Clearly) was published by West Publishing Company in 1984. An historically important work is THAYER, PRELIMINARY TREATISE ON EVIDENCE (1898). Professor Thayer's treatise was of tremendous importance in organizing, presenting, and conceptualizing the law of evidence at the turn of the century.

For a much more practical approach to the application of the rules of evidence in trial practice, see GOLDSTEIN, TRIAL TECHNIQUE (1935); BELLI, MODERN TRIALS (1954) (the 2d. ed. was recently published by the West Publishing Company); and BERGMAN, TRIAL ADVOCACY IN A NUTSHELL (1979).

Finally, law school libraries, many university libraries, and even some community libraries contain legal encyclopedias in their reference sections. For encyclopedia review, see 31A C.J.S. Evidence and 32B AmJur2d, Federal Rules of Evidence (which also has a separate section on general evidence law, see Vol. 29).

10. BLACK'S LAW DICTIONARY, supra at 546.

11.   For an excellent article on the use of computer simulations at trial, see Harper, "Computer Evidence Is Coming," 70 ABA JOURNAL 80 (Nov., 1984).   See also Marcotte, "Animated Evidence," 75 ABA JOURNAL 52 (December, 1989). As to the use of videotape evidence at trial, see Joseph, "Demonstrative Videotape Evidence," 22 TRIAL 60 (June, 1986).

REVIEW AND DISCUSSION QUESTIONS

1.   Do the Federal Rules of Evidence govern state court proceedings?   What is the importance of the federal rules?

2.   Describe the two basic types of evidence. Develop your own examples of each.

3.   Distinguish real evidence and demonstrative evidence. Give examples of both.

4.   Does your state have codified rules of evidence? If so, how do they compare with selected portions of the Federal Rules of Evidence?   Are there advantages to codification? If so, what are they?

5.   How does the process of taking "judicial notice" aid trial efficiency and administration? Is such a process fair?

Chapter Three

RELEVANCY

Rule 401[1]
DEFINITION OF "RELEVANT EVIDENCE"

"Relevant evidence" means evidence having any tendency to make the existence of any fact that is of consequence to the determination of the action more probable or less probable than it would be without the evidence.

Rule 402[2]
RELEVANT EVIDENCE GENERALLY ADMISSIBLE, IRRELEVANT EVIDENCE INADMISSIBLE

All relevant evidence is admissible, except as otherwise provided by the Constitution of the United States, by Act of Congress, by these rules, or by other rules prescribed by the Supreme Court pursuant to statutory authority.

Evidence which is not relevant is not admissible.

The Concept of Relevancy

The concept of relevant evidence is critically important to the understanding of basic trial evidence. The general rule is that relevant evidence is admissible and irrelevant evidence is inadmissible. However, while relevant evidence is generally admissible, it is important to remember that there are occasions when relevant evidence may be excluded by the court. This issue is discussed later in this chapter.

Relevancy v. Materiality

The student may recall viewing on one of the many television programs concerning lawyers and trials the attorney for a party rising at trial to object: "Your honor, the evidence is irrelevant and immaterial!" There is a traditional distinction between the concepts of relevancy and materiality.

Material evidence must be relevant _and_ go to an issue properly before the court at trial. Some issues are always properly before the court at trial. A key example of evidence always in issue is the credibility of a witness. Other

issues become proper because they have been
properly framed by the pleadings of the case.
In other words, before the trial (during pretrial procedures) the parties should have listed
in documents (e.g., the complaint, answer, pretrial order) those matters to be in issue at
trial.   Evidence is material if it is relevant
and related to one of those issues.

Example.

> A, the plaintiff, sues D, the
> defendant, for failure to pay a sum
> of money agreed upon in a purchase
> agreement.   If the only defense
> raised by D is that he never entered
> into the agreement, evidence that D
> paid the agreed upon sum would be
> immaterial.

Today, the trend is to consider relevancy
and materiality as one concept with materiality
being viewed as but a part of the general
concept of relevancy.   The Federal Rules do not
refer to the term   "materiality."   However, Rule
401 does define relevant evidence as "evidence
having any tendency to make the existence of any
fact *that is of consequence to the determination
of the action* more probable or less probable
than it would be without the evidence" (emphasis
added).   Materiality is part of the concept of
relevancy under the federal rules, in the sense

that the fact must be "of consequence to the determination of the action."

A Further Look at
The Definition of Relevant Evidence

The Rule 401 definition of relevant evidence appears immediately above. Attorneys refer to evidence which has such tendency to make the existence of a fact more probable or less probable as evidence having *probative value*.

Whether evidence has probative value is a question for the judge, and he or she must be guided by common sense and logic.[3] Practically, if the evidence assists in a reasonable manner in determining a fact, it should have probative value.

Example.

> Evidence that the defendant, when stopped by the police, had in his possession both marked bills and identifiable negotiable instruments from the National Bank of Commerce is relevant to the question of whether the defendant robbed the bank, as charged.

Problems as to Admissibility

Federal Rule 402 makes it clear that relevant evidence is admissible unless otherwise excluded by law. We will look to such key exclusions in subsequent chapters (e.g., the hearsay rule). Additionally, the judge has discretionary power to exclude relevant evidence:

Rule 403[4]
EXCLUSION OF RELEVANT
EVIDENCE ON GROUNDS OF PREJUDICE,
CONFUSION, OR WASTE OF TIME

Although relevant, evidence may be excluded if its probative value is substantially outweighed by the danger of unfair prejudice, confusion of the issues, or misleading the jury, or by considerations of undue delay, waste of time, or needless presentation of cumulative evidence.

The judge is given the discretion to weigh, or *balance*, the probative value of evidence against the dangers of unfair prejudice, etc. If the inherent dangers in the evidence "substantially outweigh" the probative value, the evidence may be excluded by the court.

Example.

> In Chapter 2, an example of the decapitation of the victim was used. If the severed head is sought to be admitted into the trial, the judge, in his or her discretion, may well exclude the evidence. Such evidence will likely shock or inflame the jury. The danger of unfair prejudice may well be seen to substantially outweigh any probative value.

It is important to remember that the decision to exclude the evidence rests within the sound discretion of the judge. While the court's decision to exclude or not exclude may be appealed, the ruling is not likely to be overturned unless there was a clear abuse of discretion of the judge.

The Question of Character

Rule 404[5]
CHARACTER EVIDENCE
NOT ADMISSIBLE TO PROVE
CONDUCT; EXCEPTIONS; OTHER CRIMES

(a) Character Evidence Generally. Evidence of a person's character or a trait of character is not admissible for the purpose of proving action in conformity therewith on a particular occasion, except:

(1) Character of accused. Evidence of a pertinent trait of character offered by an accused, or by the prosecution to rebut the same;

(2) Character of victim. Evidence of a pertinent trait of character of the victim of the crime offered by an accused, or by the prosecution to rebut the same, or evidence of a character trait of peacefulness of the victim offered by the prosecution in a homicide case to rebut evidence that the victim was the first aggressor;

(3) Character of witness. Evidence of the character of a witness, as provided in Rules 607, 608, and 609.

(b) Other Crimes, Wrongs, or Acts. Evidence of other crimes, wrongs, or acts is not admissible to prove the character of a person in order to show action in conformity therewith. It may, however, be admissible for other purposes, such as proof of motive, opportunity, intent, preparation, plan, knowledge, identity, or absence of mistake or accident.

The use of character evidence as circumstantial evidence at trial poses some important evidentiary concerns. A party may wish to introduce evidence of good character (e.g., honesty) or bad character (e.g., violent tendencies) to create the inference that during the incident in question an individual actually conformed his or her conduct to the particular character trait. While it may seem logical that one will conform his or her conduct to his or her character traits, it is also clear that significant prejudicial dangers exist in the use of such evidence. Will such evidence distract the jury from concentrating on the question of what actually happened during the incident in question? Will the jury be tempted to reward the "good" and penalize the "bad"? Because of the significant dangers of jury confusion of issues and prejudice, the use of character evidence is regulated.

Character Evidence in Criminal Cases

Federal Rule 404 is clear that character evidence is generally not admissible "to prove conduct," that is, it is generally not admissible to show that one "acted in conformity therewith on a particular occasion." However, this rule is not absolute.

While the prosecutor is not allowed to introduce evidence of the defendant's bad character, the defendant is allowed, if he or she so elects, to introduce evidence of good character. This is so, provided that such evidence is relevant to the charges against the defendant (i.e., it is evidence "of a pertinent trait," as Federal Rule 404 states).

Example.

> The defendant is charged with larceny. Evidence of his reputation for honesty in the community may be admitted. Such evidence is "of a pertinent trait."

If the defendant does elect to put a character witness on the witness stand to testify as to defendant's good character, then this "opens the door" (as attorneys say) for the prosecution to provide rebuttal evidence. If the defendant elects not to "open the door," then the prosecutor is generally prohibited from using character evidence, and he or she may not comment to the jury on the defendant's failure "to open the door."

Character Evidence of the Victim.

As to evidence of the victim's character, Federal Rule 404 states that evidence "of a pertinent trait" may be admissible to prove the conformity of the victim's actions.

Example.

> The defendant is claiming self-defense as the defense in his murder trial. The defendant may introduce evidence of the victim's violent tendencies to create an inference that the victim was the aggressor during the incident in question.[6]

Sex Offense Cases and Victim's Past Behavior

As stated above, Federal Rule 404 allows the admission of evidence "of a pertinent trait" of the victim's character to prove the conformity of the victim's actions. In certain sex offense cases (e.g., rape cases), consent serves as a basic defense at trial, and, until recent years, the general view was that the defendant could introduce evidence of the victim's sexual character as character evidence to create an inference that the victim consented to sexual intercourse during the incident in question. This view has changed with a number of states now prohibiting such evidence of the victim's sexual character.

The Federal Rules of Evidence also deals with the issue, attempting to reconcile conflicting policy interests to encourage the privacy of the victim and victim's cooperation with the need to conduct a fair trial. This is done by the application of a complex, special rule, Rule 412 (see Appendix A).[7]

Basically, Federal Rule 412 prevents the use of reputation evidence and opinion evidence concerning "the past sexual behavior" of the victim. Evidence of specific instances of sexual behavior is also generally inadmissible, although such evidence may be admissible if one of the three circumstances listed in Rule 412 exists:

(1)   It is constitutionally required; or

(2)   It concerns past sexual behavior by the alleged victim with individuals other than the accused, and it is offered by the accused to show that the accused was not the source of the semen or injury to the alleged victim; or

(3)   It concerns past sexual behavior by the alleged victim with the accused, and it is offered by the accused to show that the victim

consented to the particular sexual behavior "with respect to which such offense is alleged."

Even if one of the three circumstances exists in a case, the evidence is not automatically admissible. Prior written notice, a private ("in chambers") court hearing, and the court's prior approval for the admission of the evidence is required.[8] This must be done pursuant to the detailed procedure stated in subdivisions (c)(1), (c)(2) and (c)(3) of Rule 412. The court's prior approval for the admission of the evidence is secured only if the accused's evidence is relevant and the evidence's probative value "outweighs the danger of unfair prejudice" to the alleged victim.

Use of Evidence of Other Crimes

Federal Rule 404 presents the general rule that evidence of "other crimes, wrongs, or acts" is not admissible "to prove the character of a person in order to show action in conformity therewith." However, some important subtleties exist.

Evidence of "other crimes, wrongs, or acts" may be admissible, not to show that the defendant was "bad" and "acted in conformity therewith," but for *other purposes*, such as to establish "motive, opportunity, intent, preparation, plan, knowledge, identity, or absence of mistake or accident."

Example.

> Proof of the defendant's past crimes
> may establish a pattern or manner of
> committing offenses by the defendant
> (attorneys often use the word
> "modus operandi"). The "modus
> operandi" of the defendant when
> compared with the manner of
> committing the offense in the
> incident in question may be used to
> establish the *identity* of the
> defendant as the guilty party. For
> example, the defendant is shown to
> have committed four prior rapes.
> The rapes have all occurred in a
> certain park, at a certain time,
> with the defendant using a
> particular disguise, technique and
> weapon. The manner of committing
> the rape in the incident in question
> was the same.[9]

Of course, where the prosecutor introduces
evidence of the defendant's alleged past crimes,
the defendant is allowed to introduce evidence
that he or she did not commit the past crimes.
Also, while the prosecutor need not show that
the defendant committed the past crimes "beyond
a reasonable doubt," he or she should have
"sufficient evidence for the jury to find that
the defendant in fact committed the extrinsic
offense" and that there is no undue prejudice in

admitting the evidence.[10] The Supreme Court has submitted a proposed rule for Congressional consideration, which would amend Rule 404(d) to require notice from the prosecutor to the accused as to the general nature of such Rule 404(d) evidence the prosecutor intends to introduce at trial (see the note at the end of Appendix A for additional information regarding this proposed amendment). Such a change will provide the defendant with the opportunity to prepare his or her defense to the prosecutor's use of evidence of other crimes.

Character Evidence in Civil Cases

The general rule is that character evidence is not admissible in civil cases to show that a party "acted in conformity therewith on a particular occasion."

Example.

Evidence of the defendant's reputation as a "bad driver" or "speedster" should not be admissible to prove that the defendant was negligent in the particular incident in question.

The general view does not allow a party to introduce evidence of good character, followed by rebuttal evidence (i.e., the election which "opens the door" in the criminal case).

It should be remembered, however, that where a party's character or reputation is directly *in issue* at trial, such evidence may be admissible. In other words, the character evidence is not being offered to show that a party "acted in conformity therewith on a particular occasion." The evidence is being offered to establish character or reputation that is an issue itself.

Example.

> A basic rule in libel and slander cases (defamation actions) is that truth is a defense to the party being sued. If the plaintiff is suing the defendant because the defendant publicly called the plaintiff "a whore, a harlot," plaintiff's character is in issue. Therefore, character evidence may be allowed by either party. Additionally, if in the slander case the plaintiff is claiming damages for loss to reputation, then plaintiff's reputation is in issue, and reputation evidence may be allowed.

Character Evidence of a Witness

As previously stated, the credibility of a witness is always in issue. Therefore, the credibility of a witness may be attacked at trial.

In line with this rule, character evidence of a witness referring to untruthfulness is generally admissible at trial. Of course, if a witness' credibility is attacked, the attorney for the other party may rebut with evidence of truthful character.[11]

Proof of Character

Federal Rule 404 deals with the admissibility of character evidence. Federal Rule 405 states the proper "methods of proving character:"

Rule 405[12]

METHODS OF PROVING CHARACTER

(a) Reputation or opinion. In all cases in which evidence of character or a trait of character of a person is admissible, proof may be made by testimony as to reputation or by testimony in the form of an opinion. On cross-examination, inquiry is allowable into relevant specific instances of conduct.

(b) Specific Instances of Conduct. In cases in which

character or a trait of character of
a person is an essential element of
a charge, claim, or defense, proof
may also be made of specific
instances of conduct.

Rule 405 presents three "methods of
proving character" in those situations where
character evidence is admissible: testimony as
to reputation, testimony as to opinion, and
testimony as to specific instances of conduct.

As to the use of testimony of specific
instances of conduct, this method is generally
limited to situations where character "is an
essential element" of the case or on cross-
examination.

Basically, evidence of character is
provided by testimony as to reputation or
opinion testimony. Testimony as to reputation
is the traditional method used to bring in
direct, circumstantial evidence of character.
In general form, reputation testimony involves
the character witness testifying as to the
reputation of the defendant *in the community*.
With opinion testimony, the character witness
does not testify as to reputation in the
community, he or she testifies as to his or her
personal opinion of the defendant's character.

Example.

> The character witness testifies, "It is my opinion that the defendant, John Smith, is a peace-loving, good person." Although opinion testimony is available under the Federal Rules of Evidence, the student should be aware that many states do not permit the use of such evidence as a method of proving character.

Habit Evidence

Many of us have certain habits which guide our actions.

Example.

> We may drive a specific route every day to get from home to work and back.

Additionally, organizations may have routine practices.

Example.

> A gas station receives payment for self-service gasoline in advance of pumping.

Is evidence of such habits and routine practices relevant to establish conduct? While in many states the answer is "no," the answer is "yes" under the Federal Rules of Evidence:

Rule 406[13]
HABIT; ROUTINE PRACTICE

Evidence of the habit of a person or of the routine practice of an organization, whether corroborated or not and regardless of the presence of eyewitnesses, is relevant to prove that the conduct of the person or organization on a particular occasion was in conformity with the habit or routine practice.

Subsequent Repairs

Assume that you are the plaintiff's attorney in a civil case. Your client was severely injured when a sign belonging to the defendant fell on your client in front of the defendant's business. The day after the accident the defendant re-hung the sign with chain rather than wire. The defendant is on the witness stand, and you are asking various questions leading to a question or questions regarding the method of re-hanging the sign. You want the defendant to testify as to the use of the chain rather than the wire. May you ask a question designed to produce such testimony? Probably not, if the remedial measure is being offered to show that the chain should have been used in the first place. Simply put, you can not use such evidence as evidence that the defendant was negligent.

The rule for the inadmissibility of evidence of subsequent repairs or remedial measures is grounded in public policy, specifically, an interest in encouraging repairs, and, therefore, preventing further injuries. The Federal Rules of Evidence continue this basic rule in Rule 407:

Rule 407[14]
SUBSEQUENT REMEDIAL MEASURES

When, after an event, measures are taken which, if taken previously, would have made the event less likely to occur, evidence of the subsequent measures is not admissible to prove negligence or culpable conduct in connection with the event. This rule does not require the exclusion of evidence of subsequent measures when offered for another purpose, such as proving ownership, control, or feasibility of precautionary measures, if controverted, or impeachment.

The student should remember, however, that the rule may allow such evidence when offered for the other purposes, if controverted, or for purposes of impeachment.[15]

Example.

If there is a question as to the ownership or control of the sign, evidence of the defendant's re-hanging may be admissible to help establish the defendant's ownership or control over the property.

Evidence of Compromise, Offers to Compromise and Payment of Expenses

Public policy concerns affect the admissibility of evidence of compromise, offers to compromise and payment of expenses.

Public policy encourages settlements of disputes. This policy, along with the fact that compromises and attempts to compromise do not necessarily establish liability, serve as the basis for a general rule of evidence making such evidence inadmissible as proof of liability. Federal Rule 408 continues the basic rule.[16] Additionally, because of a policy to encourage payment of an injured person's expenses and, therefore, to encourage humanitarian actions, "evidence of furnishing or offering or promising to pay medical, hospital, or similar expenses occasioned by an injury is not admissible to prove liability for the injury."[17]

Liability Insurance

Insurance evidence may have a prejudicial effect on the defendant's case. If the jury is made aware of the existence of insurance coverage, it may be encouraged to render a verdict or provide a substantial award for the injured plaintiff. The Federal Rules of Evidence follow basic law:

Rule 411[18]
LIABILITY INSURANCE

Evidence that a person was or was not insured against liability is not admissible upon the issue whether the person acted negligently or otherwise wrongfully. This rule does not require the exclusion of evidence of insurance against liability when offered for another purpose, such as proof of agency, ownership or control, or bias or prejudice of a witness.

Pleas and Plea Discussions

Public policy favors meaningful plea discussions. To encourage such discussions and to prevent highly prejudicial evidence from being admitted, a basic rule of evidence exists to restrict the admissibility of plea offers and related statements. This is established in the Federal Rules of Evidence with Rule 410:

Rule 410[19]
INADMISSIBILITY OF PLEAS,
PLEA DISCUSSIONS,
AND RELATED STATEMENTS

Except as otherwise provided in this rule, evidence of the following is not, in any civil or criminal proceeding, admissible against the defendant who made the plea or was a participant in the plea discussions:

(1) A plea of guilty which was later withdrawn;

(2) A plea of nolo contendere;

(3) Any statement made in the course of any proceedings under Rule 11 of the Federal Rules of Criminal Procedure or comparable state procedure regarding either of the foregoing pleas; or

(4) Any statement made in the course of plea discussions with an attorney for the prosecuting authority which do not result in a plea of guilty or which result in a plea of guilty later withdrawn. However, such a statement is admissible (i) in any proceeding wherein another statement made in the course of the same plea or plea discussions has been introduced and the statement ought in fairness be considered contemporaneously with it, or (ii) in a criminal proceeding for perjury or false statement if the statement was made by the defendant under oath, on the record and in the presence of counsel.

A properly accepted guilty plea is not restricted by Rule 410. In general, Rule 410 restricts evidence of withdrawn guilty pleas, offers to plead and related statements.[20]

NOTES

1.   FED. R. EVID. 401.

2.   FED. R. EVID. 402.

3.   See Wagner v. State, Ind., 474 N.E.2d 476 (1985).

4.   FED. R. EVID. 403.

5.   FED. R. EVID. 404.

6.   See State v. Miranda, 176 Conn. 107, 405 A2d 622 (1978) for an excellent discussion of this use of evidence.

7.   FED. R. EVID. 412.

8.   For a review of the constitutional justification for such exclusion of evidence, see Doe v. U.S., 666 F.2d 43 (4th Cir. 1981).

9.   Of course, the common aspects of the prior offenses and the crime for which the defendant is being tried must have sufficient uniqueness to set them off from crimes committed by other persons.   See U.S. v. Bailleaux, 685 F.2d 1105 (9th Cir. 1982).

10.   United States V. Beechum, 582 F.2d 898 (5th Cir. 1978).

11.   FED. R. EVID. 404, 607, 608. See also, FED. R. EVID. 609, as to ability to attack the credibility of a witness by showing evidence of prior felony convictions.

12.   FED. R. EVID. 405.

13.   FED. R. EVID. 406.

14.   FED. R. EVID. 407.

15.   As to impeachment, see Kenny v. Southeastern Pennsylvania Transp. Authority, 581 F.32d 351 (3rd Cir. 1978), cert. denied 439 U.S. 1073.

16.   FED. R. EVID. 408.

17.   FED. R. EVID. 409.

18.   FED. R. EVID. 411. Note that exclusion is not required for "another purpose," e.g., bias. In Charter v. Chleborad, 551 F.2d 246 (8th Cir. 1977), a defense witness worked in part for the insurer of the defendant and evidence of insurance was admissible.

19.   FED. R. EVID. 410.

20.   See U.S. v. Albane, 414 F. Supp. 67 (1976).

REVIEW AND DISCUSSION QUESTIONS

1. What is the general rule as to the admissibility of relevant evidence? Distinguish "relevancy" from "materiality."

2. What is the significance of Rule 403? Does the rule give too much discretion to the judge? Why or why not? Explain.

3. Why is character evidence generally inadmissible?

4. Is there a difference between the admissibility of character evidence in criminal cases and civil cases? Explain.

5. Discuss the availability of the various methods to proving character (i.e., the application of Rule 405). Do you support the restrictions found in Rule 412? Explain your position.

6. While the federal courts generally admit evidence of habit and routine practice, many state courts do not. Should such evidence be available? Why or why not? Explain.

7. Discuss the public policy concerns affecting the admissibility of evidence of subsequent repairs, compromise, offers to

compromise, and payment of expenses. Is this good policy? Explain.

8. Why is evidence of insurance generally not admissible upon the issue of wrongful conduct?

9. Review Rule 410. Does the rule strike a good balance among conflicting needs of our justice system? Explain your position.

Chapter Four

WITNESS COMPETENCY

Rule 601[1]
GENERAL RULE OF COMPETENCY

Every person is competent to
be a witness except as otherwise
provided in these rules. However,
in civil actions and proceedings
with respect to an element of a
claim or defense as to which state
law supplies the rule of decision,
the competency of a witness shall be
determined in accordance with state
law.

An Overview of Witness Competency

A competent witness is a person allowed by
the law to testify in a case. The early law
limited to a much greater extent the number of
persons allowed to be witnesses. Our modern law
tends to narrow the grounds of incompetency,
leaving to the trier of fact the determination

of the "weight" and credibility to be given to the testimony received.

Example.

> At one time under the common law a person who had a financial interest in the outcome of the case might be disqualified as a witness (e.g., the party to a civil action or the party's business partner). Today, the person is not incompetent to testify. However, the trier of fact can consider the interest of the party in determining what weight and credibility to give to the testimony.

The grounds for incompetency of witnesses vary with the jurisdiction. An example of one state statute on witness incompetency is that found in the Indiana Code:

> I.C. 34-1-14-5. Who are incompetent. Except as otherwise provided by statute, the following persons shall not be competent witnesses:
>
> (1) Persons insane at the time they are offered as witnesses, whether they have been so adjudged or not.

(2) Attorneys, as to confidential communications made to them in the course of their professional business, and as to advice given in such cases.

(3) Physicians, as to matter communicated to them, as such, by patients, in the course of their professional business, or advice given in such cases.

(4) Clergymen, as to confessions or admissions made to them in course of discipline enjoined by their respective churches.

(5) Husband and wife, as to communications made to each other.[2]

Federal Incompetency Law

Federal Rule 601 makes it clear that federal incompetency law (as established in other rules in Article VI of the Federal Rules of Evidence) does not apply in all federal court cases. State incompetency law may apply instead in certain civil actions in federal court where state law must supply "the rule of decision." An example of such a situation is the federal diversity jurisdiction action (federal diversity jurisdiction is described in Chapter Eleven).

Where federal incompetency law does apply, a liberal law exists. For example, unlike many states, the federal rules do not mention a presumption of incompetency for children, nor do the rules discuss a witness mental incompetency.

The Requirements of Personal
Knowledge and Oath or Affirmation

Rule 602[3]
LACK OF PERSONAL KNOWLEDGE

A witness may not testify to a matter unless evidence is introduced sufficient to support a finding that the witness has personal knowledge of the matter. Evidence to prove personal knowledge may, but need not, consist of the witness' own testimony. This rule is subject to the provisions of Rule 703, relating to opinion testimony by expert witnesses.

Rule 603[4]
OATH OR AFFIRMATION

Before testifying, every witness shall be required to declare that the witness will testify truthfully, by oath or affirmation administered

in a form calculated to awaken the
witness' conscience and impress the
witness' mind with the duty to do
so.

Except for expert witness testimony
(discussed in Chapter Six), the Federal Rules of
Evidence require a witness to have "personal
knowledge of the subject matter" about which he
or she testifies. Basically, personal knowledge
means direct sensory perception of the facts,
e.g., seeing A slash B with the knife, hearing V
scream, smelling the marijuana, etc.[5] The
standard for determining whether for not an
individual has personal knowledge of a
particular matter is one of reasonableness. In
other words, if a reasonable person could
conclude that personal knowledge exists, then it
should be found to exist. The witness should
then be allowed to testify.

Additionally, before testifying, the
witness must "declare that he will testify
truthfully, by oath or affirmation." An oath to
God is unnecessary, as an affirmation (which
does not mention God, but refers to perjury) is
sufficient.

From a practical point of view, the
requirement in Federal Rule 603 provides some
flexibility to the court in dealing with

children and mental incompetents. The witness must understand the need to tell the truth. If the witness can not understand this obligation, the witness does not possess a minimum competency to testify. Also, a witness may be so poor in expressing himself or herself as to preclude the relevancy of the testimony (Rule 401) or promote such confusion or prejudice (Rule 403) as to allow exclusion of the testimony by the judge.

The Special Issue of Children and Witness Competency

The preceding paragraph raises an issue of special concern in evidence. Certainly, the Federal Rules of Evidence do not expressly prohibit a child from being a witness. However, in view of the requirement that a witness understand the obligation to testify truthfully, it may be necessary to make a special inquiry of a child witness' competence.

Example.

The following quote is from the Supreme Court of Indiana in *Tuggle v. State*, 457 N.E.2d 1094 (Ind. 1984):

Defendant first contends that the trial court erred in finding that the victim was competent to testify.

The record shows that she was nine years old and in the third grade at school at the time of the trial. Our statute establishes a presumption of incompetence for children under ten years of age "unless it appears that they understand the nature and obligation of an oath." Ind. Code 34-1-14-5 (Burns 1983 Supp.).

In this case, the victim was questioned by both the prosecutor and defense counsel about her understanding of an oath and the difference between telling the truth and telling a lie. She testified that she knew the difference between the truth and a lie. She stated that she knew she would "get in trouble" and "be grounded" or "go to jail" if she told a lie. She also said that she understood that taking an oath meant that you promised to tell the truth. The following colloquy then took place between the victim and the trial judge:

THE COURT: "..., in school, does your teacher ever let you just make up stories and write them for entertainment?"

THE WITNESS: "Yes."

THE COURT: "You understand that this is not the schoolroom, this is different here, that you can't make up stories or pretend stories, do you understand?"

THE WITNESS: "Yes."

THE COURT: "And the oath that I gave you when I had you raise your right hand and swear to tell the truth, that means that you have to tell the truth and nothing but the truth, can you do that?"

THE WITNESS: "Yes."

THE COURT: "You won't make up any pretending stories?"

THE WITNESS: "No."

THE COURT: "As I understood it, you said that you would get grounded, if you lied, by your Mom?"

THE WITNESS: "Yes."

THE COURT: "Would it be wrong for you to lie about something even knowing that you might not get caught at it?"

THE WITNESS: "Yes."

THE COURT: "Do you think that is wrong or right?"

THE WITNESS: "Wrong."

This was sufficient evidence to show that the victim knew the difference between telling a lie and telling the truth and knew that she would be punished for telling a lie.[6]

Interpreters

Rule 604[7]
INTERPRETERS

An interpreter is subject to the provision of these rules relating to qualification as an expert and the administration of an oath or affirmation to make a true translation.

Obviously, if a witness speaks a foreign language and can not be understood by the trier of fact, he or she needs an interpreter. One is not an incompetent witness because he or she speaks a foreign language.

It is important for the student to remember that the interpreter holds an important position. The trier of fact relies on the truthfulness of the interpretation. Therefore, the interpreter must be sworn to make a true translation. This means that the interpreter can be subject to perjury for failing to translate truthfully. Also, Rule 604 requires that the interpreter qualify as an expert. This means that the interpreter must be capable intellectually of properly performing the important role.

Competency of Judges and Jurors as Witnesses

Under Federal Rule 605, a judge is incompetent to testify at a trial over which he or she presides.[8] This is not the view in all jurisdictions. Some states leave the decision to testify to the judge's personal discretion. The student should note that the prohibition is to the presiding judge. A judge is not an incompetent witness merely because he or she is a judge; he or she may testify at other trials.

Federal Rule 606 presents the modern view that, assuming a party objects, a juror "may not testify as a witness before that jury in the trial of the case in which the juror is sitting."[9] Not all states, however, prevent the juror from so testifying.[10]

Competency of Attorneys as Witnesses

An attorney is not an incompetent witness. The general rule is that he or she may be called to testify at a trial in which the attorney is representing a party. However, if an attorney is called as a witness in such a situation, he or she faces some particular concerns which could preclude testimony as to certain matters or preclude continued representation of the party:

(1) If the attorney is called by the adverse party, the attorney-client privilege may arise (along with the attorney's ethical obligation "to maintain the confidences of the client").[11] The attorney-client privilege is discussed in Chapter Eleven.

(2) If the attorney is called to testify on behalf of the client, another ethical obligation may arise. The mandatory Disciplinary Rules of the attorneys' Code of Professional Responsibility present the ethical obligation.

Under DR 5-101, an attorney is not allowed to enter into employment if the attorney knows or should know that he or she will be called as a witness.[12] There are some exceptions to this basic rule. For example, an attorney may enter into the employment relationship where the testimony will concern uncontested matters or formal issues (where "substantial evidence" will not be submitted in opposition to the attorney's testimony). Additionally, the attorney may enter unto the employment if to do otherwise would work a "substantial hardship" against the client due to a special value of the attorney to his or her client in the case.[13]

Also, under DR 5-102, the attorney, who already took a case, not expecting to be called as a witness, should withdraw as the attorney in the case, when the attorney realizes that he or she will (or should) be called to testify on behalf of the client (the same exceptions apply as under DR 5-101).[14]

The basic rationale for the requirements is that an attorney does not serve his or her client well as a witness. This is so because, as a witness, an attorney may be more easily impeached for bias in favor of the client. Additionally, the roles of advocate and witness simply do not mix. As indicated in an Ethical Consideration of the Code of Professional Responsibility, EC 5-9, "(t)he roles of an advocate and of a witness are inconsistent; the function of an advocate is to advance or argue the cause of another, while that of a witness is to state facts objectively."[15]

NOTES

1.   FED. R. EVID. 601.

2.   Ind. Code 34-1-14-5. The student should note that the incompetency in some categories is partial, as to certain testimony only.

3.   FED. R. EVID. 602.

4.   FED. R. EVID. 603.

5.   See generally U.S. v. Lyon, 567 F.2d 777 (8th Cir. 1977), cert. denied 465 U.S. 918.

6.   Tuggle v. State, 457 N.E.2d 1094, 1906 (Ind. 1984).

7.   FED. R. EVID. 604.

8.   FED. R. EVID. 605.

9.   FED. R. EVID. 606.

10.   See Phillips v. VanHorn, 68 N.W. 452 (Iowa 1896). But note, few people with personal knowledge of a case will be allowed to sit as jurors after the "voir dire."

11.   Code of Prof. Responsibility DR 4-101.   In August, 1983, the American Bar Association approved a new code of professional responsibility entitled "Model Rules of Professional Conduct" (Model Rules).   The individual states (through their high courts) decide on whether they will adopt the Model Rules for attorneys practicing within their

jurisdictions. Most states have adopted or are considering the adoption of the new rules. The new Model Rules do affect the concenpt of confidentiality. This is noted further in Chapter Eleven. Model Rule 1.6 deals primarily with the issue. However, the new rules do not significantly vary the import of the requirement prohibiting an attorney from serving as a witness for his or her client. Therefore, the discussion in this chapter regarding this aspect of the Rules of Professional Responsibility holds true.

12. Code of Prof. Responsibility, DR 5-101(B).

13. Id.

14. Code of Prof. Responsibility, DR 5-102.

15. Code of Prof. Responsibility, EC 5-9. See also MacArthur v. Bank of New York, 524 F.Supp. 1205 (S.D.N.Y. 1981).

REVIEW AND DISCUSSION QUESTIONS

1.   Does your state's witness incompetency law differ significantly from federal law? If so, how does it differ?

2.   Is the modern trend to narrow the grounds of incompetency (leaving to the trier of fact the determination of the "weight" and

credibility to be given to the testimony received) preferable to the early law's broader limitations of competent persons to testify? Why or why not?

3. Review the Rule 602 and Rule 603 requirements of witnesses. How may they be used in dealing with children and mental incompetents?

4. If the presiding judge in a case has relevant information, why not let him or her testify (i.e., make the decision one within the court's discretion)? Compare Rule 605 with your state's incompetency law.

5. If an attorney is called as a witness in a case where he or she is representing a party, why does the attorney face some particular concerns? What are those concerns? Explain. Has your state's high court adopted the more recently proposed "Model Rules of Professional Conduct?"

FOCUS II:

CHILDREN AS WITNESSES - THE CONFRONTATION CLAUSE AND CHILDREN TESTIFYING OUTSIDE THE PHYSICAL PRESENCE OF THE DEFENDANT

Issue: Chapter Four considered the special issue of children and witness competency. Another important issue involving children as witnesses is the constitutionality of statutes allowing children in child abuse cases to testify against a defendant outside of the defendant's physical presence. Do such laws violate the Confrontation Clause of the Sixth Amendment? The Supreme Court decided this issue in its 1990 decision in *Maryland v. Craig*.

Maryland v. Craig

497 U.S. - , 111 L Ed.2d 666, 110 S.Ct. 3157 (1991)

Justice O'Connor delivered the opinion of the Court.

This case requires us to decide whether the Confrontation Clause of the Sixth Amendment categorically prohibits a child witness in a child abuse case from testifying against a defendant at trial, outside the defendant's physical presence, by one-way closed circuit television.

In October, 1986, a Howard County grand jury charged respondent, Sandra Ann Craig, with child abuse, first and second degree sexual offenses, perverted sexual practice, assault, and battery. The named victim in each count was Brooke Etze, a six-year-old child who, from August 1984 to June 1986, had attended a kindergarten center owned and operated by Craig.

In March, 1987, before the case went to trial, the State sought to invoke a Maryland statutory procedure that permits a judge to receive, by one-way closed circuit television, the testimony of a child witness who is alleged to be a victim of child abuse.[1] To invoke the procedure, the trial judge must first "determin[e] that testimony by the child victim in the courtroom will result in the child suffering serious emotional distress such that the child cannot reasonably communicate." Md.Cts. & Jud.Proc.Code Ann. Sec. 9-102(a)(1)(ii) (1989). Once the procedure is invoked, the child witness, prosecutor, and defense counsel withdraw to a separate room; the judge, jury, and defendant remain in the courtroom. The child witness is then examined and cross-examined in the separate room, while a video monitor records and displays the witness' testimony to those in the courtroom. During this time the witness cannot see the defendant.

The defendant remains in electronic communication with defense counsel, and objections may be made and ruled on as if the witness were testifying in the courtroom.

In support of its motion invoking the one-way closed circuit television procedure, the State presented expert testimony that Brooke, as well as a number of other children who were alleged to have been sexually abused by Craig, would suffer "serious emotional distress such that [they could not] reasonably communicate," Sec 9-102(a)(1)(ii), if required to testify in the courtroom. App. 7-59. The Maryland Court of Appeals characterized the evidence as follows:

> "The expert testimony in each case suggested that each child would have some or considerable difficulty in testifying in Craig's presence. For example, as to one child, the expert said that what 'would cause him the most anxiety would be to testify in front of Mrs. Craig....' The child 'wouldn't be able to communicate effectively.' As to another, an expert said she 'would probably stop talking and she would withdraw and curl up.' With respect to two others, the testimony was that one would 'become highly agitated, that he may refuse to talk

or if he did talk, that he would choose his subject regardless of the questions' while the other would 'become extremely timid and unwilling to talk.'" 316 Md. 551, 568-569, 560 A.2d 1120, 1128-1129 (1989).

Craig objected to the use of the procedure on Confrontation Clause grounds, but the trial court rejected the contention, concluding that although that statute "take[s] away the right of the defendant to be face to face with his or her accuser," the defendant retains the "essence of the right of confrontation," including the right to observe, cross-examine, and have the jury view the demeanor of the witness. App. 65-66. The trial court further found that, "based upon the evidence presented... the testimony of each of these children in a courtroom will result in each child suffering serious emotional distress... such that each of these children cannot reasonably communicate." *Id.*, at 66. The trial court then found Brooke and three other children competent to testify and accordingly permitted them to testify against Craig via the one-way closed circuit television procedure. The jury convicted Craig on all counts, and the Maryland Court of Special Appeals affirmed the convictions, 76 Md.App. 250, 544 A.2d 784 (1988).

The Court of Appeals of Maryland reversed and remanded for a new trial. 316 Md. 551, 560 A.2d 1120 (1989). The Court of Appeals rejected Craig's argument that the Confrontation Clause requires in all cases a face-to-face courtroom encounter between the accused and his accusers, *id.*, at 556-562, 560 A.2d, at 1122-1125, but concluded:

> "[U]nder (Md.) Sec. 9-102(a)(1)(ii), the operative 'serious emotional distress' which renders a child victim unable to 'reasonably communicate' must be determined to arise, at least primarily, from face-to-face confrontation with the defendant. Thus, we construe the phrase 'in the courtroom' as meaning, for sixth amendment and confrontation purposes, 'in the courtroom in the presence of the defendant.' Unless prevention of 'eyeball-to-eyeball' confrontation is necessary to obtain the trial testimony of the child, the defendant cannot be denied that right." *Id.*, at 556, 560 A.2d, at 1127.

Reviewing the trial court's finding and the evidence presented in support of the Sec. 9-102 procedure, the Court of Appeals held that, "as [it] read *Coy* [v. Iowa, 487 U.S. 1012, 108 S.Ct.

2798, 101 L.Ed.2d. 857 (1988)], the showing made by the State was insufficient to reach the high threshold required by that case before Sec. 9-102 may be invoked." *Id.* 316 Md., at 554-555, 560 A.2d, at 1121 (footnote omitted).

We granted certiorari to resolve the important Confrontation Clause issues raised by this case. 493 U.S.-, 110 S.Ct. 834, 107 L.Ed.2d 830 (1990).

The Confrontation Clause of the Sixth Amendment, made applicable to the States through the Fourteenth Amendment, provides: "In all criminal prosecutions, the accused shall enjoy the right ... to be confronted with the witnesses against him."

We observed in *Coy v. Iowa* that "the Confrontation Clause guarantees the defendant a face-to-face meeting with the witnesses appearing before the trier of fact." 487 U.S., at 1016, 108 S,Ct., at 2800 .... This interpretation derives not only from the literal text of the Clause, but also from our understanding of its historical roots. See *Coy, supra,* 487 U.S., at 1015-1016 (Confrontation Clause intended to prevent conviction by affidavit); *Green, supra,* 399 U.S. at 156....

We have never held, however, that the Confrontation Clause guarantees criminal defendants the *absolute* right to a face-to-face

meeting with witnesses against them at trial.
Indeed, in *Coy v. Iowa*, we expressly "le[ft] for
another day ... the question whether any
exceptions exist" to the "irreducible literal
meaning of the Clause: 'a right to *meet face to
face* all those who appear and give evidence *at
trial.*'" 487 U.S., at 1021 (quoting *Green,
supra*, 399 U.S., at 175 (Harlan, J.,
concurring)). The procedure challenged in *Coy*
involved the placement of a screen that
prevented two child witnesses in a child abuse
case from seeing the defendant as they testified
against him at trial. See 487 U.S., at 1014-
1015. In holding that the use of this procedure
violated the defendant's right to confront
witnesses against him, we suggested that any
exception to the right "would surely be allowed
only when necessary to further an important
public policy"-*i.e.*, only upon a showing of
something more than the generalized,
"legislatively imposed presumption of trauma"
underlying the statute at issue in that case.
Id., at 1021; see also *id.*, at 1025 (concurring
opinion). We concluded that "[s]ince there had
been no individualized findings that these
particular witnesses needed special protection,
the judgment [in the case before us] could not
be sustained by any conceivable exception." *Id*,
at 1021. Because the trial court in this case
made individualized findings that each of the
child witnesses needed special protection, this

case requires us to decide the question reserved in *Coy*.

The central concern of the Confrontation Clause is to ensure the reliability of the evidence against a criminal defendant by subjecting it to rigorous testing in the context as an adversary proceeding before the trier of fact. The word "confront," after all, also means clashing of forces or ideas, thus carrying with it the notion of adversariness. As we noted in our earliest case interpreting the Clause:

> "The primary object of the constitutional provision in question was to prevent depositions or *ex parte* affidavits, such as were sometimes admitted in civil cases, being used against the prisoner in lieu of a personal examination and cross-examination of the witness in which the accused has an opportunity, not only of testing the recollection and sifting the conscience of the witness, but of compelling him to stand face to face with the jury in order that they may look at him, and judge by his demeanor upon the stand and the manner in which he gives his testimony whether he is worthy of

belief." *Mattox, supra,* 156 U.S.,
at 242-243.

As this description indicates, the right
guaranteed by the Confrontation Clause includes
not only a "personal examination, *id,* at 242,
but also "(1) insures that the witness will give
his statements under oath-thus impressing him
with the seriousness of the matter and guarding
against the lie by the possibility of a penalty
for perjury; (2) forces the witness to submit to
cross-examination, the 'greatest legal engine
ever invented for the discovery of truth'; [and]
(3) permits the jury that is to decide the
defendant's fate to observe the demeanor of the
witness in making his statement, thus aiding the
jury in assessing his credibility." *Green* 399
U.S., at 158.

The combined effect of these elements of
confrontation-physical presence, oath, cross-
examination, and observation of demeanor by the
trier of fact-serves the purposes of the
Confrontation Clause by insuring that evidence
admitted against an accused is reliable and
subject to the rigorous adversarial testing that
is the norm of Anglo-American criminal
proceedings. ....

We have recognized, for example, the face-
to-face confrontation enhances the accuracy of
factfinding by reducing the risk that a witness
will wrongfully implicate an innocent person.

See *Coy,* 487 U.S., at 1019-1020 ("It is always
more difficult to tell a lie about a person 'to
his face' than 'behind his back.' .... That
face-to-face presence may, unfortunately, upset
the truthful rape victim or abused child; but by
the same token it may confound and undo the
false accuser, or reveal the child coached by a
malevolent adult"); *Ohio v. Roberts,* 448 U.S.
56, 63, n.6 (1980); see also 3 W. Blackstone,
Commentaries *373-374. We have also noted the
strong symbolic purpose served by requiring
adverse witnesses at trial to testify in the
accused's presence. See *Coy, supra,* 487 U.S.,
at 1017 ("[T]here is something deep in human
nature that regards face-to-face confrontation
between accused and accuser as 'essential to a
fair trial in a criminal prosecution'") (quoting
Pointer v. Texas, 380 U.S. 400, 404, 85 S.Ct.
1065, 1068, 13 L.Ed.2d 923 (1965)).

Although face-to-face-confrontation forms
"the core of the values furthered by the
Confrontation Clause," *Green, supra,* 399 U.S.,
at 157, we have nevertheless recognized that it
is not the *sine qua non* of the confrontation
right. See *Delaware f. Fensterer,* 474 U.S. 15,
22, 106 S.Ct. 292, 295, 88 L.Ed.2d 15 (1985)
(*per curiam*) ("[T]he Confrontation Clause is
generally satisfied when the defense is given a
full and fair opportunity to probe and expose
infirmities [such as forgetfulness, confusion,
or evasion] through cross-examination, thereby

calling to the attention of the factfinder the reasons for giving scant weight to the witness' testimony"); *Roberts, supra,* 448 U.S., at 69 (oath, cross-examination, and demeanor provide "all that the Sixth Amendment demands: 'substantial compliance with the purposes behind the confrontation requirement'") (quoting *Green supra,* 399 U.S., at 166); see also *Stincer, supra,* 482 U.S. at 739-744 (confrontation right not violated by exclusion of defendant from competency hearing of child witnesses, where defendant had opportunity for full and effective cross-examination at trial)....

For this reason, we have never insisted on an actual face-to-face encounter at trial in *every* instance in which testimony is admitted against a defendant. Instead, we have repeatedly held that the Clause permits, where necessary, the admission of certain hearsay statements against a defendant despite the defendant's inability to confront the declarant at trial. See *e.g., Mattox,*156 U.S., at 243 ("[T]here could be nothing more directly contrary to the letter of the provision in question than the admission of dying declarations"); *Pointer, supra,* 380 U.S. at 407 (noting exceptions to the confrontation right for dying declarations and "other analogous situations"). In *Mattox,* for example, we held that the testimony of a government witness at a former trial against the defendant, where the witness was fully cross-examined but had died after the first trial, was admissible in evidence against the defendant at his second trial. See 156 U.S., at 240-244. We explained:

"There is doubtless reason for saying that ... if notes of [the witness's] testimony are permitted to be read, [the defendant] is deprived of the advantage of that personal presence of the witness before the jury which the law has designed for his protection. But general rules of law of this kind, however beneficent in their operation and valuable to the accused, must occasionally give way to considerations of public policy and the necessities of the case. To say that a criminal, after having once been convicted by the testimony of a certain witness, should go scot free simply because death has closed the mouth of that witness, would be carrying his constitutional protection to an unwarrantable extent. The law in its wisdom declares that the rights of the public shall not be wholly sacrificed in order that an incidental benefit may be preserved to the accused." *Id.*, at 243.

We have accordingly stated that a literal reading of the Confrontation Clause would "abrogate virtually every hearsay exception, a result long rejected as unintended and too extreme." *Roberts,* 448, U.S., at 63. Thus, in certain narrow circumstances, "competing interests, if 'closely examined,' may warrant dispensing with confrontation at trial." *Id.,* at 64 (quoting *Chambers v. Mississippi,* 410 U.S. 284, 295, 93 S.Ct. 1038, 35 L.Ed.2d 297 (1973), and citing *Mattox, supra.*). We have recently held, for example, that hearsay statements of nontestifying co-conspirators may be admitted against a defendant despite the lack of any face-to-face encounter with the accused. See *Bourjaily v. United States,* 483 U.S. 171, 107 S.Ct. 2775, 97 L.Ed.2d 144 (1987); *United States v. Inadi,* 475 U.S. 387, 106 S.Ct. 1121, 89 L.Ed.2d 390 (1986). Given our hearsay cases, the word "confront," as used in the Confrontation Clause, cannot simply mean face-to-face confrontation, for the Clause would then, contrary to our cases, prohibit the admission of any accusatory hearsay statement made by an absent declarant-a declarant who is undoubtedly as much a "witness against" a defendant as one who actually testifies at trial.

In sum, our precedents establish that "the Confrontation Clause reflects a *preference* for face-to face confrontation at trial," *Roberts, supra,* 448 U.S., at 63 (emphasis added; footnote omitted), a preference that "must occasionally give way to considerations of public policy and the necessities of the case," *Mattox, supra,* 156 U.S., at 243. "[W]e have attempted to harmonize the goal of the Clause-placing limits on the kind of evidence that may be received against a defendant-with a societal interest in accurate factfinding, which may require consideration of out-of-court statements." *Bourjaily, supra,* 483 U.S., at 182. We have accordingly interpreted the Confrontation Clause in a manner sensitive to its purposes and sensitive to the necessities of trial and the adversary process. See, *e.g., Kirby,* 174 U.S., at 61 ("It is scarcely necessary to say that to the rule that an accused is entitled to be confronted with witnesses against him the admission of dying declarations is an exception which arises from the necessity of the case"); *Chambers, supra,* 410 U.S., at 295 ("Of course, the right to confront and to cross-examine is not absolute and may, in appropriate cases, bow to accommodate other legitimate interest in the criminal trial process"). Thus, though we reaffirm the importance of face-to-face confrontation with witnesses appearing at trial, we cannot say that such confrontation is an indispensable element of the Sixth Amendment's guarantee of the right to confront one's accusers. Indeed, one commentator has noted that "[i]t is all but universally assumed that there are circumstances that excuse compliance with the right of confrontation." Graham, The Right of Confrontation and the Hearsay Rule: Sir Walter Raleigh Loses Another One, 8 Crim.L.Bull. 989, 107-108 (1972).

This interpretation of the Confrontation Clause is consistent with our cases holding that other Sixth Amendment rights must also be interpreted in the context of the necessities of trial and the adversary process. See *e.g.* *Illinois v. Allen,* 397 U.S. 337, 342-343, 90 S.Ct. 1057, 1060, 25 L.Ed.2d 353 (1970) (right to be present at trial not violated where trial judge removed defendant for disruptive behavior); *Ritchie,* 480 U.S., at 51-54 ... (right to *cross-examination not violated where* State denied defendant access to investigative files); *Taylor v. United States,* 484 U.S. 400, 410-416, 108 S.Ct. 646, 98 L.Ed.2d 798 (1988) (right to compulsory process not violated where trial judge precluded testimony of a surprise defense witness); *Perry v. Lecke,* 488 U.S. 272, 280-285, 109 S.Ct. 594, 102 L.Ed.2d 624 (1989) (right to effective assistance of counsel not violated where trial judge prevented testifying defendant from conferring with counsel during a short break in testimony). We show no reason to treat the face-to-face component of the confrontation right any differently, and indeed we think it would be anomalous to do so.

That the face-to-face confrontation requirement is not absolute does not, of course, mean that it may easily be dispensed with. As we suggested in *Coy*, our precedents confirm that a defendant's right to confront accusatory witnesses may be satisfied absent a physical, face-to-face confrontation at trial only where denial of such confrontation is necessary to further an important public policy and only where the reliability of the testimony is otherwise assured. See *Coy*, 487 U.S., at 1021 . . . .

Maryland's statutory procedure, when invoked, prevents a child witness from seeing the defendant as he or she testifies against the defendant at trial. We find it significant, however, that Maryland's procedure preserves all of the other elements of the confrontation right: the child witness must be competent to testify and must testify under oath; the defendant retains full opportunity for contemporaneous cross-examination; and the judge, jury, and defendant are able to view (albeit by video monitor) the demeanor (and body) of the witness as he or she testifies. Although we are mindful of the many subtle effects face-to-face confrontation may have on an adversary criminal proceeding, the presence of these other elements of confrontation-oath, cross-examination, and observation of the witness' demeanor-adequately ensures that the testimony is both reliable and subject to rigorous adversarial testing in a manner functionally equivalent to that accorded live, in-person testimony. These safeguards of reliability and adversariness render the use of such a procedure a far cry from the undisputed prohibition of the Confrontation Clause: trial by *ex parte* affidavit or inquisition .... Rather, we think these elements of effective confrontation not only permit a defendant to "confound and undo the false accuser, or reveal the child coached by a malevolent adult," *Coy,* 487 U.S., at 1020, but may well aid a defendant in eliciting favorable testimony from the child witness. Indeed, to the extent the child witness' testimony may be said to be technically given out-of-court (though we do not so hold), these assurances of reliability and adversariness are far greater than those required for admission of hearsay testimony under the Confrontation Clause. See *Roberts,* 448 U.S., at 66. We are therefore confident that use of the one-way closed-circuit television procedures, where necessary to further an important state interest, does not impinge upon the truth-seeking or symbolic purposes of the Confrontation Clause.

The critical inquiry in this case, therefore, is whether use of the procedure is necessary to further an important state interest. The State contends that it has a substantial interest in protecting children who are allegedly victims of child abuse from the trauma of testifying against the alleged perpetrator and that its statutory procedure for receiving testimony from such witnesses is necessary to further that interest.

We have of course recognized that a State's interest in "the protection of minor victims of sex crimes from further trauma and embarrassment" is a "compelling" one. *Globe Newspaper Co. v. Superior Court,* 457 U.S. 596, 607, 102 S.Ct. 2613, 73 L.Ed.2d 248 (1982).... "[W]e have sustained legislation aimed at protecting the physical and emotional well-being of youth even when the laws have operated in the sensitive area of constitutionally protected rights." *Ferber, supra,* 458 U.S., at 757. In *Globe Newspaper,* for example, we held that a State's well-being of a minor victim was sufficiently weighty to justify depriving the press and public of their constitutional right to attend criminal trials, where the trial court makes a case-specific finding that closure of the trial is necessary to protect the welfare of the minor. See 457 U.S., at 608-609. This Term, in *Osborne v. Ohio,* 495 U.S.-, 110 S.Ct. 1691, 109 L.Ed.2d 98 (1990), we upheld a state statute that proscribed the possession and viewing of child pornography, reaffirming that "'[i]t is evident beyond the need for elaboration that a State's interest in "safeguarding the physical and psychological well-being of a minor" is "compelling."'" *Id.*, at -, 110 S.Ct. at 1696 (quoting *Ferber, supra,* 458 U.S., at 756, 757, 102 S.Ct. at 3354-55).

We likewise conclude today that a State's interest in the physical and psychological well-being of child abuse victims may be sufficiently important to outweigh, at least in some cases, a defendant's right to face his or her accusers in court. That a significant majority of States has enacted statutes to protect child witnesses from the trauma of giving testimony in child abuse cases attests to the widespread belief in the importance of such a public policy. See *Coy,* 487 U.S., at 1022-1023 .... Thirty-seven States, for example, permit the use of videotaped testimony of sexually abused children; 24 States have authorized the use of one-way closed circuit television testimony in child abuse cases, and 8 States authorize the use of a two-way system in which the child witness is permitted to see the courtroom and the defendant on a video monitor and in which the jury and judge is permitted to view the child during the testimony.

The statute at issue in this case, for example, was specifically intended "to safeguard the physical and psychological well-being of child victims by avoiding, or at least minimizing, the emotional trauma produced by testifying." *Widermuth v. State,* 310 Md 496,

518, 530 A.2d 275, 286 (1987). The *Wildermuth*
court noted:

> "In Maryland, the Governor's
> Task Force on Child Abuse in its
> Interim Report (Nov. 1984)
> documented the existence of the
> [child abuse] problem in our State.
> Interim Report at 1. It brought the
> picture up to date in its Final
> Report (Dec. 1985). In the first
> six months of 1985, investigations
> of child abuse were 12 percent more
> numerous than during the same period
> of 1984. In 1979, 4,615 cases of
> child abuse were investigated; in
> 1984, 8,321. Final Report at iii.
> In its Interim Report at 2, the
> Commission proposed legislation
> that, with some changes, became Sec.
> 9-102. The proposal was 'aimed at
> alleviating the trauma to a child
> victim in the courtroom atmosphere
> by allowing the child's testimony to
> be obtained outside of the
> courtroom.' *Id.*, at 2. This would
> both protect the child and enhance
> the public interest by encouraging
> effective prosecution of the alleged
> abuser." *Id.*, at 517, 530 A2d, at
> 285.

Given the State's traditional and "'transcendent interest in protecting the welfare of children,'" *Ginsberg*, 390 U.S. at 640, 20 L.Ed.2d 195, 88 S.Ct. 1274 (citation omitted), and buttressed by the growing body of academic literature documenting the psychological trauma suffered by child abuse victims who must testify in court, see Brief for American Psychological Association as Amicus Curiae 7-13; G. Goodman *et at*, Emotional Effects of Criminal Court Testimony on Child Sexual Assault Victims, Final Report to the National Institute of Justice (presented as conference paper at annual convention of American Psychological Assn., Aug 1989), we will not second-guess the considered judgment of the Maryland Legislature regarding the importance of its interest in protecting child abuse victims from the emotional trauma of testifying. Accordingly, we hold that, if the State makes an adequate showing of necessity, the state interest in protecting child witnesses from the trauma of testifying in a child abuse case is sufficiently important to justify the use of a special procedure that permits a child witness in such cases to testify at trial against a defendant in the absence of face-to-face confrontation with the defendant.

The requisite finding of necessity must of course be a case-specific one: the trial court must hear evidence and determine whether use of the one-way closed circuit television procedure is necessary to protect the welfare of the particular child witness who seeks to testify. .... The trial court must also find that the child witness would be traumatized, not by the courtroom generally, but by the presence of the defendant. .... Denial of face-to-face confrontation is not needed to further the state interest in protecting the child witness from trauma unless it is the presence of the defendant that causes the trauma. In other words, if the state interest were merely the interest in protecting child witnesses from courtroom trauma generally, denial of face-to-face confrontation would be unnecessary because the child could be permitted to testify in less intimidating surroundings, albeit with the defendant present. Finally, the trial court must find that the emotional distress suffered by the child witness in the presence of the defendant is more than de minimus, *i.e.*, more than "mere nervousness or excitement or some reluctance to testify." *Wildermuth*, 310 Md, at 524, 530 A.2d, at 289, see also *State v. Mannion*, 19 Utah 505, 511-512,57 P 542, 543-544 (1989). We need not decide the minimum showing of emotional trauma required for use of the special procedure, however, because the Maryland statute, which requires a determination that the child witness will suffer "serious emotional distress such that the child cannot reasonably communicate," Sec. 9-102(a)(1)(ii), clearly suffices to meet constitutional standards.

To be sure, [the] face-to-face confrontation may be said to cause trauma for the very purpose of eliciting truth, *cf. Coy, supra,* at 1019 1020, 101 L.Ed.2d 857, 108 S.Ct. 2798, but we think that the use of Maryland's special procedure, where necessary to further the important state interest in preventing trauma to child witnesses in child abuse cases, adequately ensures the accuracy of the testimony and preserves the adversary nature of the trial. .... Indeed, where face-to-face confrontation causes significant emotional distress in a child witness, there is evidence that such confrontation would in fact *disserve* the Confrontation Clause's truth-seeking goal. See, *e.g., Coy, supra,* at 1032, 101 L.Ed.2d 857, 108 S.Ct. 2798 (Blackmun, J., dissenting) (face-to-face confrontation "may so overwhelm the child as to prevent the possibility of effective testimony, thereby undermining the truth-finding function of the trial itself"); Brief for American Psychological Association as Amicus Curiae 18-24; *State v. Sheppard,* 197 NJ Super 411, 416, 484 A2d 1330, 1332 (1984); Goodman & Helgeson, Child Sexual Assault: Children's Memory and the Law, 40 U. Miami L.Rev. 181, 203-204 (1985); Note, Videotaping Children's Testimony: An Empirical View, 85 Mich.L.Rev. 809, 813-820 (1987).

In sum, we conclude that where necessary to protect a child witness from trauma that would be caused by testifying in the physical presence of the defendant, at least where such trauma would impair the child's ability to communicate, the Confrontation Clause does not prohibit use of a procedure that, despite the absence of face-to-face confrontation, ensures the reliability of the evidence by subjecting it to rigorous adversarial testing and thereby preserves the essence of effective confrontation. Because there is no dispute that the child witnesses in this case testified under oath, were subject to full cross-examination, and were able to be observed by the judge, jury, and defendant as they testified, we conclude that, to the extent that a proper finding of necessity has been made, the admission of such testimony would be consonant with the Confrontation Clause.

The Maryland Court of Appeals held, as we do today, that although face-to face confrontation is not an absolute constitutional requirement, it may be abridged only where there is a "'case-specific finding of necessity.'" 316 Md., at 564, 560 A.2d, at 1126 (quoting *Coy, supra,* 487 U.S., at 1025 (concurring opinion)). Given this latter requirement, the Court of Appeals reasoned that "[t]he question of whether a child is unavailable to testify...should not be asked in terms of inability to testify in the ordinary courtroom seating, but in the much narrower terms of the witness's inability to

testify in the presence of the accused." 316
Md., at 564, 560 A.2d, at 1126 (footnote
omitted). "[T[he determinative inquiry required
to preclude face-to-face confrontation is the
effect of the presence of the defendant on the
witness or the witness's testimony." *Id.*, at
565, 560 A.2d, at 1127. The Court of Appeals
accordingly concluded that, as a prerequisite to
use of the Sec. 9-102 procedure, the
Confrontation Clause requires the trial court to
make a specific finding that testimony by the
child in the courtroom *in the presence of the
defendant* would result in the child suffering
serious emotional distress such that the child
could not reasonably communicate. *Id.*, at 566,
560 A.2d, at 1127. This conclusion, of course,
is consistent with our holding today.

In addition, however, the Court of Appeals
interpreted our decision in *Coy* to impose two
subsidiary requirements. First, the court held
that "Sec. 9-102 ordinarily cannot be invoked
unless the child witness initially is questioned
(either in or outside the courtroom) in the
defendant's presence." *Id.*, at 566, 560 A.2d,
at 1127; see also *Wildermuth*, 310 Md., at 523-
524, 530 A.2d, at 289 (personal observation by
the judge should be the rule rather than the
exception). Second, the court asserted that
before using the one-way television procedure, a
trial judge must determine whether a child would
suffer "severe emotional distress" if he or she

were to testify by *two-way* closed circuit television. 316 Md., at 567, 560 A.2d, 1128.

Reviewing the evidence presented to the trial in support of the finding required under Sec. 9-102 (a)(1)(ii), the Court of Appeals determined that "the finding of necessity required to limit the defendant's right of confrontation through invocation of Sec. 9-102...was not made here." *Id.*, at 570-571, 560 A.2d, at 1129. The Court of Appeals noted that the trial judge "had the benefit only of expert testimony on the ability of the children to communicate; he did not question any of the children himself, nor did he observe any child's behavior on the witness stand before making his ruling. He did not explore any alternatives to the use of one-way closed-circuit television." *Id.*, at 568, 560 A.2d, at 1128 (footnote omitted). The Court of Appeals also observed that "the testimony in this case was not sharply focused on the effect of the defendant's presence on the child witnesses." *Id.*, at 569, 560 A.2d, at 1129. Thus, the Court of Appeals concluded:

"Unable to supplement the expert testimony by responses to questions put by him, or by his own observations of the children's behavior in Craig's presence, the judge made his Sec, 9-102 finding in terms of what the experts had said.

He ruled that 'the testimony of each of these children *in a courtroom* will [result] in each child suffering serious emotional distress...such that each of these children cannot reasonably communicate.' He failed to find-indeed, on the evidence before him, *could not have found*-that this result would be the product of testimony in a courtroom but in the defendant's televised presence. That, however, is the finding of necessity required to limit the defendant's right of confrontation through invocation of Sec. 9-102. Since that finding was not made here, and since the procedures we deem requisite to the valid use of Sec. 9-102 were not followed, the judgment of the Court of Special Appeals must be reversed and the case remanded for a new trial." *Id.,* at 570-571, 560 A.2d, at 1129 (emphasis added).

The Court of Appeals appears to have rested its conclusion at least in part on the trial court's failure to observe the children's behavior in the defendant's presence and its failure to explore less restrictive alternatives to the use of the one-way closed circuit television procedure. See *id.*, at 568-571, 560 A.2d, at 1128-1129. Although we think such evidentiary requirements could strengthen the grounds for use of protective measures, we decline to establish, as a matter of federal constitutional law, any such categorical evidentiary prerequisites for the use of the one-way television procedure. The trial court in this case, for example, could well have found, on the basis of the expert testimony before it, that testimony by the child witnesses in the courtroom in the defendant's presence "will result in [each] child suffering serious emotional distress such that the child cannot reasonably communicate." Sec. 9-102(a)(1)(ii). See *id.*, at 568-569, 560 A.2d, at 1128-1129; see also App. 22-25, 39, 41, 43,44-45, 54-57. So long as a trial court makes such a case-specific finding of necessity, the Confrontation Clause does not prohibit a State from using one-way closed circuit television procedure for the receipt of testimony by a child witness in a child abuse case. Because the Court of Appeals held that the trial court had not made the requisite finding of necessity under its interpretation of "the high threshold required by [*Coy*] before Sec. 9-102 may be invoked," 316 Md., at 554-555, 560 A.2d, at 1121 (footnote omitted), we cannot be certain whether the Court of Appeals would reach the same conclusion in light of the legal standard we establish today. We therefore vacate the judgment of the Court of

Appeals of Maryland and remand the case for further proceedings not inconsistent with this opinion.

It is so ordered.

NOTES

1. Section 9-102 of the Court and Judicial Proceedings Article of the Annotated Code of Maryland (1989) provides in full:

"(a)(1) In a case of abuse of a child as defined in Sec. 5-701 of the Family Law Article or Article 27, Sec. 35A of the Code, a court may order that the testimony of a child victim be taken outside the courtroom and shown in the courtroom by means of a closed circuit television if:

"(i) The testimony is taken during the proceeding; and

"(ii) The judge determines that testimony by the child victim in the courtroom will result in the child suffering serious emotional distress such that the child cannot reasonably communicate.

"(2) Only the prosecuting attorney, the attorney for the defendant, and the judge may question the child.

"(3) The operators of the closed circuit television shall make every effort to be unobtrusive.

"(b)(1) Only the following persons may be in the room with the child when the child testifies by closed circuit television:

"(i) The prosecuting attorney;

"(ii) The attorney for the defendant;

"(iii) The operators of the closed circuit television equipment; and

"(iv) Unless the defendant objects, any person whose presence, in the opinion of the court, contributes to the well-being of the child, including a person who has dealt with the child in a therapeutic setting concerning the abuse.

"(2) During the child's testimony by closed circuit television, the judge and the defendant shall be in the courtroom.

"(3) The judge and the defendant shall be allowed to communicate with the persons in the room where the child is testifying by any appropriate electronic method.

"(c) The provisions of this section to not apply if the defendant is an attorney pro se.

"(d) This section may not be interpreted to preclude, for purposes of identification of a defendant, the presence of both the victim and the defendant in the courtroom at the same time."

For a detailed description of the Sec. 9-102 procedure, see *Wildermuth v. State,* 310 Md. 496, 503-504, 530 A.2d 275, 278-279 (1987). Additional notes (notes 2-4) to the *Craig* decision have been omitted.

Chapter Five

EXAMINATION OF THE WITNESS

Rule 611[1]
MODE AND ORDER OF INTERROGATION AND PRESENTATION

(a) Control by court. The court shall exercise reasonable control over the mode and order of interrogating witnesses and presenting evidence so as to (1) make the interrogation and presentation effective for the ascertainment of the truth, (2) avoid needless consumption of time, and (3) protect witnesses from harassment or undue embarrassment.

(b) Scope of cross-examination. Cross-examination should be limited to the subject matter of the direct examination and matters affecting the credibility of the witness. The court may, in the exercise of discretion, permit inquiry into additional matters as if on direct examination.

(c) Leading questions. Leading questions should not be used on the direct examination of a witness except as may be necessary to develop the witness' testimony. Ordinarily leading questions should be permitted on cross examination. When a party calls a hostile witness, an adverse party, or a witness identified with an adverse party, interrogation may be by leading questions.

A Flexible Approach to Witness Examination

Rule 611 presents the basic federal law as to the process of examining a witness. In line with the general liberal thrust of the Federal Rules of Evidence, Rule 611 provides a flexible approach to examining the witness.

Direct Examination & Cross-Examination

The terms "direct examination" and "cross examination" have already been discussed in Chapter One. However, at this point, it is necessary to look more specifically to the form of examination of the witness in the course of the party's direct examination and cross-examination.

The Direct Examination

The process of examination begins with a party calling the particular witness. Pursuant to Rule 603 (discussed in Chapter Four), the oath or affirmation is administered, and the questioning commences.

Leading Questions

A leading question is instructional in nature. It informs the witness of the expected response.[2] In other words, a leading question is one which is simply *too* *suggestive* of the answer.

Example.

> At the murder trial of John Doe, the prosecutor asks her witness: "Did John Doe, the defendant, then pick up the rifle and point it at Jane Smith?"

Some attorneys and judges view a leading question as one which will invoke either a "yes" or "no" response. While this standard is somewhat imprecise, it does emphasize that leading questions are heavily suggestive of the answers.

The basic common law rule is that leading questions are not allowed on the direct examination. This traditional rule is subject to some exceptions. The chief exceptions are the following:

(1) Leading questions are used for what attorneys call "preliminary matters," that is, relatively trivial or undisputed matters.

Example.

> Attorney for party A asks the witness: "Are you the John Doe who resides in Hammond, Indiana?"

(2) Leading questions are also available for "hostile" (i.e., adverse or unwilling) witnesses called on direct examination.

(3) Leading questions may be used where the witness is a young child or suffers from lack of recall or confused state of mind.

Rule 611 and Leading Questions
On Direct Examination

Under Rule 611(c) leading questions "should not be used on direct examination." This rule continues the traditional view as to the undesirability of the use of leading questions during the direct examination. However, the use of the word "should" rather than "shall" underscores that Rule 611(c) is to be considered in line with the discretion granted to the judge in 611(a). Rule 611(c) interprets the "hostile" witness exception broadly as including "a hostile witness, an adverse party, or a witness identified with an adverse party" (e.g., a partner of the defendant).

The Cross-Examination

As indicated in Chapter One, a party's cross-examination follows the adverse party's direct examination of the witness.

Leading Questions

Trial attorneys are quick to point out that leading questions are indispensable to a good cross-examination. In fact, it is rare (and, as the great trial attorneys believe, simply wrong) for an attorney to even ask a question on cross-examination for which he or she is not aware of the answer. The traditional rule is that leading questions are available on cross-examination.

Rule 611 and Leading Questions on Cross-Examination

The traditional rule allowing leading questions on cross-examination is continued in Rule 611(c): "Ordinarily leading questions should be permitted on cross-examination." The use of the world "ordinarily" in Rule 611(c) is significant. A party may call a hostile witness on direct examination. For example, party A may call party B as a witness during party A's presentation of his case (i.e., a direct witness). If this occurs, then party B's attorney may cross-examine his or her own client. A judge does have the discretion under Rule 611 to prevent the use of leading questions in such a situation.

The Scope of
Cross-Examination

There are two basic views concerning the proper scope of cross-examination. One view, the majority one, is restrictive, and the other view is not.

The restrictive view (sometimes called the "American" rule) is that cross-examination should be limited to the matter (i.e., the issues) initially brought out in the direct examination.[3] What this means to the cross-examining attorney is that, if the witness has other relevant knowledge about the case, the attorney must wait to develop the evidence during his or her client's presentation of case. The other view (sometimes called the "wide-open" rule or "English" rule) considers the proper scope of cross-examination as unlimited by the matter raised in the direct examination.[4]

Rule 611 and the Scope
Of Cross-Examination

Rule 611(b) presents the restrictive view on the scope of cross-examination, with the addition of a final sentence providing judicial discretion as to a wider scope of cross-examination: "The court may, in the exercise of discretion, permit inquiry into additional matters as if on direct examination."[5]

Rule 611, 614 &
Judicial Discretion

Reference has been made to the fact that the judge exercises discretion in the progress of the trial. The student should remember this point. It is emphasized in Rule 611(a). The judge has "reasonable control" over the conduct of the trial, and he or she may exercise this discretion with the three Rule 611(a) objectives in mind.

The judge also has discretion in the development of the evidence, as the Federal Rules of Evidence continue the traditional powers of the court to call and interrogate witnesses.

Rule 614[6]
CALLING AND INTERROGATION
OF WITNESSES BY COURT

(a) Calling by court. The
court may, on its own motion or at
the suggestion of a party, call
witnesses, and all parties are
entitled to cross-examine witnesses
thus called.

(b) Interrogation by court.
The court may interrogate witnesses,
whether called by itself or by a
party.

(c) Objections. Objections
to the calling of witnesses by the
court or to interrogation by it may
be made at the time or at the next
available opportunity when the jury
is not present.

Rule 614(c) provides a mechanism by which
an attorney may avoid the awkward position of
objecting to the judge's calling of a witness or
to the judge's witness interrogation in front of
the jury. Under the rule, objections "may be
made...at the next available opportunity when
the jury is not present."

Exclusion of Witnesses

The student should consider the situation where the plaintiff has called his or her first witness in the presentation of the case. Witness I takes the stand to testify. May the other trial witnesses sit in the courtroom and hear the testimony of witness I? The general rule is that exclusion of witnesses may be allowed in the discretion of the court (generally considered upon motion for exclusion by one of the parties). Of course, exclusion does not apply to a party. An obvious purpose of the rule is to prevent a witness from being "educated" by the testimony of others.

Federal Rule 615 presents the rule in federal courts as to the exclusion of witnesses:

Rule 615[7]
EXCLUSION OF WITNESSES

At the request of a party the court shall order witnesses excluded so that they cannot hear the testimony of other witnesses, and it may make the order on its own motion. This rule does not authorize exclusion of (1) a party who is a natural person, or (2) an officer or employee of a party which is not a natural person designated as its representative by its attorney, or (3) a person whose presence is shown by a party to be essential to the presentation of the party's cause.

While a number of states leave the decision of exclusion to the judge, Rule 615 makes it mandatory "at the request of a party." Rule 615 continues the basic rule of the right of a party to remain in the courtroom. To do otherwise would raise constitutional due process and right of confrontation issues. Corporations, under exception (2), may designate an officer or employee as its representative, who may stay. Also, under exception (3), one "whose presence is shown by a party to be essential" may stay in the courtroom.[8]

Witness Memory Problems

A witness cannot just enter the witness stand with a writing and testify from the writing. That is just not how facts are developed at trial. However, writings may be used in the witness examination in two basic situations. Attorneys use the terms "present recollection revived" and "past recollection recorded" to refer to the two situations.

Present Recollection Revived

Present recollection revived is the process by which a witness' memory is "refreshed." In other words, the witness, for whatever reason, has forgotten a point and needs to look to a writing to refresh his or her recollection of the facts. The writing must refresh the witness' recollection so that he or she may then continue on with the testimony without the need for further use of writing. The writing itself is not admitted into evidence by the party using it.

Example.

The following interchange occurs in a criminal trial:

Prosecutor:

Mr. Doe, you testified that you were behind the counter, as salesperson, of John's Gun Shoppe when Ms. Roe purchased the single-barrel shotgun. As best as you are able to recollect, please tell the jury the time of day and date on which the purchase occurred.

Witness Doe:

It was late afternoon, a little before closing.

Prosecutor:

Do you recollect the date of purchase?

Witness Doe:

I am sorry; I do not recall the date, sometime in Spring.

Prosecutor:

Mr. Doe, I am now showing you State's Exhibit C for identification, and I want you to look it over. Does this writing refresh your recollection of the matter?

Witness Doe:

The writing does refresh my recollection.

Prosecutor:

I'll take the writing back. Thank you. Now, with your memory refreshed, please tell the jury the date upon which the purchase of the shotgun was made.

Witness Doe:

April 4, 1990.

Prosecutor:

Mr. Doe, I thank you.

Of course, the other party may review the writing, and, while the offering party may not admit the writing, the other party may do so (at least relevant parts of the writing). This may occur, for example, where the writing might discredit the witness' testimony.

Example.

> The writing was a sales invoice, bearing the date April 4, 1990, but it was an invoice from Diane's House of Mirrors.

The right of the adverse party to review and admit the writing is provided for in the Federal Rules of Evidence under Rule 612.

Past Recollection Recorded

Past recollection recorded is the process which may be available to a party when the present recollection revived process has been attempted, without success. In other words, the writing does not refresh the recollection of the witness. If the writing meets certain standards, it may be admitted as evidence itself. In general, the writing must have been made when the facts were clear and fresh in the mind of the witness, and the witness must establish that the writing was accurate when made.

Many legal scholars view past recollection recorded as an exception to the hearsay rule, and there is further discussion of the process as an exception in Chapter Eight.

Witness Impeachment

Witness impeachment is the process of establishing that a witness' testimony is not worthy of weight and credibility.[9] The impeachment of a witness is an important aspect of good cross-examination. The trier of fact determines what weight and credibility to give to a witness' testimony. If you can successfully "impeach" a witness, you negatively affect the witness' testimony, enhancing your position at the trial.

There are a variety of ways to impeach a witness. One has already been noted in Chapter Three, i.e., to establish character evidence of untruthfulness. This may also involve a showing of conviction for past crimes.

The jurisdictions vary as to what crimes may be shown for such impeachment. The federal rule is found in Rule 609 (see Appendix A).[10]

Rule 609 follows what is the better view among the jurisdictions. It limits impeachment by evidence of criminal conviction to the following categories of crimes:

(1) Serious crimes "punishable by death or imprisonment in excess of one year" (i.e., felonies); or

(2) Crimes which "involved dishonesty or false statement, regardless of the punishment." Here, examples include the crimes of perjury and larceny/theft.

There is a distinction in Rule 609 between a witness who is an accused and a witness who is not accused of a crime in the particular case. Under Rule 609(a), the credibility of a witness other than the accused may be attacked by showing that such witness has been convicted of a crime "punishable by death or imprisonment in excess of one year" (subject to Rule 403 dictates). The credibility of the accused may be so attacked if the court first determines that "the probative value of admitting the evidence outweighs its prejudicial effect on the accused." While the distinction may not seem significant, in view of the fact that Rule 403 allows the court to weigh probative value, there is an important difference. Rule 403 allows the court to exclude evidence "if its probative value is *substantially* outweighed by the danger of unfair prejudice," etc. This degree need not be shown for the court, under Rule 609(a), to exclude the evidence as to the accused.

While the judge is given some discretion in admitting the evidence, there is a basic ten year "time limit" imposed under Rule 609(b). If the witness has been pardoned, under Rule 609(c), impeachment for the pardoned crime is unavailable. While the court maintains discretion in the criminal trial, evidence of juvenile adjudications are generally not available to impeach a witness (Rule 609(d)).

A witness may also be impeached by a showing of bias or prejudice.

Example.

> Witness Doe is party A's brother (bias in favor of party A) or party A's chief business competitor (prejudice against party A).

Showing that the witness was paid for testifying is also generally allowed. However, the value of this means of impeachment will vary significantly with the particular case. The jury may well expect certain witnesses, e.g., the physician witness, to be well-paid.

Another impeachment route often employed by attorneys is to attack the memory or perception of a witness.

Example.

> Establishing the witness' poor sight, poor memory, poor hearing, lack of opportunity to see or hear (e.g., the witness was standing down the hall and too far away from the victim's apartment to hear the conversation), etc.

If possible, an attorney will also seek to impeach a witness by showing a prior inconsistent statement (oral or written). There is some variance among the jurisdictions as to the necessary "foundation" to be initially laid in such a situation. In other words, to what extent must a witness first be given the opportunity to admit, deny or explain the inconsistency and must the contents of a written inconsistent statement first be shown to a witness?[11] The Federal Rules of Evidence take a liberal position as to the necessary foundation.

Rule 613[12]
PRIOR STATEMENT OF WITNESSES

(a) Examining the witness concerning prior statement. In examining a witness concerning a prior statement made by the witness, whether written or not, the statement need not be shown nor its contents disclosed to the witness at that time, but on request the same shall be shown or disclosed to opposing counsel.

(b) Extrinsic evidence of prior inconsistent statement of witness. Extrinsic evidence of a prior inconsistent statement by a witness is not admissible unless the witness is afforded an opportunity to explain or deny the same and the opposite party is afforded an opportunity to interrogate the witness thereon, or the interests of justice otherwise require. This provision does not apply to admissions of a party-opponent as defined in Rule 801(d)(2).

Under the federal rule, the statement need not be shown to the witness, although it must be shown to the opposing counsel on request to help avoid fabrications. Basically, subject to some judicial discretion, what is necessary is the provision of "an opportunity to explain or deny" the inconsistency.

Impeachment of Own Witness

The traditional rule was that a party could not impeach a witness he or she called. Several exceptions developed to the traditional rule (e.g., where the witness is a hostile witness). Today, the tendency among the jurisdictions is to significantly limit or abandon the traditional rule.[13] The traditional rule was abandoned in the federal courts with Rule 607.

Rule 607[14]
WHO MAY IMPEACH

The credibility of a witness may be attacked by any party, including the party calling the witness.

Rehabilitation

Of course, where one party has sought to impeach a witness, the other party may try to rehabilitate the witness' credibility. This is the process of restoring the trier of fact's confidence in the witness' testimony. The rehabilitation method used depends upon the impeachment method used. For example, if a prior inconsistent statement is shown, the other party may seek to explain the inconsistency away. Also, for example, if character evidence for untruthfulness is used, the other party may provide character evidence for truthfulness in rehabilitation.

NOTES

1.   FED. R. EVID. 611.

2.   See BLACK'S LAW DICTIONARY 1034 (4th ed. 1968).

3.   See Finch v. Weiner, 109 Conn. 616, 145 A. 31 (1929).

4.   See Boller v. Confrances, 42 Wis.2d 170, 166 N.W.2d 129 (1969).

5.   See U.S. v. Pilcher, 672 F.2d 875 (11th Cir. 1982).

6.   FED. R. EVID. 614.

7.   FED. R. EVID. 615.

8.   Exception (3) may include such people as agents of a principal or perhaps

certain experts. The basis for the exception must be "shown by a party." See Notes of Advisory Committee on Proposed Rules, Fed. Rules of Evid. Rule 615, 28 U.S.C.A. <u>Note</u>. U.S.C.A. stands for United States Code Annotated, which is published by West Publishing Company. It sets forth the federal law. As to the Federal Rules of Evidence, it presents the rules and the Advisory Committee Notes. It also provides excellent case summaries (i.e., annotations) of court cases interpreting the rules. It is a fine source of the law, and the student is encouraged to review the U.S.C.A. volumes, particularly Vol. 28.

9. See BLACK'S LAW DICTIONARY supra at 887.

10. FED. R. EVID. 609.

11. See Ladd, "Some Observations on Credibility: Impeachment of Witnesses," 52 CORNELL L.Q. 239 (1967).

12. FED. R. EVID. 613.

13. See "Notes of Advisory Committee on Proposed Rules" to Fed. Rule 613, Fed. Rules of Evid. Rule 613, 28 U.S.C.A.

14. FED. R. EVID. 607.

REVIEW AND DISCUSSION QUESTIONS

1. Give an example of a "leading question." What is the federal rule as to leading questions on direct examination? How does the federal rule compare with the state court practice in your jurisdiction?

2. Does Rule 611 present the restrictive view or the "wide-open" view of the proper scope of cross-examination? Explain.

3. What is the judicial discretion available under Rules 611 and 614?

4. Distinguish "present recollection revived" from "past recollection recorded."

5. What is the purpose of witness impeachment? Make a list of those ways to impeach a witness. Consider Rule 609. Do you believe the rule provides the best approach to impeachment by evidence of past crimes? Explain.

Chapter Six

OPINION TESTIMONY AND
THE EXPERT WITNESS

The Issue of Opinion Testimony

May a witness testify as to his or her opinion in a matter, or must the witness limit the testimony to the facts, leaving to the trier of fact the determination of the necessary conclusions?

Answer. It is preferable that a witness testify as to the facts only, and this is the basic rule. However, the rule is not absolute, and witness opinions are allowed in *limited* situations.

This chapter considers the proper scope of witness opinion testimony.

The Lay Witness and the Expert Witness Distinction

The extent to which a witness may present an opinion at trial depends upon whether the witness is a "lay witness" or an "expert witness." To be an expert witness, a witness must qualify as an expert in a relevant field. The requirements as to qualification as an expert are discussed later in this chapter. Those who do not qualify as experts are lay witnesses.

Opinion Testimony
By Lay Witnesses

As stated above, the basic rule is that lay witnesses may not state their opinions as to a matter. They must testify as to the facts only. However, in many situations the only natural way to express oneself is by way of an opinion (e.g., "John Doe looked in pain.").[1] Recognizing this reality, the law has not totally banned the use of lay witness opinion testimony.

The traditional view as to the use of lay witness opinion is that it is limited to those situations where the witness testifies as to that which he or she has perceived, *and* the opinion testimony is necessary because it is impossible (or nearly so) to testify otherwise (i.e., the opinion testimony is the best existing evidence).[2]

Legal conclusions are not allowed (e.g., "John Doe was negligent;" "The defendant breached the contract."). Only *factual* conclusions may be allowed, if the situation falls within the jurisdiction's standard.

It is not feasible to list all situations in which lay witness opinion may be allowed. A large volume of cases exist on the subject. Some common, non-exclusive categories of allowable witness opinions are listed below.

Example.

(1) Opinions as to mental and physical condition or health (e.g., "John was mentally and physically sick," "John Doe was drunk.").[3]

(2) Opinions as to the identity of a person (e.g., "I know the defendant's voice and that was the defendant speaking to me on the telephone.").

This category includes the identification of handwriting, where the witness is familiar with same.[4]

(3) Opinions drawn from sensory perception (e.g., "I heard a crash.").[5]

(4) Opinions concerning such matters as speed, weight, height, distance, duration of time (i.e., measurements).[6]

Opinion Testimony by Lay Witnesses
And the Federal Rules of Evidence

Rule 701 of the Federal Rules of Evidence presents the federal law as to lay witness opinion testimony.

Rule 701[7]
OPINION TESTIMONY BY LAY WITNESSES

If the witness is not testifying as an expert, the witness' testimony in the form of opinions or inferences is limited to those opinions or inferences which are (a) rationally based on the perception of the witness and (b) helpful to a clear understanding of his testimony or the determination of a fact in issue.

Unlike the traditional view, where the opinion testimony must be necessary to be allowed, Rule 701 merely requires that the opinion testimony be "helpful to a clear understanding" of the testimony "or the determination of a fact in issue." Rule 701 continues the traditional requirement that the lay witness opinion must be based upon facts perceived by the witness (i.e., personal, direct knowledge).[8]

The Expert Witness

Rule 702[9]
TESTIMONY BY EXPERTS

If scientific, technical, or other specialized knowledge will assist the trier of fact to understand the evidence or to determine a fact in issue, a witness qualified as an expert by knowledge, skill, experience, training, or education, may testify thereto in the form of an opinion or otherwise.

Who Is an Expert Witness and
To What May the Expert Testify

Under Rule 702, an expert witness is one who qualifies as an expert "by knowledge, skill, experience, training, or education." If so qualified, the expert witness may testify as to "scientific, technical, or other specialized knowledge," as long as such testimony will *assist* the judge or jury "to understand the evidence or to determine a fact in issue."

The expert's testimony need only be of assistance to the trier of fact. This liberal approach to the use of expert witness testimony contrasts with the more restrictive view held by a number of states that expert witness testimony should be used only where such testimony is *necessary*, i.e., where the subject matter is simply beyond the comprehension of lay people.[10]

The Bases of the Expert Witness' Opinion

Rule 703[11]
BASES OF OPINION TESTIMONY BY EXPERTS

The facts or data in the particular case upon which an expert bases an opinion or inference may be those perceived by or made known to the expert at or before the hearing. If of a type reasonably relied upon by experts in the particular field in forming opinions or inferences upon the subject, the facts or data need not be admissible in evidence.

Under Rule 703, "facts or data ...upon which an expert bases an opinion" may come from a variety of sources:

(1) The personal observations of the expert witness;

(2)   Matters made known to the expert witness at the trial; and

(3)   Matters made known to the expert witness before the trial.

Again, the Federal Rules of Evidence take a liberal approach, as Rule 703 enlarges permissible sources for facts and data.[12]

The Personal Observations of the Expert Witness

The expert witness may base his or her opinion upon facts personally observed. For example, in an automobile accident case, the doctor who treated the plaintiff may serve as an expert witness, testifying as to his or her opinion of injury based upon matters observed in treating the plaintiff, or, in a breach of warranty case, a mechanic who repaired an automobile may testify as to his or her opinion of defect based on personal observations in repairing the car.

Matters Made Known to the Expert Witness at Trial

The expert witness may base his or her opinion upon facts presented at trial. This is generally done either through the use of the traditional "hypothetical question," or by having the expert witness listen to the other witnesses testifying at trial.

The Hypothetical Question

With the hypothetical question, the attorney provides the expert witness with a presentation of those facts in evidence from which the expert witness can formulate his or her opinion.

Method.

The attorney for the party calling the expert witness asks the expert witness a question formulated somewhat as follows: "Mr. Doe, assuming the existence of the following facts: A, B, C, D, E (the attorney lists the facts), do you have an opinion?"

The hypothetical can be quite long. The process has been criticized as being cumbersome and tedious to the jury. However, although criticism has been strong, and movement away from the use of the hypothetical question has occurred, its use is still common. In some states its use is still the only method allowed for providing the expert witness' testimony.[13] Of course, in federal court it is but one method generally available to a party. Even in federal court, however, the use of the hypothetical is common. Although not necessarily required (see Rule 705 below), an attorney in federal court may choose to elicit the expert's opinion by means of the hypothetical because this can be generally done in a light favorable to the client.

Listening to the Other Witnesses Testifying at Trial

Where the expert witness is not excluded from the courtroom (pursuant to Rule 615), he or she may remain to listen to the testimony of the other witnesses. Under Rule 703 (and subject to Rule 705 discussed below), the expert witness may generally present his or her opinion based upon the testimony heard. This is an expansion of the traditional law, and it is at variance with the existing law in a number of states.

Method.

The attorney for the party calling the expert witness enters into the following (or similar) questioning of the expert witness:

Attorney:

"Mr. Doe, have you remained in the courtroom during these proceedings?"

Expert:

"Yes, I have."

Attorney:

"Have you heard the testimony given by the witnesses in this case?"

Expert:

"Yes."

Attorney:

"Based upon the facts developed in the testimony of the witnesses, do you have an opinion?"

Expert:

"Yes, I do."

Attorney:

"What is your opinion?"

Matters Made Known to the Expert Witnesses before Trial

Under Rule 703, the expert witness may base his or her opinion upon facts made known to him or her by the attorney of a party (or others) *before trial*. This process is not available in a number of states, and it is at variance with the traditional view that the expert's opinion must be based on evidence developed at the trial.

Disclosure of Facts or Data

Rule 705[14]
DISCLOSURE OF FACTS OR DATA
UNDERLYING EXPERT OPINION

The expert may testify in terms of opinion or inference and give reasons therefore without prior disclosure of the underlying facts or data, unless the court requires otherwise. The expert may in any event be required to disclose the underlying facts or data on cross-examination.

In many state courts, before an expert witness may indicate his or her opinion, the facts upon which the expert relies must be disclosed. Under Rule 705, such prior disclosure is not required "unless the court requires otherwise." Assuming that the judge does not exercise his or her discretion to require the prior disclosure, the attorney on direct examination may request the opinion of the expert witness, without disclosure of the factual basis for same. While this may not be done as a practical matter, since an opinion without a factual basis may be viewed by the jury as too weak, it may be done. Therefore, absent exercise of judicial discretion, the hypothetical is unnecessary. Of course, on cross-examination, the expert may be "required to disclose the underlying facts or data."

Opinion on Ultimate Issue

Rule 704[15]
OPINION ON ULTIMATE ISSUE

(a) Except as provided in subdivision (b), testimony in the form of an opinion or inference otherwise admissible is not objectionable because it embraces an ultimate issue to be decided by the trier of fact.

(b) No expert witness testifying with respect to the mental state or condition of a defendant in a criminal case may state an opinion or inference as to whether the defendant did or did not have the mental state or condition constituting an element of the crime

charged or of a defense thereto.
Such ultimate issues are matters for
the trier of fact alone.

The traditional law applied the so-called
"ultimate issue rule," which prohibited a
witness from giving his or her opinion on an
"ultimate issue" in the case (e.g., the
"liability" of a party, the defendant's "guilt,"
the "negligence" of the physician, etc.),
because the resolution of such issue was to be
left to the trier of fact.[16]

Under Rule 704, except as to the instance
described in (b), such testimony is "not
objectionable because it embraces an ultimate
issue to be decided by the trier of fact."
Still, not all such testimony will necessarily
be admissible in federal court. Such testimony
is still governed by other requirements of the
federal rules, particularly, the testimony must
be "helpful to" (Rule 701) or "assist" (Rule
702) the trier of fact, and, under Rule 403
(discussed in Chapter Four), the court may
exclude evidence that is a "waste of time."
Therefore, if the expert merely testifies,
establishing that she is an expert, and in her
opinion, the defendant is "guilty," such
testimony may be excluded as unhelpful or a
waste of time.

Court Appointed Experts

While the parties may choose to call expert witnesses of their own selection, Rule 706 of the Federal Rules of Evidence provides the court with the discretionary power to appoint its own expert. This is begun on the court's own motion or the motion of any party (Rule 706(a)). It is hoped that such appointment (or even the possibility of such appointment) will assist the parties in reaching settlement and give incentive to the parties to choose good experts of their own.

NOTES

1. See "Notes of Advisory Committee on Proposed Rules" to Federal Rule 701, Fed. Rules of Evid. Rule 701, 28 U.S.C.A.

2. For excellent language on the matter, see Justice Foster's influential dissent in Hardy v. Merrill, 56 N.H. 227 (1875). For a modern view, see Teen-Ed, Inc. v. Kimball Intern., Inc., 620 F.2d 399 (3rd Cir. 1980).

3. See State v. Garver, 190 Or. 291, 225 P.2d 771 (1950); Gerrich v. State, 451 N.E.2d 327 (Ind. 1983).

4. See FED. R. EVID. 901 as to the admissibility of handwriting testimony.

5. See "Ability to See, Hear, Smell or Otherwise Sense as Proper Subject of Opinion By Lay Witness," 10 A.L.R. 3d 258 (1966).

6. See Patton v. Hendrikson, 79 Nev. 197, 380 P.2d 916 (1963) (Speed).

7. FED. R. EVID. 701.

8. "Notes of Advisory Committee on Proposed Rules" to Federal Rule 701, supra.

9. FED. R. EVID. 702.

10. See Long v. State, Okla., 274 P.2d 553 (1954).

11. FED. R. EVID. 703.

12. "Notes of Advisory Committee on Proposed Rules" to Federal Rule 703, supra.

13. See 56 A.L.R. 3d 300 for an examination of the general rules in regard to the use of hypotheticals in civil cases among the states.

14. FED. R. EVID. 705.

15. FED. R. EVID. 704.

16. See United States v. Spaulding, 293 U.S. 498, 79 L.Ed 617, 55 S.Ct 273 (1935), where the Court held that doctors could not give their

opinion as to whether an insured had suffered "total permanent disability," since such was an ultimate issue for the jury. See also "Notes of Advisory Committee on Proposed Rules" to Federal Rule 704, supra.

REVIEW AND DISCUSSION QUESTIONS

1. Distinguish the availability under the federal rules of opinion testimony by lay witnesses and opinion testimony by expert witnesses.

2. The federal rules present a liberal view of the bases of expert witness opinion testimony allowed at trial. Is the flexibility too great? Does the flexibility enhance the attempt to do justice? Explain.

3. What are the permissible bases of expert witness opinion testimony in your state? Do they differ from the Federal Rules of Evidence? If so, how do they differ?

4. Interview an attorney in your area. What is his or her attitude as to the use of hypothetical questions at trial? Ask him or her to provide you with some examples of interesting hypothetical questions heard at trial.

5.   Why were "ultimate issue" opinions prohibited under the traditional law? Should they still be prohibited? Why/why not? Explain.

6.   What are the advantages of the availability of court appointed experts (Rule 706)? Do you believe that the rule will help improve the quality of experts testifying at trial? Why/why not? Explain.

Chapter Seven

THE HEARSAY RULE

The Hearsay Concept

A witness may testify in various ways and with various effects:

(1)   The witness may testify as to his or her personal observations, providing direct evidence.

Example.

> As first set forth in Chapter Two, X is a witness in a murder trial.   X takes the stand and testifies: "I saw Y (the defendant) pick up an ax from the garage floor and swing it at Z (the victim), chopping off Z's head with one swing."

(2)   The witness may testify as to his or her personal observations, providing circumstantial evidence.

Example.

As first set forth in Chapter Two, X, the witness in the murder trial, takes the stand and testifies: "I was standing outside Y's (the defendant's) garage. I heard a scream, and I entered the garage. I saw Z (the victim) lying on the floor, Z's head severed from the rest of the bloody body, and Y was standing over Z's body, holding a bloody ax."

(3) The witness may testify (in limited situations, see Chapter Six) as to his or her opinion.

Example.

X, the witness in the murder trial, takes the stand and testifies: "Y (the defendant) was mentally and physically sick."

(4) The witness may testify (in some situations) as to knowledge of factual matters received by the witness from other sources.

Example.

X, the witness in the murder trial, takes the stand and testifies: "I held Z (the victim) in my arms until

> he died; just before he died Z told
> me: 'Y (the defendant) knifed me!'"

This example introduces us to the issue of hearsay, perhaps the most complicated issue in evidence law.

The Hearsay Rule

The general rule is that hearsay is not admissible unless one of the many exceptions applies. The general rule is established for the federal courts in Rule 802 (see Appendix A).[1]

The general rule appears to be both simple and straight forward. However, it is often difficult to determine the following:

(1)   Does hearsay exist in the particular case?

(2)   If hearsay does exist, does one of the many exceptions to the hearsay rule apply?

If hearsay does not exist, then, of course, the hearsay rule is inapplicable. Even if hearsay does exist, it may still be admissible if it falls within one of the many exceptions. The exceptions will be reviewed in the next chapter. In this chapter, we shall look to the definition of hearsay. In other words, in this chapter we will deal with the first of the inherent problems posed by the application of the hearsay concept. If the student understands the definition of hearsay, then he or she can deal effectively with the issue of whether it applies in a given fact situation.

Defining Hearsay

The federal law defines hearsay in Rule 801 (see Appendix A). [2]

Rule 801(c) defines hearsay as "a statement, other than one made by the declarant while testifying at the trial or hearing, offered in evidence *to prove the truth of the matter asserted*" (emphasis added).

The student should consider the following key points:

(1) "*Statement.*" The statement to which hearsay applies is not limited to oral reports. The statement (as described in Rule 801(a)) may be "an oral or written assertion." Also, it may be "nonverbal conduct..., if it is intended by the person as an assertion." Such "nonverbal conduct" involves those situations where the declarant, rather than using words, expresses himself or herself by physical conduct. Of course, the nonverbal conduct must be intended by the declarant as an assertion.

Example.

The declarant shakes his head up and down (i.e., the nonverbal conduct). He does this in response to the police officer's question, "Did you shoot this person?" In other words, rather than answering, "Yes, I shot him!" (i.e., rather than using words), the declarant uses nonverbal conduct to communicate. This is hearsay, just as answering, "Yes, I shot him!" would have been hearsay.

(2) *"Declarant."* The declarant is the person making the out-of-court statement (Rule 801(b)).

(3) *"To Prove the Truth of the Matter Asserted."* The rule applies only where the statement is "offered in evidence to prove the truth of the matter asserted" (Rule 801(c)). This is a fundamental aspect of the rule. If this is not the purpose of offering the statement into evidence, then the hearsay rule does not apply to prevent admissibility.

While it may not be readily apparent, evidence may well be offered for purposes other than to establish the truth of the facts in the statement. For example, a statement by a declarant may be offered into evidence simply to show that the statement was made, not that what was said is true.

Example.

As stated in Chapter Three, defamation (libel or slander) is a cause of action. Plaintiff may sue the defendant for the defendant's defamatory remarks (e.g., defendant publicly calls the plaintiff "a drug addict and a whore"). Obviously, to succeed in her suit, the plaintiff must establish that the remarks were made by the defendant. In seeking to do this, the plaintiff puts witness X on the stand. X will testify: "Y (the defendant) told me that Z (the plaintiff) is a drug addict and a whore." Is such a statement by the witness hearsay? No, it is not hearsay. The plaintiff is not offering the testimony to show that the facts are true! The plaintiff must show the opposite to win her suit, since truth is a defense in a defamation action. The plaintiff seeks instead to establish merely that the statement was made.

The declarant's statement may also be offered into evidence to establish its effect on the person receiving the statement. As such, the statement is not being offered "to prove the truth of the matter asserted."

Example.

> Prosecutor Jones calls X, a witness
> in the murder trial, to the stand. X
> testifies: "I heard Z (the victim)
> tell Y (the defendant) that he was a
> yellow, low-down, sleazy creep!" Is
> such a statement hearsay? No, not
> if the statement is offered by
> Prosecutor Jones to show the anger
> of the defendant, i.e., to establish
> the motive from which the decision
> (intent) to kill Z developed.

Rule 801(d) and Non-Hearsay

Rule 801(d) establishes special non-hearsay categories for the federal courts:

(1) "**Prior statement by witness**." Prior inconsistent statements were discussed previously in Chapter Five as a means to impeach a witness. Certainly, if a party uses a prior inconsistent statement to attack (or a prior consistent statement to rehabilitate) a witness' credibility, then the party is not offering the prior statement "to prove the truth of the matter asserted" (i.e., there is no hearsay problem). However, under the federal rules certain prior statements of a declarant testifying as a witness at trial are expressly excluded as hearsay and may be used "to prove the truth of the matter asserted."

Therefore, if a declarant-witness makes a prior inconsistent statement under oath, the statement is admissible, not only to impeach, but to prove the truth so asserted (Rule 801(d)(1)(A)).[3] Also, a declarant-witness' prior consistent statements (under oath or not) may be used "to rebut an express or implied charge against the declarant of recent fabrication or improper influence or motive" (Rule 801(d)(1)(B)).[4] Finally, under Rule 801(d)(1)(C), a prior statement by a declarant-witness identifying "a person made after perceiving the person" is excluded from the hearsay rule, and such evidence is admissible to prove the truth asserted.[5]

(2) **"Admission by party opponent**." Admissions are "statements by a party, or someone identified with him in legal interest, of the existence of a fact which is relevant to the cause of his adversary."[6]

Example.

> X, the witness in an automobile accident case, takes the stand and testifies: "I went up to D's (the defendant's) car after the collision, and D said: 'I'm sorry, I went right through the red light!'" D's statement as to his liability is an admission.

Traditionally, admissions have been considered as exceptions to the hearsay rule. However, under Rule 801(d)(2), they are treated as non-hearsay to begin with. The practical effect is the same in either case, such admissions are not subject to exclusion under the hearsay rule.

Under Rule 801(d)(2), five categories of admissions are identified as the non-hearsay:

(1) The party's own statement (see example above).

(2) A statement in which the party "has manifested an adoption or belief in its truth." This involves the situation where a party fails to deny something which one would expect the party to deny (an admission by silence).

Example.

> The defendant was at a private social gathering with his girlfriend. His girlfriend made the statement: "We hid stacks of money." The defendant failed to deny the statement. In *United States v. Hoosier*, 542 F.2d 687 (6th Cir. 1976), the court found that this statement by the defendant was admissible as an admission. It

found that the defendant had adopted the statement by his silence.

It is necessary to look to the circumstances in each case to determine what the probable behavior of a person would be (i.e., to deny the statement or not).[7]

(3)   A statement by someone authorized by a party to make the statement. Lawyers call the application of such admissions "vicarious admissions." If a party authorizes someone to speak for him or her, then the statements of that third person can be reasonably deemed the statements (i.e., the admissions) of the authorizing party.

Example.

> Corporation X, Y, Z, Inc. hires John Doe as its President. John Doe is authorized to speak for X, Y, Z, Inc., and his statements are binding on X, Y, Z, Inc.

(4)   Statements by a party's "agent or servant concerning a matter within the scope of the agency or employment, made during the existence of the relationship." This goes to the question of unauthorized statements made by employees of a party during the employment relationship (still vicarious admissions).

Example.

> The defendant (X, Y, Z, Inc.) hired John Doe to deliver its baked goods by truck. After an accident, John Doe makes the statement: "I'm sorry, I just didn't see the stop sign!" Is such a statement a Rule 801(d)(2) admission? It's not an authorized statement in the strictest sense, since John Doe was hired (authorized) to drive, not make statements, and a number of state courts would not allow the statement as an admission against X, Y, Z, Inc. However, the liberal federal rules lead the trend to make the statement admissible as an admission.[8] The student should remember that the statement must concern an act "within the scope" of the employee's employment with the party, and it must be made "during the existence of the relationship" of employment (i.e., not after the truck driver, John Doe, leaves his employment with X, Y, Z, Inc.). Why? There is less reliability (perhaps John Doe was fired by X, Y, Z, Inc. or is otherwise upset with the company).

(5) Statements by a party's co-conspirator made "during the course and in furtherance of the conspiracy."

Example.

>A and B enter an agreement (conspire) to rob C. A and B are co-conspirators. A's statements are admissions against B (and vice versa), provided the statements are made "during the course" of the conspiracy (i.e., before the robbery was committed or the person making the statements withdrew from the conspiracy) and also "in furtherance of the conspiracy" (i.e., the statements relate to the promotion of the crime, the robbery).[9]

The Rationale for the Hearsay Rule

As stated at the beginning of this chapter, the general rule is that hearsay is not admissible, unless one of the many exceptions applies. This then is the hearsay rule.

The many exceptions to the hearsay rule will be discussed in Chapter Eight. However, before looking to exceptions (and as an assistance in understanding the exceptions) it is useful to consider the basic rationale for the existence of the hearsay rule.

In general, the hearsay rule exists because hearsay tends to lack trustworthiness. The declarant's statement is not made under oath. Therefore, it is made with no fear of perjury prosecution. Also, the declarant makes his or her statement outside of the trial or hearing, where his or her demeanor can not be observed by the trier of fact. There is no opportunity for cross-examination of the declarant (i.e., to impeach the declarant). Additionally, the witness may restate the declarant's words incorrectly.[10] As such, hearsay lacks basic reliability; and, hence, the prohibitory rule exists.

Still, some forms of hearsay are more reliable than other forms. In those cases where the hearsay is deemed to be sufficiently reliable, hearsay exceptions have developed, and the hearsay becomes admissible.

NOTES

1.   FED. R. EVID. 802.

2.   FED. R. EVID. 801.

3.   See United States v. Coran, 589 F.2d 70 (1st Cir. 1978).

4.   See "Notes of Advisory Committee on Proposed Rules" to Federal Rule 801, Fed. Rules of Evid. Rule 201, 28 U.S.C.A.

5.   Id.

6.   BLACK'S LAW DICTIONARY 68 (4th ed. 1968).

7.   See United States v. Flecha, 539 F.2d 874 (2d Cir. 1976); see also 48 ALR FED 721.

8.   See "Notes of Advisory Committee on Proposed Rules" to Federal Rule 801, supra.

9.   Id.

10.   For a good discussion of the reasons for the hearsay rule, see Donnelly v. United States, 228 U.S. 243, 57 L.Ed. 820, 33 S.Ct. 449 (1913).

REVIEW AND DISCUSSION QUESTIONS

1.   Review the Rule 801 hearsay definition. Consider the following fact situation:

> The plaintiff sues the defendant grocery store for injuries received in a fall the plaintiff experienced in the store. The plaintiff fell after stepping in ketchup on the floor of the store. The plaintiff alleges, in part, that the store failed to warn her of the presence of the ketchup.

The defendant puts a witness on the stand who is asked by the defendant what she heard the store manager yell to the plaintiff just before the plaintiff stepped in the ketchup. Plaintiff's counsel objects on the grounds of hearsay. If allowed to testify, the witness will answer that the manager said, "Lady, please don't step in the ketchup!" As judge in the trial, will you sustain the objection? Why/why not? Explain.

Note: See *Safeway Stores, Inc. v. Combs*, 273 F.2d 295 (5th Cir. 1960).

2.   Why does the hearsay rule exist? Explain.

3.   A and B are partners in an office supply business. The plaintiff is suing the partnership (partners) for non-payment of monies owed to the plaintiff. B tells the plaintiff before suit, "The partnership owes you the $1,500 for the inventory." Is such a statement hearsay under the Federal Rules of Evidence? Why/why not? Explain.

4.   Rule 801(d) establishes for federal courts non-hearsay categories. As such, what can statements falling in those categories be used for at trial? Explain.

Chapter Eight

EXCEPTIONS TO THE HEARSAY RULE

The Effect of an Exception

A statement by the declarant falling within one of the many hearsay exceptions is not excluded by the Rule 802 hearsay rule.[1]

The Availability Distinction

Traditionally, hearsay exceptions are divided into two basic categories:

(1)   Those exceptions which exist *only if the declarant is unavailable*; and

(2)   Those exceptions which exist *even though the declarant is available* to testify.

The two categories reflect a distinction made as to the reliability of the evidence. The exceptions requiring unavailability are viewed as less reliable. Therefore, before the law allows them to apply the declarant must be unavailable to testify. However, some hearsay provides a greater degree of trustworthiness, so that it is not excluded even where the declarant is available to testify.

The Availability
Distinction and the Federal Rules

The Federal Rules of Evidence conveniently present the exceptions in separate rules, based upon the availability of the declarant. Rule 803 presents those statements which are not excluded by the Rule 802 hearsay rule "even though the declarant is available as a witness." Rule 804 presents those statements which are not excluded "if the declarant is unavailable."

The definition of "unavailability" is found in Rule 804(a) (see Appendix A).[2] Basically, the unavailability must be genuine and not based upon the "wrongdoing of the proponent" of declarant's statement. It includes those situations where a declarant is exempted by a privilege, refuses to testify; claims memory failure, is unable to testify because of death or physical/mental infirmity, or is absent and "the proponent of a statement" fails to procure the declarant's attendance by "reasonable means."

The Rule 803 Hearsay Exceptions

Under Rule 803 (see Appendix A) the availability of a witness is not important.[3] In reviewing Rule 803, the student should consider the following points:

1. Subdivisions (1) and (2) are directly related exceptions.

Subdivision (2), (the "Excited Utterance" exception), follows the traditional approach. If an event causes the declarant to be placed in a state of excitement, then statements "relating to" the "startling event or condition" made while the declarant was excited are excepted from the hearsay rule.

Example.

> The declarant states: "No, No! The motorcycle just ran the stop sign and drove into the bus!"

Such hearsay is viewed as more reliable because the declarant's statement is spontaneous, devoid of time for fabricating a false statement.[4]

Subdivision (1), "Present Sense Impression," is an expansion of the "excited utterance" exception. Here, nearness in time is essential, but excitement is not. Again, the closeness in time to the event offers the reliability.[5]

Example.

> The declarant nonchalantly turns his head after viewing an accident and says to his friend: "The motorcycle

just ran the stop sign and drove
into the school bus."

2.   Subdivision (3), the "Then Existing
Mental,   Emotional,   or   Physical   Condition"
exception,   refers   generally   to   the   situation
where the declarant states his or her present
(not past) state of mind or physical condition.[6]
Obviously, spontaneity plays a role here, as
well.

Example.

The   declarant   (the   defendant   in   a
murder   case)   states: "I   hate   Jane
(the victim)."

3.   Subdivision   (4),   "Statements   for
Purposes of Medical Diagnosis or Treatment,"
recognizes that people under the care of medical
personnel generally tell the truth (i.e., they
want   proper   diagnosis   and   treatment).
Therefore, the subdivision (4) defined exception
exists, even though spontaneity may be lacking.

Example.

The   declarant,   after   his   automobile
accident,   goes   to   his   doctor   and
tells the doctor: "I have terrible
pain in my right arm and shoulder."

4.   In   Chapter   Five   a   distinction   was
made between "present recollection revived" and

"past recollection recorded." As stated then, "past recollection recorded" is considered an exception to the hearsay rule. Rule 803 (5) presents the federal rule which follows the general practice among the states.[7]

Under the federal rule, complete lack of memory is not required, but "insufficient recollection" to allow the witness "to testify fully and accurately" is required. The time issue continues to be important, as the writing must "have been made or adopted by the witness when the matter was fresh in the witness' memory." This (again) is viewed as making the hearsay more reliable.

5. Subdivision (6), "Records of Regularly Conducted Activity," the so-called business records exception to the hearsay rule, is an often used exception. In fact, without it, much information might be lost to substantive consideration by the trier of fact. On the other hand, as critics of the exception contend, it does afford an opportunity to admit possibly self-serving material.

The item which one seeks to admit under this exception must have the following attributes:

(a) It must be "kept in the course of a regularly conducted business activity" (e.g., an account ledger);

(b)   It must be "the regular practice of that business activity to make" the record; and

(c)   The record must be "made at or near the time by, or from information transmitted by, a person with knowledge."

The student should note that Rule 803(6) broadly defines the word "business." The term includes any business, institution, association, profession, occupation, and calling of every kind, *whether or not conducted for profit.*

In practice, the exception allows the custodian of records to establish the above attributes. Therefore, the records may be admitted as substantive evidence through a witness with possibly *no personal knowledge* of the relevant matter.[8]

6.   Subdivision (7), "Absence of Entry in Records Kept in Accordance With the Provisions of Paragraph (6)," establishes that the non-existence of something may be established by the absence of such information in a business record, kept in accordance with paragraph 6 of Rule 803. This is a reasonable expansion of the use of the business records exception.

7.   Subdivision (8), "Public Records and Reports," is the public records exception to the hearsay rule. This, along with subdivision (9),

"Records of Vital Statistics," and subdivision (10), "Absence of Public Record or Entry," provide for entry at trial of great numbers of official records.

The exceptions recognize that the public is better served if officials are not often called from their agencies to testify in court. Also, such hearsay is considered more reliable, since public officials are presumed to act properly.[9]

In general, admissibility under the exceptions requires that the public records be prepared "pursuant to duty imposed by law." The proving of the "nonoccurrence or nonexistence" of a fact by showing absence of entry under subdivision (7) is expanded to include public records under subdivision (10).[10] The scope of this important exception is further discussed in Focus III, immediately following this Chapter.

8. Recognizing the reliability of "regularly kept records" of religious organizations (e.g., records of "births, marriages, deaths, legitimacy, ancestry, relationships by blood or marriage, or other similar facts of personal or family history"), subdivision (11) creates an exception for "Records of Religious Organizations." Likewise, factual statements in "marriage, baptismal, and similar certificates" make up the subdivision (12) exception to the hearsay rule.

9. Traditional law has long accepted into evidence family record entries from Bibles, tomb stones, etc.. This hearsay exception is continued in subdivision (13), "Family Records."[11]

10. Subdivision (14), "Records of Documents Affecting an Interest In Property," and subdivision (15), "Statements in Documents Affecting an Interest in Property," provide exemptions for recordable public records as proof of the "content of the original recorded document," as well as its execution/delivery, and all relevant statements therein.[12]

11. Subdivision (16), "Statements in Ancient Documents," provides an exemption from the hearsay rule for statements in documents at least 20 years of age. In other words, "ancient documents" are documents meeting the 20 year age requirement (under the common law the age requirement was 30 years).

The ancient document must be authenticated to fit within this exception (i.e., it must be shown to be what its proponent claims it to be[13]). Many types of documents fall within this exception (e.g., letters, newspaper articles, maps,).[14]

12. An exception for "market reports, commercial publications" and "learned treatises" is found in subdivision (17), "Market Reports,

Commercial Publications," and subdivision (18), "Learned Treatises," respectively.

Under subdivision (17), the reports and publications must be "generally used and relied upon by the public or by persons in particular occupations," such reliance serving as a basis for the trustworthiness of the hearsay.

Example.

> Securities listings in the *Wall Street Journal*[15] or trade publications.[16]

Under subdivision (18), "learned treatises" (e.g., scholarly texts) are admissible as an hearsay exception "on a subject of history, medicine, or other science or art." Prior to the federal rules, very few states allowed such an exception. The liberal approach here allows such hearsay in, provided the work is "established as a reliable authority." This reliability can be shown "by the testimony or admission of the witness or by other expert testimony or by judicial notice." The availability of judicial notice is exceptional, conceivably allowing certain famous treatises into evidence without the need to call an expert witness. Judicial notice is discussed in detail later in the text.[17]

13. The issue of reputation is raised in subdivisions (19), (20), (21), and (23).

Subdivision (19), the "Reputation Concerning Personal or Family History" exception, liberally allows as substantive evidence reputation evidence "concerning a person's birth, adoption, marriage, divorce, death, legitimacy, relationship by blood, adoption, or marriage, ancestry, or other similar fact of...personal or family history."[18]

Example.

> Community reputation as to the defendant's marriage.

Subdivision (20), the "Reputation Concerning Boundaries or General History" exception, allows for the use of community reputation evidence in land boundary disputes and to prove "events of general history."[19]

Subdivision (21), "Reputation as to Character," follows traditional law to allow as an exception to the hearsay rule community reputation evidence of a person's character, when that is an issue in a case. It is essential to note, however, that subdivision (21) is an exception to the hearsay rule only. The use of character evidence is subject to any and all other limitations in the federal rules (e.g., the Rule 404 requirements discussed in Chapter Three).

Subdivision (23), "Judgment as to Personal, Family or General History, or Boundaries," provides as exception for the use of previous civil court judgments as to the matters noted in the subdivision title, to the extent that such matters "would be provable by evidence of reputation."

14. Subdivision (22), "Judgment of Previous Conviction," provides for the limited availability of evidence of a final judgment of prior conviction to prove a fact in a <u>current</u> case.

Example.

> The plaintiff sues the defendant in state civil court for damages resulting from a wrong by the defendant (e.g., a rape or a battery). The defendant has already been convicted of the rape or the battery in criminal court. The plaintiff now seeks to use evidence of the prior conviction to sustain her claim in the civil action. The question becomes whether or not she can use such evidence. If the jurisdiction follows the federal rule in subdivision (22), then the

answer to the question is in the affirmative (at least as to the rape conviction, which is assumed to be a felony)."

The traditional law viewed such evidence as inadmissible hearsay. However, as discussed previously in Chapter One, the burden of proof in the criminal case is greater than that required in the civil case (i.e., beyond a reasonable doubt v. the preponderance of the evidence). With this consideration, the direction of modern authority is to allow such evidence. Subdivision (22) does so, but only as to felony convictions. The limitation as to felony convictions recognizes that misdemeanor cases are often not defended because of their relatively minor status.[20]

Subdivision 22 deals with the admissibility of prior conviction evidence. Evidence of the defendant being found innocent in a criminal case is not admissible in a later civil case.[21] Also, evidence of a civil judgment is not admissible in later criminal prosecution. Why? It is because of the difference in burden of proof. Evidence of acquittal means only that the prosecutor did not meet the high burden of proof required. Also, evidence of a civil judgment merely establishes that the lower burden was met, but it does not mean that the defendant is guilty "beyond a reasonable doubt."

15. The Federal Rules of Evidence, after listing the basic exceptions discussed above, then provide for a residual (or "catchall") exception in subdivision (24), "Other Exceptions." This final residual exception provides the potential for expansion of the noted exceptions by giving to the judge the ability to, in effect, fashion new exceptions to the hearsay rule. The judge may do so if he or she determines "that (A) the statement is offered as evidence of material fact; (B) the statement is more probative on the point for which it is offered than any other evidence which the proponent can procure through reasonable efforts; and (C) the general purposes of these rules and the interests of justice will be best served by admission of the statement into evidence."[22]

The Rule 804 Hearsay Exceptions

Under Rule 804 (see Appendix A), the availability of a witness is important.[23]

As noted at the beginning of this chapter, these exceptions requiring unavailability do so because they are based on situations viewed as somewhat less reliable than the situations serving as the bases for the Rule 803 exceptions. In reviewing Rule 804, the student should consider the five exception categories and compare them with the Rule 803 exceptions. Are the Rule 804 exceptions less reliable? If so, in what way(s)? Additionally, in reviewing the rules, the student should consider the following points:

1. Subdivision (1), the "Former Testimony" exception, refers to hearsay in the form of witness testimony given at "another hearing of the same or a different proceeding" or in a deposition taken "in the course of the same or another proceeding." Such former testimony, which would have been taken under oath, is admissible as an exception to the hearsay rule, where the witness is *unavailable*, and "the party against whom the testimony is now offered, or, in a civil action or proceedings a predecessor in interest, had an opportunity and similar motive to develop the testimony by direct, cross, or redirect examination."

Example.

> The defendant drove his automobile through a red light, striking John Doe and Tom Smith as they were crossing the street. John Doe sued the defendant and after trial was awarded a judgment. John Doe has now disappeared. Tom Smith also sued the defendant. He has obtained a copy of a transcript of John Doe's testimony against the defendant. May he use the testimony in his trial

against the defendant? The answer is in the affirmative, assuming the defendant ("the party against whom the testimony is now offered") had an opportunity to cross-examine John Doe in the earlier trial, and John Doe is genuinely unavailable.

2. Subdivision (2), "Statement Under Belief of Impending Death," deals with the federal presentation of the traditional, "dying declaration" exception to the hearsay rule.

The common law limited the use of the exception to homicide cases. Subdivision (2) continues this limitation in the criminal area, but it expands the basic law by allowing use of the exception in civil actions. It is important to note that the declarant must make his or her statement "while believing that the declarant's death was imminent." Also, the statement must deal with the "cause or circumstances of what the declarant believed to be impending death."

Example.

> X, the witness in the murder trial, takes the stand and testifies: "I held Z (the victim) in my arms until he died; just before he died Z told me, 'Y (the defendant) knifed me!'" The student must remember that Z must believe that death was

"imminent." In most jurisdictions, Z must actually die. In federal court, Z must be "unavailable" (commonly by death, but not necessarily).

3.   Subdivision (3), "Statement Against Interest," should not be confused with the admission (discussed earlier). An admission is made by a party; a statement (also called a "declaration") against interest is made by a non-party. The statement must be "so far contrary to the declarant's ... interest" such "that a reasonable man in the declarant's position would not have made the statement unless believing it to be true."

Example.

The plaintiff hires the declarant, John Doe, to drive him to the next town. During the drive, John Doe collides with the defendant's truck. A witness at the accident scene is told by the declarant that he (John Doe, the declarant) ran a red light. The declarant is unavailable. May the defendant use the witness and get in the declarant's statement? Assuming that John Doe tended to subject himself to civil liability, the answer is "yes."

Traditional law would not allow as a statement against interest declarant's statement "against penal interest" (e.g., declarant's statement that he, not the defendant, committed the robbery). Such exculpating statements are allowed under the federal rules, provided, "corroborating circumstances clearly indicate the trustworthiness of the statement."[24]

4. Subdivision (4), "Statement of Personal or Family History," and subdivision (5), "Other Exceptions," make up the final exceptions under Rule 804.

Subdivision (4) has two parts. Part (A) allows as an exception statements by the declarant of his own personal or family history. Part (B) allows declarant's statements concerning the personal or family history of others, where the declarant qualifies by intimate association "as to be likely to have accurate information concerning the matter declared."

Subdivision (5) is of identical language and purpose as Rule 803(24), only unavailability is required. As with Rule 803(24), subdivision (5) provides the potential for expansion of the noted exceptions by giving to the judge the ability to, in effect, fashion new exceptions to the hearsay rule.

Hearsay Within Hearsay

Rule 805[25]
HEARSAY WITHIN HEARSAY

Hearsay included within hearsay is not excluded under the hearsay rule if each part of the combined statements conforms with an exception to the hearsay rule provided in these rules.

"Hearsay within hearsay" (also called "double hearsay") involves the situation where a hearsay statement includes another hearsay statement, i.e., a chain of hearsay exists. This is quite common in the business records and official records area.

Example.

The plaintiff and the defendant are involved in an automobile accident. Police officer Smith goes to the scene of the accident. The defendant tells the police officer that he (the declarant) ran the red light. The police officer duly records the statement in her police report. Hearsay within hearsay? Yes. One person provided the information, and another person recorded it. Each must be looked to separately. The defendant's statement is admissible as an admission; the police report qualifies as an official or business record exception. Under Rule 805, the record is not excluded under the hearsay rule since "each part of the combined statements conforms with an exception to the hearsay rule."

If the informer and the recorder are both acting as part of the same business ("acting in the routine of the business") and, therefore, under the same business obligations, there is no double hearsay problem.[26]

Example.

Salesperson of X, Y, Z, Inc. reports her weekly sales to A, the X, Y, Z, Inc. bookkeeper, who duly enters the data in the company books. There is no need for a showing of independent qualifications here as both are under the same obligation of accuracy.

NOTES

1.   Of course, this does not mean that statements fitting within one of the exceptions are necessarily admissible. They must still

meet all other applicable requirements of the rules of evidence for admissibility. See Focus III for a further discussion of this fact.

2. FED. R. EVID. 804(a).

3. FED. R. EVID. 803.

4. See "Notes of Advisory Committee on Proposed Rules" to Federal Rule 803, Fed. Rules of Evid. 803, 28 U.S.C.A.

5. See Houston Oxygen Co. v. Davis, 139 Tx. 1, 161 S.W.2d 474 (1942). Also see United States v. Blakey, 607 F.2d 779 (7th Cir. 1979), which cites Houston Oxygen and discusses the issue of the necessity of "substantial contemporaneity" of the event.

6. See "Notes of Advisory Committee on Proposed Rules" to Fed. Rule 803, supra.

7. See United States v. Kelly, 349 F.2d 720 (2nd Cir. 1965).

8. Authority exists that the witness need not be the recorder of the information if he/she is able to establish the attributes. See United States v. Jones, F.2d 251 (5th Cir. 1977). For an example of similar state law, see Baker v. Wagers, 472 N.E.2d 218 (Ind.App. 1984).

9. "Notes of Advisory Committee on Proposed Rules" to Fed. Rule 803, supra.

10. Id.

11. Id.

12. Id.

13. "Authenticity" will be fully discussed in the next chapter to the handbook.

14. "Notes of Advisory Committee on Proposed Rules" to Fed. Rule 803, supra.

15. United States v. Anderson, 532 F.2d 1218 (9th Cir. 1976), cert. den. 429 U.S. 839.

16. See First National Bank of Chicago v. Jefferson Mortgage Co., 576 F.2d 479 (3rd Cir. 1978), allowing a trade publication to show securities market price trends.

17. See "Notes of Advisory Committee on Proposed Rules" to Fed. Rule 803, supra.

18 Many states will not allow community reputation evidence beyond that of marriage. Id.

19. Id.

20. Id.

21. See United States v. Viserto, 592 F.2d 531 (2nd Cir. 1979).

22. See "Notes of Advisory Committee on Proposed Rules" to Fed. Rule 803, supra. See also 36 ALR FED 742.

23. FED. R. EVID. 804(b).

24. For a discussion of the "against penal interest" concept, see United States v. Alvarez, 584 F.2d 694 (5th Cir. 1978).

25. FED. R. EVID. 805.

26. "Notes of Advisory Committee on Proposed Rules" to Fed. Rule 805, Fed. Rules Evid. Rule 805, 28 U.S.C.A.

REVIEW AND DISCUSSION QUESTIONS

1. What is the affect of the declarant's availability on the use of exceptions to the hearsay rule? Do you understand the definition of the term "unavailability?"

2. On a sheet of paper list all Rule 803 hearsay exceptions. List one under the other down the left side of the sheet of paper. On the right side of the sheet of paper, across from each exception, write down a factual example of each exception.

3. How might the "Records of Regularly Conducted Activity" exception to the hearsay rule allow for the introduction of self-serving statements?

4. What basis for trustworthiness exists for "ancient documents?" Explain.

5. Is the "Judgment of Previous Conviction" statement fair? Why should the convicted defendant face the introduction of such evidence in the civil case?

6. Witness X is walking through the woods. She comes upon Z (the victim). Z has been badly assaulted with a blunt object. X holds Z in her arms, and Z tells X: "Y (the defendant) attacked me!" Z thereupon falls into a coma, where he remains. Y is charged with aggravated battery/attempted murder. At trial, is Z's statement admissible as a "Statement Under Belief of Impending Death?" Explain. Are other facts needed? If so, what additional facts might affect the outcome of the decision on the availability of the exception?

7. Are statements "against penal interest" a part of the allowable statement against interest exception in your state? Should such statements be a part of the exception. Explain.

FOCUS III:

THE CHALLENGE IN APPLYING HEARSAY EXCEPTIONS -
FOCUSING ON THE RULE 803(8) PUBLIC RECORDS AND
REPORTS EXCEPTION

Issues: What is the scope of the Rule 803(8)
Public Records and Reports Exception?
Specifically, are the conclusions and opinions
of a public official contained in a report
admissible? The following case provides the
student with a view as to court interpretation
in regard to this matter. Also, the following
case emphasizes that escaping the prohibition in
the hearsay rule (by finding an exception) does
not guarantee admissibility. Hearsay is but one
basis for the exclusion of evidence. Other
bases can be used to exclude evidence even when
the hearsay rule prohibition is successfully
navigated by the proponent of the evidence.

Hines v. Brandon Steel Decks, Inc.

886 F.2d 299 (11th Cir. 1989)

CLARK, Circuit Judge.

This is a wrongful death action brought in
federal court on the basis of diversity
jurisdiction. On appeal, we address the

propriety of the district court's refusal, during the trial, to admit into evidence the opinions and conclusions contained in an OSHA investigative report. In light of the Supreme Court's intervening decision of *Beech Aircraft v. Rainey,* - U.S. - , 109 S.Ct. 439, 102 L.Ed.2d 445 (1988), we remand this case to the district court for reconsideration.

BACKGROUND

Prior to January 1987, Brandon Steel Decks, Inc. (Brandon Steel), was a roof decking contractor, headquartered in Brandon, Florida. As a decking contractor, Brandon Steel installed metal roof decking on buildings. On January 8, 1987, Emory Singletary, son of the owner of the company, arrived in Cordele, Georgia, along with Richard Burrows and Bill Wood, regular employees of Brandon Steel, to begin work on a decking contract at the Southeastern Frozen Foods plant then under construction in Cordele. Conn-Delmar Steel Erectors, Inc. (Conn-Delmar), contracted to do the structural steel work on the building and was already present on the job site when Mr. Singletary and his employees arrived.

Upon arriving in Cordele, Mr. Singletary found that Conn-Delmar was running behind schedule and had completed relatively little of the structural steel work. Consequently, there was very little decking work for Brandon Steel to do. Nonetheless, the Brandon Steel employees proceeded to complete the decking work on a relatively low portion of the building. Having completed all of the decking work that could be done given the lack of a completed structural frame, Singletary returned to Florida to await completion of the structural steel. Upon learning of Singletary's plans to return to Florida, Bill Meredith, president of Conn-Delmar, agreed with Singletary that Bill Wood and Richard Burrows would stay on the site for a few days as employees of Conn-Delmar to assist with the completion of the structural frame of the building. Wood and Burrows then worked for Conn-Delmar on January 10 and 11, 1987, and were paid in cash by Bill Meredith for the work done on those days.

Conn-Delmar completed a substantial portion of the structural frame of the building by January 11, 1987, and on the morning of January 12, 1987, several men attempted to land bundles of steel roof decking on the top of the frame of the structural steel. The men involved in the landing of the decking on that morning were Bill Wood, Richard Burrows, Quinten Holcomb (Conn-Delmar's foreman), Robert Griffin and Pete Hines (Conn-Delmar employees). Although Conn-Delmar's equipment was used, the work being done was under Brandon Steel's contract. Thus, a dispute exists over which company was in charge of this work and which company employed Richard Burrows and Bill Wood on that particular morning. Other disputes involve which individuals were directing the crane and who made the decision to land the decking in a certain area.

In any event, the first bundle of decking that was landed on the superstructure that morning was placed directly in the center of a span of bar joists. This placement of the decking was admittedly dangerous; the proper place to land decking is at the intersection of a bar joist and a girder. When the crane operator landed the second bundle on top of the first bundle, the superstructure collapsed and both Mr. Hines and Mr. Burrows fell to their deaths. The next day, an investigator from Occupational Safety and Health Administration (OSHA), arrived on the scene of the accident, interviewed several people and prepared an official report.

On July 15, 1987, Wanda P. Hines commenced this action by filing a complaint against Brandon Steel in the United States District Court for the Middle District of Georgia. Brandon Steel timely answered, and the case proceeded to trial on July 11, 1988. During trial, Brandon Steel tendered into evidence the report prepared by the OSHA inspector. The report stated, among other things, that Brandon Steel did not employ any of the individuals allegedly negligent in this case, and exercised no control over the operations which resulted in the death of plaintiff's decedent. Plaintiff's counsel objected on the grounds that the conclusions and opinions in the report were not admissible under Federal Rule of Evidence 803(8)(C).

The district court applied Rainey v. Beech Aircraft Corp., 827 F.2d 1498 (11th Cir.1987) (in banc) to resolve the issue. Under the Eleventh Circuit *Rainey* decision, opinions and conclusions contained in public reports were not admissible under Rule 803(8)(C). Thus, the district court held that only so much of the OSHA report as dealt with specific findings of fact would be admitted and that all conclusions and opinions would be excluded. Accordingly, the parties struck out the following "opinions" and "conclusions" recounted in the OSHA report:

1. Mr. Richard Burrows was a Conn-Delmar employee "loaned" from Brandon Steel;

2. Conn-Delmar was the employer of both (deceased) men at the time of the accident;

3. Conn-Delmar's foreman controlled the work;

4. It was Conn-Delmar's idea that the decking be placed on the joists that morning;

5. No evidence exists that Brandon Steel had control over the work being done at the time of the accident;

6. At no time did any Brandon Steel employees have control over the operation.

The rest of the report was admitted into evidence and published to the jury without emphasis or comment from either party. After closing arguments and instructions, the jury returned a verdict in favor of the plaintiff in the amount of $620,000.00. The district court entered judgment in accordance with the jury's verdict on July 21, 1987. Brandon Steel timely field this appeal. While the appeal was pending, the Supreme Court unanimously reversed the Eleventh Circuit *Rainey* decision. - U.S. -, 109 S.Ct. 439, 102 L.Ed.2d 445 (1988). Specifically, the Supreme Court held that "factually based conclusions or opinions are not on the account excluded from the scope of Rule (803(8)(C)." 109 S.Ct. at 446.

DISCUSSION

Rule 803(8)(C) allows into evidence public reports that (1) set forth factual findings (2) made pursuant to authority granted by law (3) that the judge finds trustworthy. Fed.R.Evid. 803(8)(C). In addition, public reports, otherwise admissible under Rule 803(3)(C), may nonetheless be excluded in whole or in part if the trial court finds that they are either irrelevant or more prejudicial than probative. See *Rainey*, 109 S.Ct. at 448-49; *United States v. MacDonald*, 688 F.2d 224, 230 (4th Cir. 1982), *cert. denied*, 459 U.S. 1103, 103 S. Ct. 726, 74 L.Ed.2d 951 (1983). The district court has broad discretion to admit or exclude evidence during trial and the decision to exclude certain evidence will not be reversed absent a clear showing of abuse of that discretion. *Balogh's of Coral Gables, Inc. v. Getz*, 798 F.2d 1356, 1358, (11th Cir. 1986) (*in banc*).

In this case, however, the district court did not exercise discretion in excluding certain portions of the OSHA report. Rather, the court understandably relied on the Eleventh Circuit *in banc Rainey* opinion and held that the opinions and conclusions contained in the report were *per se* inadmissible under Rule 803(3)(C). This rationale has since been explicitly rejected by the Supreme Court. Under these circumstances, we have no choice but to remand the case to the district court for reconsideration of the report's admissibility in light of the Supreme Court's recent reversal of *Rainey*.

In order to aid the district court on remand in determining the admissibility, either in whole or in part, of the OSHA report, we discuss some factors that the district court may wish to consider.

A. LEGAL VERSUS FACTUAL CONCLUSIONS

In footnote thirteen of the Supreme Court *Rainey* opinion, the Court cautioned that it expressed no view as to whether a legal conclusion as opposed to a factual conclusion was admissible under Rule 803(8)(C):

> We emphasize that the issue in this case is whether Rule 803(8)(C) recognizes any difference between statements of "fact" and "opinion." There is no question in this case of any distinction between "fact" and "law." We thus express no opinion on whether legal conclusions contained in an official report are admissible as "findings of act" under Rule 803 (8)(C).

Rainey, 109 S.Ct. at 450 n. 13. In his concurring opinion in the Eleventh Circuit *Rainey* case, Judge Tjoflat suggested that, indeed, legal conclusions contained in reports would not fall within Rule 803(8)(C) as a "finding." "The common meaning of finding ... comports with investigative conclusions (i.e., the results derived from the examination of facts), but not with idle speculation or legal conclusions: 'a finding does not include legal conclusions that may have been reached by an investigator and is necessarily something more than a mere recitation of evidence...'" *Rainey,* 827 F.2d at 1510 (citation omitted). We agree that Rule 803(8)(C) does not provide for the admissibility of the legal conclusions contained within an otherwise admissible public report. Thus, one approach that the district court might take is to determine whether any of the excluded portions of the OSHA report contain legal conclusions that fall outside the purview of Rule 803(8)(C). Legal conclusions are inadmissible because the jury would have no way of knowing whether the preparer of the report was cognizant of the requirements underlying the legal conclusion and, if not, whether the preparer might have a higher or lower standard than the law requires.

We caution, however, that the amorphous line between "factual" and "legal" conclusions may obscure a practical analysis under this rubric. While a legal conclusion encompasses "the idea that the State will habitually sanction and enforce a legal relation of a specific content," a factual conclusion is one of a number of "contingencies on which the State predicates this relation." Isaacs, *Law and the Facts,* 22 Colum.L.Rev. 1 (1922). Another way of looking at this inquiry is: Would the conclusion, if made by the district court, be subject to the clearly erroneous standard of review on appeal? If so, then the conclusion is factual; if not, then the conclusion is legal.

In addition, for those conclusions which are a mixed question of law and fact, a potential framework for analysis would be to ask whether the investigator made a finding of the 'ultimate facts" underlying the legal conclusion.

B. TRUSTWORTHINESS

We further note that most cases analyzing the admissibility of reports under 803(8)(C) do not frame the issue in terms of factual versus legal conclusions. Instead, almost all of the courts frame the inquiry in terms of trustworthiness. Comment, *The Trustworthiness of Government Evaluation Reports under Federal Rule of Evidence 803(8)(C)*, 96 Harv.L.Rev. 492, 497-98 (1982). The Advisory Comments to the rule set forth several considerations to aid in determining the trustworthiness of a public report: the timeliness of the investigation; the skill and experience of the investigator, whether the investigator held any sort of hearing; and the investigator's impartiality. These considerations are not meant to be exhaustive. Advisory Committee's Notes on Fed.R.Evid. 803(8), 28 U.S.C.App., p. 725.

Under these factors, the district court might consider whether the OSHA investigator's "expertise" includes that necessary to decide questions of agency and whether this factor goes to the admissibility of the report or merely to its weight. *Cf. Fraley v. Rockwell*

International Corp., 470 F.Supp. 1264, 1267 (S.D. Ohio 1979) (document properly excluded where prepared by inexperienced investigator in highly complex field of investigation); *United States v. School District of Ferndale,* 577 F.2d 1339, 1354-55 (6th Cir. 1978) (fact that HEW examiner not an expert goes to weight and not to admissibility; therefore examiner's findings were erroneously excluded as untrustworthy). Furthermore, the district court might consider how the fact that no hearing was held in making the report affects its trustworthiness. *See Denny v. Hutchinson Sales Corp.,* 649 F.2d 816, 821-22 (10th Cir. 1981) (Civil Rights Commission's findings on discrimination properly excluded where ex parte investigation lacked formal procedures such as opportunity to cross-examine witnesses); *McKinnon v. Skill Corp.,* 638 F.2d 270, 278 (1st Cir. 1981) (Consumer Product Safety Commission Reports properly excluded as untrustworthy where they contained double hearsay on issues of defect, causation and negligent design); *Miller v. Caterpillar Tractor Company,* 697 F.2d 141, 144 (6th Cir. 1983) (report excluded because relied upon hearsay statements of witnesses interviewed by investigator).

In addition, the OSHA investigator stands in a unique position because federal law generally prohibits him or her from testifying in private civil litigation. *See* 29 C.F.R. Sec.

2.20 *et seq.* While the inability to cross-examine the investigator cannot *per se* invalidate the report since Rule 803(8) does not depend on the availability of the declarant, it is nonetheless a proper factor to take into consideration when deciding trustworthiness. *See Wilson v. Attaway*, 757 F.2d 1227, 1245 (11th Cir. 1985) (report excluded for a variety of reasons including failure to afford possibility of cross-examination); *see generally The Trustworthiness of Government Evaluation Reports*, 96 Harv.L.Rev. at 499.

C. CUMULATIVE, IRRELEVANT OR PREJUDICIAL

Finally, the district court might consider whether the report should be excluded under any of the other Rules of Evidence. For instance, if sufficient evidence existed on the question of agency, then the report may be cumulative and excludable under Fed.R.Evid. 403. *See Johnson v. Yellow Freight System, Inc.*, 734 F.2d 1304, 1309-10 (8th Cir.), *cert. denied*, 469 U.S. 1041, 105 S.Ct. 525, 83 L.Ed.2d 413 (1984). The report might also be excluded as irrelevant or as more prejudicial than probative. Fed. R. Evid. 402 & 403; *see MacDonald*, 688 F.2d at 230 (although otherwise admissible under Rule 803(8)(C), report properly excluded where it would not help jury ultimate issue of case and would be confusing).

CONCLUSION

The foregoing considerations are merely suggestive; we leave the initial determination of the admissibility of the OSHA report to the sound discretion of the district court. The case is therefore REMANDED to the district court to consider the admissibility of the OSHA report in light of *Beech Aircraft v. Rainey,* - U.S. -, 109 S.Ct. 439, 102 L.Ed.2d 445 (1988), and such other factors as the court deems appropriate.

REMANDED.

CHAPTER NINE

NON-TESTIMONIAL WRITINGS

The Use of Non-Testimonial Writings

Much of the discussion to this point has dealt with the use of testimonial evidence at trial. In this chapter, the focus will shift to the use of non-testimonial writings.

This chapter will consider the evidence law issues of authentication of writings, the best evidence rule, the rule of completeness, and the parole evidence rule. Additionally, this chapter will look to the issue of voice identification, as the Federal Rules of Evidence provide in one rule the requirements for both authentication and voice identification.

Authentication of Writings

A basic rule of evidence is that a writing must be authenticated before it is admitted into evidence.

Rule 901 of the Federal Rules of Evidence presents the federal court requirement for authentication (see Appendix A).[1] Rule 901(a) provides the basic explanation of the requirement of authentication. Under this rule, sufficient evidence must be shown "to support a finding that the matter in question is what its proponent claims." If such evidence is shown, the precondition to admissibility is met. However, even though admitted, the jury is not bound to accept the genuineness of the writing received.

At old common law, authentication required testimony of genuineness by witnesses who signed the writing (so-called "subscribing" or "attesting" witnesses). Today, this requirement has generally been abolished, except in rare cases, e.g., in establishing the genuineness of a will at probate. Rule 903 abolishes the old requirement, subject to state law to the contrary (e.g., state probate law).

Rule 903[2]
SUBSCRIBING WITNESS
TESTIMONY UNNECESSARY

The testimony of a subscribing witness is not necessary to authenticate a writing unless required by the laws of the jurisdiction whose laws govern the validity of the writing.

Means to Authentication
Of Writings under Rule 901

A variety of means now exist for the authentication of writings. Rule 901(b) illustrates key examples:

(1) **Testimony of Witness With Knowledge**" (Rule 901 (b)(1)). This example of authentication includes testimony by witnesses who *signed* the writing (e.g., the parties to the contract). It also includes the testimony by witnesses who *saw* the parties to the contract sign it.

(2) **Nonexpert Opinion on Handwriting**" (Rule 901(b)(2)). In discussing lay witness opinions (in Chapter Six), common categories of allowable lay witness opinions were listed. One category was lay opinions as to the identity of a person, and handwriting identification was noted. Rule 901(b)(2) is clear in that handwriting identification by the nonexpert conforms with Rule 901. This is so, provided there is witness "familiarity not acquired for purposes of litigation."

Example.

The witness Jones has been corresponding with the defendant for a number of years. She has familiarity with the defendant's handwriting, which was not recently developed for purposes of suit.

(3) **"Comparison by Trier or Expert Witness"** (Rule 901(b)(3)). A properly qualified expert may give an opinion as to the genuineness of a writing. This is commonly done by comparison technique. In other words, a specimen of writing which is admittedly authentic is provided to an expert. The expert is also given the contested writing, and a comparison is made. The expert may demonstrate the basis of his or her opinion to the jury (e.g., certain loops, crosses, dots, etc. exist).

A lay witness, even with familiarity, *not being an expert*, may not do such a comparison. He or she may only look at a writing and give a lay opinion as to the identity of the writer. However, an interesting aspect of evidence law is that while a lay witness may not make a comparison, the jury may take properly authenticated writings into the jury room and compare them.

(4) **"Distinctive Characteristics and the Like"** (Rule 901(b)(4)). Characteristics and circumstances may be used to authenticate a writing.

Example.

The writer may use certain distinctive styles, words, phrases, etc.. The writing may contain a special practice or code identifying the writer.[3]

(5) **"Public Records or Reports"** (Rule 901(b)(7)). Public agency records may be authenticated by showing custody, i.e., by showing evidence that the record is from a public agency.[4] Subdivision (7) of Rule 901 applies to all forms of records, including "data compilations" (i.e., computer/electronic data).

(6) **"Ancient Documents or Data Compilations"** (Rule 901(b)(8)). It is possible to authenticate a document based upon the document's age. The Federal Rules of Evidence expand upon the common law authentication base by allowing authentication of a document or "data compilations" (see above, e.g., computer data), if the document is not suspicious, "was in a place where it, if authentic, would likely be," and is at least 20 years old.

(7) **"Process or System"** (Rule 901(b)(9)). Records may be authenticated by showing an "accurate" process or system for production.

Example.

A computer printout may be authenticated by establishing that the process for the production of the printout produces "an accurate result."[5]

Self-Authentication of Writings

Some records or documents are subject to "self-authentication." This means that the writings do not need "extrinsic evidence of authenticity" as a *pre-condition* to admissibility.

If a party seeks to admit such a self-authenticating writing, then the other party to the case may challenge the authenticity of the writing, but he or she carries the burden of doing so.

The Federal Rules of Evidence expand the traditional law as to self-authentication by allowing for an increased number of such instances. Rule 902 of the federal rules (see Appendix A) establishes those several instances.[6]

Official public documents (the originals) may be self-authenticating under Rule 902(1)-(3), provided they meet certain signature requirements or are under seal. However, it is more often the case to produce a copy of a public document than the original, as original documents are usually kept by the particular agency. Certified copies of public records are much more common. Self-authentication in such form is governed by Rule 902(4). Generally, the self-authentication of certified copies involves the custodian of the record certifying that the copy is of the original on file with the public agency.

"Acknowledged documents" (i.e., notarized documents) are self-authenticating under Rule 902(8). Under federal law, self-authenticating acknowledged documents are not limited just to those documents dealing with the ownership of land.[7]

The liberal approach of the Federal Rules of Evidence is again demonstrated by the expansion of the instances of self-authentication to the following:

(1) Public agency "books, pamphlets, or other publications" (e.g., an agency's promulgated regulations) under Rule 902(5);

(2) Newspapers or periodicals under Rule 902(6);

(3) Trade name inscriptions such as tags, signs, or labels "affixed in the course of business and indicating ownership, control, or origin" under Rule 902(7); and

(4) Commercial paper (e.g., a promissory note) under Rule 902(9).

Voice Identification

Rule 902 deals with voice identification, as well as with the authentication of writings. Therefore, while not a "writings" issue, it is useful to deal with the question of voice identification at this point.

At times, the identity of a person who made a particular statement is of importance in a case. Here, the statement of the person must be authenticated.

Under Rule 901(b)(5), the identification may be based upon the opinion of one who had heard the speaker's voice. Rule 901(b)(6) deals with telephone conversations. As to telephone conversations, authentication may occur where the evidence shows that a call was made to the proper phone number ("assigned at the time by the telephone company to a particular person or business"), and, (1) as to a person, the person identifies himself or herself, or otherwise circumstances show the person answering to be the one called (e.g., the voice is recognized, or the person answering only knows facts which the identified person could know), or (2) as to a business, "the call was made to a place of business and the conversation related to business reasonably transacted over the telephone."[8]

The Best Evidence Rule

Not only must one generally authenticate a writing as a precondition to admissibility, but, in certain cases, one must also produce in court the original of the writing. This occurs in those situations where the so-called "best evidence rule" (or, more accurately, the "original document rule") is applicable.

Rule 1002[9]
REQUIREMENTS OF ORIGINAL

To prove the content of a writing, recording, or photograph, the original writing, recording, or photograph is required, except as otherwise provided in these rules or by Act of Congress.

The best evidence rule does not apply to a public record which meets the requirements of Rule 902 or is "testified to be correct by a witness who has compared it with the original." Rule 1005 (see Appendix A). The intent in the public record instance is to protect such originals and to avoid public inconvenience.[10]

The best evidence rule does apply "to prove the content of a writing, recording, or photograph," except as otherwise provided by law. In other words, it applies when the writing's terms are being shown. Rule 1002 represents the modern position of including recordings and photographs within the gambit of the best evidence rule.

Rule 1001 (see Appendix A) provides the relevant definitions of the terms writings, recordings, and photographs (which includes x-ray films, video tapes and motion pictures, as well as still photographs), and it distinguishes the terms "original" and "duplicate."[11] The student should consider carefully the distinction. The concept of the duplicate is important under the federal rules, as discussed below.

The Use of Duplicates

Rule 1003[12]
ADMISSIBILITY OF DUPLICATES

A duplicate is admissible to the same extent as an original

unless (1) a genuine question is raised as to the authenticity of the original or (2) in the circumstances it would be unfair to admit the duplicate in lieu of the original.

Under Rule 1003, a duplicate is admissible "to the same extent as an original," assuming that no real question as to the authenticity of the original has been raised, or under the circumstances "it would be unfair to admit the duplicate in lieu of the original" (e.g., the duplicate is of only a part of the original, and the rest of the original is needed for cross-examination).[13] This rule as to duplicates was unknown under traditional law.

The Use of Other Evidence of Contents

Rule 1004[14]
ADMISSIBILITY OF OTHER
EVIDENCE OF CONTENTS

The original is not required, and other evidence of the contents of a writing, recording, or photograph is admissible if - (1) Originals lost or destroyed. All originals are lost or have been destroyed, unless the proponent lost or destroyed them in bad faith; or (2) Original not obtainable. No original can be obtained by any available judicial process or procedure; or (3) Original in possession of opponent. At a time when an original was under the control of the party against whom offered, that party was put on notice, by the pleadings or otherwise, that the contents would be a subject of proof at the hearing, and that party does not produce the original at the hearing; or (4)Collateral matters. The writing, recording, or photograph is not closely related to a controlling issue.

The best evidence rule is not required in certain situations described in Rule 1004:

(1) **"<u>Originals Lost or Destroyed</u>."** The most common excuse for nonperformance of the best evidence rule is where the originals have been lost or destroyed. However, the loss or destruction must not have occurred in bad faith.

(2) **"Original Not Obtainable**." An original is not obtainable if it can not be obtained by "judicial process or procedure." If unobtainable in this sense, there is an excuse.

This aspect of Rule 1004 is less liberal than the law found in many jurisdictions where an original is viewed as unobtainable if it is in a non-party's possession outside the state. Since it may be possible to secure a subpoena ducus tecum out of state in a deposition, the federal law is more limited.[15]

(3) **"Original in Possession of Opponent**." If a party has notice that a writing in his or her possession will be proved at trial, he or she has no need for the protection of the best evidence rule. Therefore, if the opposing party gives such notice, and the original is not produced by the party who has the original in his or her possession and receives notice, an excuse exists for the opposing party to produce other evidence.

(4) **"Collateral Matters**." The best evidence rule does not apply where the writing, recording, or photograph "is not closely related to a controlling issue" (the so-called "collateral documents rule").

In many cases, a writing is just not all that crucial to a case to require the burden of the rule. No precise definition is possible, but

the court does have the power under this
exception to admit other evidence.[16]

The Use of Summaries

Rule 1006[17]

SUMMARIES

The contents of voluminous
writings, recordings, or photographs
which cannot conveniently be
examined in court may be presented
in the form of a chart, summary, or
calculation. The originals or
duplicates shall be made available
for examination or copying, or both,
by other parties at a reasonable
time and place. The court may order
that they be produced in court.

Where the originals are in such great
number (so "voluminous") that they become
impractical to use at trial, then summaries may
be resorted to under Rule 1006. By "summaries,"
the rule notes summaries, charts or
calculations. Of course, to prevent inaccuracy
or fabrication, the rule requires that the
summarized originals "be made available for

examination or copying, or both, by other parties at reasonable time and place."[18]

Testimony or Written Admissions

If a party against whom the writing (or recording, photograph) is offered admits in testimony or writing as to the contents, then the best evidence rule does not apply. Because of concern for accuracy, this rule does not include out-of-court or non-deposition, oral statements.[19]

The Rule of Completeness

While not a part of Article X, another rule should be cited at this point because of its importance in regulating the use of writings at trial.

Rule 106[20]
REMAINDER OF OR RELATED
WRITINGS OR RECORDED STATEMENTS

When a writing or recorded statement or part thereof is introduced by a party, an adverse party may require the introduction at that time of any other part or any other writing or recorded statement which ought in fairness to be considered contemporaneously with it.

The federal rules provide the modern and better view that a party may not be allowed to present only a part of a writing or recorded statement. If fairness requires, the party will have to produce "any other part" of the writing or recorded statement. This view presents the so-called "rule of completeness."

The Parole Evidence Rule

The parole evidence rule is important in breach of contract trials. It is a rule of exclusion, which recognizes a belief in the greater reliability of both written and later contractual expressions. The rule excludes evidence of earlier understandings (either in oral or written form) which contradicts the terms of the parties' final, written contract.

Example.

Jane Smith and Tom Jones enter into a written lease. Tom agrees to rent from Jane Apartment #301, 8544 Elmwood Drive, Hammond, Indiana. Prior to signing the lease agreement, Tom offers to install new carpets in the apartment at his expense, if Jane will discount the rent by 50% over the first three months of the rental period. Jane agrees. However, the written lease contains no provision for discount and, in fact, states the rental in the full amount beginning immediately. In a suit for breach of contract, the lease is submitted to the court. It appears to be a complete expression of the parties' agreement. Therefore, evidence of the prior 50% discount understanding will not be admissible, since it contradicts the terms of the parties final, written contract.[21]

Exceptions to the Parole Evidence Rule

The parole evidence rule excludes earlier, contradictory evidence. It does not exclude evidence of understandings arrived at subsequent to the signing of the written contract (i.e., contract modifications or cancellations). Additionally, evidence of earlier statements concerning the transaction may be admissible under certain circumstances as an exception to the rule. The key situations for exception can be classified into three categories:

(1)   Evidence of additional terms;

(2)   Evidence that clears up ambiguities; and

(3)   Evidence that establishes situations rendering a contract void or voidable.

In the first category, evidence is admissible if it establishes additional terms of the parties' agreement. The key factor here is that the evidence does not contradict the terms of the final, written contract; the evidence merely supplements the terms of the writing. Many written contracts, however, contain provisions indicating that the written terms represent the entire agreement of the parties (i.e., so-called merger clauses). Most courts respect such provisions and deny the admissibility of earlier statements to supplement.

Evidence may be admissible to clear up an ambiguity posed in the written contract.

Example.

John Doe and Harry Roe enter into a written contract wherein John agrees to sell Harry "his watch." John has two watches. Evidence of earlier understandings is admissible to clear up the ambiguity as to which of the two watches is subject to the sale.

In contract law, a variety of situations may exist to render a contract void or voidable (i.e., void at the election of the innocent party) and, therefore, unenforceable. Key examples include situations establishing fraud, duress, illegality, or mistake.[22] Evidence of such situations is admissible as an exception to the parole evidence rule.

Example.

> Tom Smith comes up to John Doe with a written contract in one hand and a gun in the other. Tom puts the gun to John's head and orders John to sign the contract or be shot. This represents physical duress which voids the contract. Evidence of the duress is admissible as an exception to the rule.

NOTES

1. FED. R. EVID. 901.

2. FED. R. EVID. 902.

3. See United States v. Wilson, 532 F.2d 641 (8th Cir. 1976), cert. den., 429 U.S. 846 (1977). See also "Notes of Advisory Committee on Proposed Rules" to Federal Rule 901, Fed. Rules of Evid. Rule 901, 28 U.S.C.A.

4. Id.

5.   Id.

6.   FED. R. EVID. 902.

7.   Id.

8.   Id.

9.   FED. R. EVID. 1002.

10.   See "Notes of Advisory Committee on Proposed Rules" to Federal Rule 1005, Fed. Rules of Evid. Rule 1005, 28 U.S.C.A.

11.   FED. R. EVID. 1001.

12.   FED. R. EVID. 1003.

13.   See "Notes of Advisory Committee on Proposed Rules" to Federal Rule 1003, Fed. Rules of Evid. Rule 1003, 28 U.S.C.A.

14.   FED. R. EVID. 1004.

15.   See "Notes of Advisory Committee on Proposed Rules" to Federal Rule 1004, Fed. Rules of Evid. Rule 1004, 28 U.S.C.A.

16.   Id.

17.   FED. R. EVID. 1006.

18.   See United States v. Conlin, 551 F.2d 534 (2nd Cir. 1977), where the court said, at 539, "(a) chart which for any reason presents

an unfair picture can be a potent weapon for harm, and permitting the jury to consider it is error."

    19.   FED. R. EVID. 1007.

    20.   FED. R. EVID. 106.

    21.   While there are some exceptions to the rule (as described in the text), its effect can be so great that the safest route is to ensure that all terms of the agreement are included in the written contract.

    22.   Other examples exist in contract law. A full analysis is beyond the proper scope of this book. The student should also be aware of the fact that the Uniform Commercial Code, Section 2-202, liberalizes the parole evidence rule in contracts involving the sale of goods. The UCC allows for the explanation or supplementation of a written contract by evidence of course of dealing, trade usage, or course of performance.

REVIEW AND DISCUSSION QUESTIONS

1.   How has the means to authenticate a writing been expanded since old common law?

2.   Do you believe that "official publications," "newspapers and periodicals," and "trade

inscriptions and the like," should be self-authenticating? Explain.

3. Review the Rule 1001 definitions of "original" and "duplicate." Within which category would a carbon copy fall? Computer printout? Photograph negative?

4. Under Rule 1007, testimony or written admissions "of the party against whom" a writing is offered is a basis for proof of the contents. Does that forego use of oral admissions? What if the particular writing is established as lost (Rule 1004)? May oral admissions then be used to establish contents?

5. What is the parole evidence rule? Create a fact situation to portray each of the three main exception categories.

Chapter Ten

PRESENTATION OF EXHIBITS, OBJECTIONS, AND CONSTITUTIONAL DIMENSIONS

In the last chapter, the focus shifted from the use of testimonial evidence to the use of non-testimonial writings as evidence. Such writings (also called documentary evidence) represent the most common form of exhibits at trial, and they are affected by the special rules discussed in Chapter Nine. In this chapter, the discussion will broaden to consider rules of evidence applicable to non-testimonial evidence in general.

The Presentation of Real Evidence

Real evidence was first described in Chapter Two. It involves the submission of some physical object which was a direct part of the situation or incident in question. Real evidence includes non-testimonial writings and other exhibits, as well (e.g., Y's ax, the murder weapon example in Chapter Two).

In general, as with all evidence, real evidence must be relevant (see Chapter Three), non-privileged (see Chapter Eleven), and conform to the requirements of the hearsay rule (see

Chapters Seven and Eight).[1] Also, the requirement for "authentication" is not limited to non-testimonial writings. Real evidence must be shown to be "what its proponent claims" (attorneys consider this authentication process as the laying of the evidentiary foundation).

Example.

> In Chapter Two, Y's ax was given as an example of real evidence. If the prosecutor seeks to admit the ax into evidence, he or she must first lay a foundation for admissibility. This process can be done in the following manner:
>
> Prosecutor: "Your honor, I would now request that the clerk (or reporter) mark this item (the prosecutor has the ax) as State's Exhibit No. I for the purpose of its identification."
>
> Note: The court clerk will mark the exhibit for purposes of identification.
>
> Prosecutor: "Mr. X (the witness in Chapter Two who heard a scream and entered Y's garage), I give you this item which has been marked by the clerk for purposes of

identification as State's Exhibit I, and I now ask you if you recognize this item?"

Witness X: "Yes, I do."

Prosecutor: "Would you please indicate how you can identify the item."

Note: Witness X will now testify that the ax is the one that the defendant Y was holding in the garage, while standing over Z's decapitated body. He will indicate that he recognizes it due to the particular characteristics or markings on the ax, and the witness will establish that it is presented in the same condition as it was when first seen.

Prosecutor: "Your honor, I now move to admit State's Exhibit No. I for identification into evidence as State's Exhibit No. I.

Note: The exhibit will be given to the defense attorney by the prosecutor for inspection. The defense attorney will have an opportunity to object (e.g., insufficient foundation laid). The court will rule on the objection, if any, and admit or not admit the exhibit. The judge will generally admit the exhibit if sufficient evidence is presented from which the jury may find that the ax is what its proponent claims it to be.[2] If the exhibit is admitted, it will then be displayed to the jury.

The Chain of Custody

Some evidence is simply not capable of easy recognition or is capable of easy tampering, loss, substitution or mistake. As to such evidence, the party wishing to admit the evidence must meet a more heightened authentication requirement. This requirement is generally referred to as the chain of custody foundation. The following quote from an Indiana case presents the general rationale for the chain of custody foundation:

> The purpose of requiring an adequate chain of custody is to connect the evidence with the proper individual and to negate any substantial likelihood of tampering, loss, substitution or mistake. .... Accordingly, the specificity and completeness of the evidentiary foundation diminishes as the nature of the proposed exhibit becomes

decreasingly susceptible to alteration, tampering or substitution. .... A blood sample, like a drug sample or a semen sample, is more than a gun and consequently the chain of custody foundation is more stringent. Nevertheless, it is not necessary to account for every minute or every hand through which the sample passes. What is required is the production of evidence from which the trial court can reasonably conclude the specimen passed through time and the various hands in a relatively undisturbed fashion to the point it is subjected to analysis.[3]

A test of reasonableness is applied in dealing with the chain of custody question.

Example.

The following evidence was found to be sufficient to authenticate blood specimens in the Indiana case *Orr v. Econo-Car of Indianapolis, Inc.*, 276 N.E.2d524 (Ind. App. 1971):

A pathologist, who had taken blood specimens from the decedents, testified that he took the blood samples and placed the samples in vials. The vials were then put into sealed envelopes with the decedents' names indicated on the appropriate vial. The envelopes were put into mailing containers and mailed to the state police laboratory. An Indiana state police technician, who analyzed the specimens of blood, testified that he had received the samples through the mail. The sealed envelopes found in the mailing containers contained the vials which bore the names of the decedents. The technician further testified that such blood specimens were the ones that he analyzed.

The Presentation of New Scientific Evidence

Recent advances in forensic science and technology (e.g., DNA profile analysis) have greatly enhanced criminal investigation. However, before the results of such science and technology can be used in court, the proponent of the evidence must lay a proper foundation.

Generally, this requires a sufficient showing for the judge to conclude that (1) the form of evidence is generally accepted by the scientific community, (2) the testing procedures used in the particular case are generally accepted as reliable, if performed in a proper manner, and (3) that the testing in the particular case was, in fact, performed properly. Additionally, Rule 403 (discussed in Chapter Three) may well be in issue. For example, if the testing involves DNA analysis, there may be an issue raised as to whether the statistics used to determine the probability of another person having the same genetic characteristics are more probative than prejudicial. The student should remember that, under Rule 403, the judge is given the discretion to weigh, or balance, the probative value of evidence against the danger of unfair prejudice. If the inherent dangers in the evidence "substantially outweigh" the probative value, the evidence may be excluded by the court.

The question of the admissibility of new scientific evidence is developed in detail in Focus IV (which can be found immediately after this chapter). Through the presentation of an Eighth Circuit Court of Appeals decision, Focus IV considers, in particular, the use of DNA evidence at trial. However, the case presented in Focus IV also discusses other evidence and the general foundational requirements for the admissibility of new scientific evidence.

The Presentation of
Demonstrative Evidence

Demonstrative evidence was also first described in Chapter Two. It is to be distinguished from real evidence in that, unlike real evidence, it merely serves as a visual/audio visual aid to the trier of fact (e.g., an anatomical model such as the plastic skeleton skull from biology class).

Because demonstrative evidence may be fabricated or otherwise inaccurately portrayed, the court requires that such evidence be shown to be accurate.

Example.

> If the plaintiff's attorney seeks to use a plastic skull as a model to aid in a physician witness' description of the plaintiff's head injuries in an automobile accident, he or she must first lay a proper foundation. This process can be done in the following manner:
>
> Note: The exhibit has already been marked by the clerk.
>
> Attorney: "Doctor Jones, I now hand you Plaintiff's Exhibit I, and I ask you to look it over (the physician studies the model exhibit).

Now, Doctor are you in a position to adequately illustrate the plaintiff's head injuries suffered as a result of the automobile accident without the use of an anatomical model?"

Witness Jones: "No, I need the use of an anatomical model, specifically a model of the human skull, to adequately describe the injuries suffered."

Attorney: "You've studied the exhibit. Please describe it."

Witness Jones: "It is a model of the human skull."

Attorney: "Is the exhibit anatomically accurate?"

Witness Jones: "Yes, it is. It is the same type of model used by me at the University of Calumet School of Medicine in teaching my medical students."

Attorney: "And you testified that it will assist you in giving your testimony today?"

Witness Jones: "Yes, so I have testified."

Attorney: "Your honor, I now wish to have Plaintiff's Exhibit No. I admitted into evidence and displayed to the jury."

Note: The exhibit will be shown to the other party's attorney, and it will be subject to his or her objection. The court will rule on its propriety as demonstrative evidence.

Objections

The Objection Requirement

Where one party has violated the rules of evidence, the opposing party should object.

The following represent common (non-exclusive) examples of objections:

(1)   The question posed to the witness by defendant's attorney is a leading question.

(2)   The question asks for inadmissible hearsay.

(3)   The question is irrelevant.

(4)   A proper foundation has not been laid for admitting the plaintiff's exhibit into evidence.

(5) An "expert" witness has not been properly qualified as an expert.

Failure to properly object will constitute a waiver, allowing otherwise improper evidence to be admitted and considered by the trier of fact.

When to Object

The basic rule is that the objection must be timely. In other words, if the objection is to a question asked, then the objection must be made when the question is posed. If the objection is to the offering into evidence of an exhibit, then the objection must be made when the evidence is offered. In other words, the objection must be made as soon as possible. It simply does not serve the attempt to do justice to allow a party to wait for a response to an improper question, and then, if the response is not to a party's liking, allow an objection and the striking of the response.

The Motion to Strike

The timeliness rule above does not mean that a motion to strike already presented evidence is never available. A motion to strike may be granted in limited situations where fairness allows it.

Example.

The question posed by a party's attorney may not be improper, but the witness' answer may present improper evidence:

Plaintiff's Attorney: "Mr. Smith, did you see the red light?"

Witness Smith: "The defendant has a lot of insurance coverage on his automobile!"

Also, evidence may be presented on condition that additional evidence be shown later at trial (attorneys call this taking proof subject to connection). For example, an expert witness may be allowed to give an opinion on facts not in evidence, with an understanding that such facts will be later proved. If the facts are not later proved, a motion to strike the expert's evidence is proper.

The Offer of Proof

The requirement of making an offer of proof is not a burden on the party making an objection. It is a burden on the party to whose proposed evidence an objection has been made. It applies where the court has *sustained* an objection.

Example.

The prosecutor is questioning Witness X on direct examination. She reaches the point in her direct at which she asks Witness X to state what he heard the defendant say as to his present state of mind concerning the victim. When the question is posed, the defense attorney objects on the grounds of inadmissible hearsay. The court thereupon sustains the objection. At this point, the prosecutor must make an offer of proof. She will ask the judge for permission to do so. Upon receiving permission, the jury will be dismissed. The prosecutor will have the court reporter note that the question was asked and that the prosecutor does not agree with the court's position sustaining the hearsay objection. The prosecutor will note for the record (or the witness will be allowed to answer the question posed) that had Witness X been allowed to answer the question, he would have said that the defendant told him: "I hate Jane (the victim)." Without an offer of proof the record is not preserved. The appellate court would have no way of knowing what evidence was withheld from the jury.

Constitutional Dimensions

The Effect of the Constitution
On Admissibility of Evidence

The rules of evidence are subject to the dictates of the Constitution. As such, evidence obtained in violation of one's constitutional rights may be inadmissible at trial.

Two major constitutional bases for the exclusion of evidence are the Fourth Amendment's prohibition against unreasonable search and seizure and the Fifth Amendment's privilege against self-incrimination.[4] The exclusion of evidence and the privilege against self-incrimination are discussed in Chapter Eleven. The remainder of this chapter will focus on the exclusion of evidence and the prohibition against unreasonable search and seizure.

The Exclusionary Rule

On February 24, 1914, the United States Supreme Court handed down its landmark decision *Weeks v. United States*, wherein it found prejudicial error in using at trial evidence seized in violation of the Fourth Amendment's prohibition against unreasonable search and seizure.[5] The so-called "exclusionary rule" was established to exclude from a criminal trial evidence obtained as a result of an illegal search and seizure. At first applicable only to the federal government, the exclusionary rule was later extended to the states (through the Fourteenth Amendment) in *Mapp v. Ohio*.[6]

Criticism of the Exclusionary Rule

The exclusionary rule has been subject to a great deal of criticism in recent years.

In his famous 1971 dissent in *Bivens v. Six Unknown Agents*, then Chief Justice Warren Burger expressed his opinion that the exclusionary rule is flawed and that, rather than using the exclusionary rule, an action for damages against the government violating one's rights (i.e., a different remedy) is necessary to safeguard constitutional rights.[7] The Chief Justice stated that a rule for the exclusion of evidence is, in fact, "unique to American jurisprudence."[8]

Other voices have been raised for a so-called "good faith" exception to the exclusionary rule, allowing evidence to be admissible to trial where it is seized as a result of a "good faith" error as to the constitutional requirements.[9]

A Good Faith Exception
To the Exclusionary Rule

On July 5, 1984, the U.S. Supreme Court decided *United States v. Leon*[10] and a companion case, *Massachusetts v. Sheppard*.[11] In addition to discussing in these cases the basis for the exclusionary rule, the Court adopted a good faith exception to it.

The Court's Clarification
Of the Exclusionary Rule's Basis

In *Leon*, the Court made it quite clear that the exclusionary rule "operates as 'a judicially created remedy designed to safeguard Fourth Amendment rights generally through its deterrent effect...'."[12] In other words, the exclusionary rule is not designed to make someone whole whose constitutional rights have been violated. It exists to deter unlawful police actions. This fact was made additionally clear in *Sheppard*, where the court refused to apply the exclusionary rules where a judge, *not the police*, made a mistake as to the constitutional propriety of a search warrant. Quoting from *Illinois v. Gates*, 103 Sup. Ct. 2317 (1983), the Court stated, "'(T)he exclusionary rule was adopted to deter unlawful searches by police, not to punish the errors of magistrates and judges.'"[13] Excluding evidence because of judicial failure does not serve the deterrent function of the rule.[14]

The Court's Application
Of a Good Faith Exception

In deciding *Leon*, the Court "concluded that, in the Fourth Amendment context, the exclusionary rule can be modified somewhat without jeopardizing its ability to perform its intended function" (i.e., police deterrence).[15] The Court stated that the question of the appropriateness of the exclusionary rule "must be resolved by weighing the costs and benefits of preventing the use in the prosecution's case-in-chief of inherently trustworthy tangible evidence...."[16] This cost-benefit analysis takes into consideration the "substantial social costs" exacted by the rule (e.g., some guilty people go free).[17] The Court stated: "Particularly when law enforcement officers have acted in objective good faith or their transgressions have been minor, the magnitude of benefit conferred on such guilty defendants offends basic concepts of the criminal justice system."[18] In basic terms, the Court made clear that, while the application of the exclusionary rule may well be appropriate in cases, it is not appropriate in the particular case before the Court: "We conclude that the marginal or nonexistent benefits produced by suppressing evidence obtained in objectively reasonable reliance on a subsequently invalidated search warrant cannot justify the substantial costs of exclusion."[19] The good faith exception found a foothold in the constitutional law of evidence.

A Possible Future Re-Assessment
Of the Good Faith Exception

In his concurring opinion to *Leon*, Justice Blackmun wrote to "underscore... the unavoidably provisional nature" of the *Leon* decision.[20] While Justice Blackmun agreed with the Court's opinion, he felt it necessary to caution law enforcement officers:

> By their very nature, the assumptions on which we proceed today cannot be cast in stone. To the contrary, they now will be tested in the real world by state and federal law enforcement, and this Court will attend to the results. If it should emerge from experience that, contrary to our expectations, the good faith exception to the exclusionary rule results in a material change in police compliance with the Fourth Amendment, we shall have to reconsider what we have undertaken here. The logic of a decision that rests on untested predictions about police conduct demands no less.[21]

The police must still meet the requirements of the fourth Amendment. *Leon* and *Sheppard* deal solely with the evidence issue posed in the application of the exclusionary rule. If police misconduct is fostered by the availability of the good faith exception, then the propriety of the exception may have to be re-assessed by the Court.

The Court's Enhancement
Of a Good Faith Exception

While Justice Blackmun's 1984 caution to the police remains viable, the Court has not shown any actual interest in abandoning the good faith exception course of jurisprudence.

In the 1987 Supreme Court decision *Illinois v. Krull*,[22] the Court enhanced the good faith exception by applying it in a case where the police in good faith relied on an Illinois statute authorizing a warrantless search of an automobile wrecking yard. The Illinois statute was later found to be unconstitutional. The Court refused to apply the exclusionary rule to the case. Instead, it stated that a good faith exception applies "when an officer's reliance on the constitutionality of a statute is objectively reasonable, but the statute is subsequently declared unconstitutional."[23] The Court found that the rationale in *Leon* and *Sheppard* applied equally in *Krull*:

> The application of the exclusionary rule to suppress evidence obtained by an officer acting in objectively reasonable reliance on a statute

would have as little deterrent on the officer's actions as would the exclusion of evidence when an officer acts in objectively reasonable reliance on a warrant. Unless a statute is clearly unconstitutional, an officer cannot be expected to question the judgment of the legislature that passed the law. If the statute is subsequently declared unconstitutional, excluding evidence obtained pursuant to it prior to such a judicial declaration will not deter future Fourth Amendment violations by an officer who has simply fulfilled his responsibility to enforce the statute.[23]

NOTES

1. In addition to these general requirements, other law may affect the admissibility of real evidence, e.g., the Fourth Amendment's search and seizure restraints reviewed later in this chapter.

2. However, other factors may well affect the judge's decision as to admissibility. For example, even if the item is what the proponent claims it to be and is relevant, the court may exercise its discretion under Rule 403 of the Federal Rules of Evidence and prevent the

admissibility where the exhibit is highly misleading, prejudicial, etc. (see Rule 403). See also the discussion regarding Rule 403 in the case presented in Focus IV. Additionally, the evidence may be excluded by the exclusionary rule in illegal search and seizure cases (discussed later in this chapter).

   3.   Fendley v. Ford, Ind.App., 458 N.E.2d 1167, 1169-1170 (1984).

   4. The violation of other constitutional requirements may also affect the admissibility of evidence at trial. For example, the taping of the defendant's incriminating statements, without defendant's knowledge, after charges were filed against the defendant, while such charges were pending, and "in the absence of" defendant's attorney, presented a violation of the defendant's Sixth Amendment right to counsel and required the exclusion at trial of such statements. Massiah v. United States, 377 U.S. 201, 12 L.Ed.2d 246, 84 S.Ct. 1199 (1964). Also, see Gilbert v. California, 388 U.S. 263, 87 S.Ct. 1951 (1967), as to the right to counsel and the exclusion of evidence. See footnotes to Chapter Eleven (the material concerning the privilege against self-incrimination).

   Additionally, the due process of law protections found in the Fifth and Fourteenth Amendments, if violated, may result in the exclusion of evidence. See the Chapter Eleven footnotes (the material concerning the privilege against self-incrimination, where the due process issue is raised). See also Manson v. Brathwaite, 432 U.S. 98, 97 S.Ct. 2243 (1977) for a view of the Due Process Clause and any effects on the exclusion of evidence of pretrial identification. For a state case example (dealing with the propriety of the "show-up") see Grossenbacher v. State, Ind., 468 N.E.2d 1053 (1984).

5.   232 U.S. 383, 58 L.Ed. 652, 34 S.Ct. 431 (1914). Note. The exclusionary rule can be raised only by the person whose rights were allegedly violated (e.g., the individual with an adequate interest on the premises searched by the police). This is a basic "standing" limitation on the exclusionary rule. See Combs v. United States, 408 U.S. 224, 33 L.Ed.2d 308, 92 S.Ct. 2284 (1972).

6.   367 U.S. 643, 6 L.Ed.2d 1081, 81 S.Ct. 1684 (1961).

7.   403 U.S. 388, 91 S.Ct. 1999 (1971).

8.   See Id.

9.   A number of government leaders, scholars, and federal and state courts have urged the U.S. Supreme Court to adopt a good faith exception to the exclusionary rule. See

United States v. Ailouny, 659 F.2d 830 (2nd Cir. 1980). Some states have enacted a good faith exception by statute. See Indiana Code (I.C.) 35-37-4-5.

10. 468 U.S. 897, 82 L.Ed.2d 677, 104 S.Ct. 3405 (1984).

11. 468 U.S. 981, 82 L.Ed.2d 737, 104 S.Ct. 3424 (1984).

12. 82 L.Ed.2d at 687.

13. 82 L.Ed.2d at 745.

14. Id.

15. 82 L.Ed. 2d at 687.

16. Id. at 688.

17. The cost-benefit analysis was also used by the Court in applying the INEVITABLE DISCOVERY EXEMPTION to the exclusionary rule in Nix v. Williams, 467 U.S. 431, 81 L.Ed.2d 377, 104 S.Ct. 2501 (1984), decided on June 11, 1984. This Sixth Amendment exclusionary rule case dealt with the admissibility of unlawfully obtained evidence as to the place of discovery and condition of a victim's body. The police had been led to the body by the defendant in violation of the person's Sixth Amendment right to counsel. However, it was clear that search parties would have found the victim's body

independently of the defendant's directions. In view of the inevitable discovery, the application of the exclusionary rule would "add nothing to either the integrity or fairness of a criminal trial" which the Sixth Amendment right to counsel is designed to aid. 81 L.Ed.2d at 389. Therefore, where such unlawfully obtained evidence would have been discovered by lawful means, the INEVITABLE DISCOVERY EXEMPTION to the EXCLUSIONARY RULE allows admission at trial. See also Murray v. United States, 487 U.S. 533 (1988).

18.   82 L.Ed.2d at 689.

19.   Id. at 698.

20.   Id. at 701.

21.   Id. at 702.

22.   480 U.S. 340, 107 S.Ct. 1160 (1987).

23.   107 S.Ct. at 1165.

24.   107 S.Ct. at 1167.

REVIEW AND DISCUSSION QUESTIONS

1.   What is the purpose for the laying of an evidentiary foundation at trial?

2.   What is the general rationale for the chain of custody foundation? Must every

moment of possession be accounted for? What is meant by a test of reasonableness as to this issue? Explain.

3. Where one party has violated the rules of evidence, the opposing party should object. A *specific* objection is required. List ten (10) specific objections which may be used at trial.

4. When should the offer of proof be used at trial?

5. What is the exclusionary rule? In your opinion, is the "good faith" exception to the exclusionary rule good policy? Explain.

6. What is the inevitable discovery exemption to the exclusionary rule? See footnote #17. Is such an exemption good policy? Explain.

FOCUS IV:

LAYING THE FOUNDATION FOR THE ADMISSION OF SCIENTIFIC EVIDENCE - THE ISSUE OF DNA EVIDENCE

Issue: What is the proper foundation for the admissibility of scientific evidence? As noted in Chapter Ten, new scientific evidence poses particular problems for the courts. One important new form of evidence is the results of DNA testing. The following case not only deals directly with the issue of the foundation required for the admissibility of the results of DNA testing, but, in discussing this matter, the court also discusses the admissibility of other forms of scientific evidence, as well.

U.S. v. Two Bulls

918 F.2d 56 (8th Cir. 1990)

LAY, Chief Justice.

Matthew Sylvester Two Bulls was charged with aggravated sexual abuse, 18 U.S.C. Sec. 1153, 2241(a)(1) (1989), and sexual abuse of a minor, 18 U.S.C. Sec. 1153, 2243 (1989), arising out of the rape of a fourteen-year-old girl on the Pine Ridge Indian Reservation in South Dakota. The police seized the underwear the girl was wearing before and after the incident. The Federal Bureau of Investigation (FBI) laboratory isolated the semen stain on her underwear by using a scientific technique called DNA (Deoxyribonucleic Acid)[1] profiling. After testing Two Bulls' blood, the government concluded that there was a very high probability that the semen on the underwear came from Two Bulls.[2] Before trial, Two Bulls made a motion for a suppression hearing challenging the admissibility of that evidence. At the pre-trial hearing the district judge ruled, after hearing the testimony of the government's first witness, that it had been sufficiently established that DNA evidence was generally accepted by the scientific community so that the evidence could be presented to the jury. After the hearing, Two Bulls entered a conditional guilty plea,[3] pursuant to a plea agreement, to a superseding Information charging sexual abuse in violation of 18 U.S.C. Sec. 1153, 2242(1) (1989). He was sentenced to 108 months in prison followed by two years of supervised release. The sentence was delayed and Two Bulls was discharged on bond pending this appeal.

On appeal, Two Bulls argues that the trial court erred because it applied Federal Rule of Evidence 702[4] in determining the admissibility of the DNA evidence instead of using the test in *Frye v. United States,* 293 F. 1013 (D.C.Cir.1923),[5] or a more rigid standard. He argues that the district court violated his due process because the pre-trial suppression hearing was incomplete.

This is a case of first impression in the federal circuit courts. *See United States v. Jakobetz,* F.Supp. 250 (D.Vt.1990). It is generally conceded that DNA profiling is relatively new and has been the subject of controversy in both the legal and scientific fields.[6]. Several state courts, however, have admitted DNA evidence. *Andrews v. State,* 533 So.2d 841 (Fla.Dist.Ct.App. 1988) (finding DNA evidence admissible using a relevancy test); *Caldwell v. State,* 260 Ga. 278, 393 S.E.2d 436 (1990) (admitting DNA evidence but not population statistics); *Cobey v. State,* 80 Md.App. 31, 559 A.2d 391 (1989) (admitting DNA evidence using *Frye* test); *State v. Schwartz,* 447 N.W.2d 422 (Minn.1989) (admitting DNA evidence if tests performed properly); *People v. Castro,* 144 Misc.2d 956, 545 N.Y.S.2d 985 (Sup.Ct. 1989) (using three step test to determine whether to admit DNA evidence); *People v. Wesley,* 140 Misc.2d 306, 533 N.Y.S.2d 643 (Albany County Ct.1988) (admitting DNA evidence under the *Frye* test); *State v. Pennington,* 327 N.C. 89, 393 S.E.2d 847 (1990) (finding DNA evidence admissible); *State v. Ford,* - S.C.-, 392 S.E.2d 781 (1990) (admitting DNA evidence and, because technique generally accepted, future *Frye* hearings unnecessary); *Glover v.*

State, 787 S.W.2d 544 (Tex.Ct.App.) (admitting DNA evidence using the *Frye* test), *review granted* (1990); *Spencer v. Commonwealth,* 238 Va. 275, 384 S.E.2d 775 (1989) (using reliability test to find DNA evidence admissible) (case one), *cert. denied,* - U.S. -, 110 S.Ct. 759, 107 L.Ed.2d 775 (1990); *Spencer v. Commonwealth,* 238 Va. 295, 384 S.E.2d 785 (1989) (admitting DNA evidence) (case two), *cert. denied,* - U.S. -, 110 S.Ct. 1171, 107 L.Ed.2d 1073 (1990). Although DNA analysis has been used in forensics only recently, it has been used for several years in diagnostics. *Andrews,* 533 So.2d at 848-49; *Caldwell,* 260, Ga. at 286, 393 S.E.2d at 441; *Ford,* - S.C. at -, 392 S.E.2d at 783. It has also been used in determining parentage. *In re Baby Girl S.,* 140 Misc.2d 299, 532 N.Y.S.2d 634 (Sur.Ct.1988) (finding it unnecessary to have hearing on DNA evidence admissibility when state statute provided for admission of blood genetic marker tests).

The Congressional Office of Technology Assessment has found that DNA tests are valid and reliable in forensics when performed and analyzed properly by skilled personnel. U.S. Congress, Office of Technology Assessment, *Genetic Witness: Forensic Uses of DNA Tests* 7-8, OTA-BA-438 (Washington, D.C.: U.S. Government Printing Office, July 1990). Commentators have also stated that "[t]here is nothing controversial about the *theory* underlying DNA typing. Indeed, this theory is so well accepted that its accuracy is unlikely even to be raised as an issue in hearings on the admissibility of the new tests." Thompson & Ford, *DNA Typing: Acceptance and Weight of the New Genetic Identification Tests,* 75 Va.L.Rev. 45, 60 (1989) (emphasis added). These same commentators have stated that:

> It would ease the burden on trial lawyers and triers of fact to make proper implementation a threshold issue for the admissibility of DNA typing tests. Before the test offered by a particular laboratory is admitted, *there should be a showing, during an evidentiary hearing, that the specific protocol employed by the laboratory is accepted as reliable by disinterested scientists familiar with the procedure.* In routine cases, then, the attorneys could focus their attention on the tractable question of whether an accepted protocol was accurately followed instead of the enormously more difficult question of whether the protocol itself is good or bad.

Id. at 58 (emphasis added).

Two Bulls asserts that a three step test should be used to determine the admissibility of DNA evidence similar to the test used in *Castro*. In *Castro*, the court stated that the three step analysis would aid in evaluating and resolving the admissibility issue. *Castro*, 144 Misc.2d at 959, 545 N.Y.S.2d at 987. The three steps are (1) whether the scientific community generally accepts the theory that DNA tests produce reliable results; (2) whether techniques currently exist in DNA testing that are generally accepted by the scientific community and which are capable of producing reliable results; and (3) whether the laboratory that performed the tests used these techniques in analyzing the samples in this case. *Id.* at 959, 545 N.Y.S.2d at 987. In *Castro*, the court focused on resolving the third question. The court observed that "'[p]erhaps the most important flaw in the *Frye* test is that by focusing attention on the general acceptance issue, the test obscures critical problems in the use of a particular technique.'" *Id.* at 960, 545 N.Y.S.2d at 987 (quoting Giannelli, *The Admissibility of Novel Scientific Evidence*: Frye v. United States, A *Half-Century Later*, 80 Colum.L.Rev. 1197, 1226 (1908)). The Court stated that:

It is the view of this court that given the complexity of the DNA multi-system identification tests and the powerful impact that they may have on a jury, passing muster under *Frye* alone is insufficient to place this type of evidence before a jury without a preliminary, critical examination of the actual testing procedures performed in a particular case.

Id. at 960, 545 N.Y.S.2d at 987.

The government argues that *Castro* stands alone and provides too stringent a standard, necessitating long drawn out testimonial procedures before trial. The government urges that Rule 702 creates a liberal rule of admissibility which now supersedes *Frye* and which is contrary to the *Castro* standards. We read it differently. The *Frye* Court stated that scientific evidence should be distinguished according to whether it was in an experimental or demonstrative stage. *Frye,* 293 F. at 1014.

In discussing the admissibility of DNA evidence, we find that *Frye* and Rule 702 both require that a proper foundation be laid for any scientific testing or laboratory procedure. *See United States v. Distler,* 671 F.2d 954, 961-62 (6th Cir.) (admitting gas chromatography analysis), *cert. denied,* 454 U.S. 827, 102 S.Ct. 118, 70 L.Ed.2d 102 (1981); *United States v. Cyphers,* 553 F.2d 1064, 1072 (7th Cir.) (finding microscopic comparison of hair samples

admissible), *cert. denied,* 434 U.S. 843, 98
S.Ct. 142, 54 L.Ed.2d. 107 (1977); *United States
v. Franks,* 511 F.2d 25, 33 (6th Cir.) (admitting
voice print analysis), *cert. denied,* 422 U.S.
1042, 95 S.Ct. 2654, 45 L.Ed.2d 693 (1975).
Regardless of which rule may be followed, we
feel Rule 702 and *Frye* both require the same
general approach to the admissibility of new
scientific evidence. Neither rule should permit
speculative and conjectural testing which fails
normal foundational requirements necessary for
the admissibility of scientific testimony or
opinion.

For example, as we discuss later, hypnosis
evidence is inadmissible unless certain
procedures are carried out, *see Sprynczynatyk v.
General Motors Corp.,* 771 F.2d 1112, 1122-24
(8th Cir.1985), *cert. denied,* 475 U.S. 1046, 106
S.Ct. 1263, 89 L.Ed.2d 572 (1986), and polygraph
testing is still inadmissible until there exists
greater scientific reliability. *See United
States v. Alexander,* 526 F.2d 161, 163-64 (8th
Cir. 1975). Blood tests are inadmissible unless
foundational evidence establishes that the
testing procedures are reliable. *Gardner v.
Meyers,* 491 F.2d 1184, 1189 (8th Cir. 1974). Any
experimental evidence requires certain proofs of
similarity or identity to be deemed admissible.

The *Castro* court held that DNA evidence
was admissible under *Frye* because (1) DNA
identification was generally accepted by the

scientific community and (2) identification techniques were generally accepted and were capable of producing reliable results. *People v. Castro*, 144 Misc.2d at 979, 545 N.Y.S.2d at 999. The court also found that a pre-trial hearing should be held to determine whether the laboratory used accepted techniques to yield results reliable enough to be admitted as a question of fact for the jury. *Id.* We fail to see that this analysis is *sui generis* or that it in any way allows intrusion of the court into deciding problems of weight vis a vis admissibility. When the evidence is so prejudicial and the admissibility seriously challenged, trial courts routinely hear motions in limine preliminary to the offer at trial.

Because DNA evidence is so new and the resulting prejudice to the defendant is sufficiently great, it is imperative that the court satisfy itself that there exists a sufficient foundational basis as to the overall admissibility of the evidence. This must be done before the government exposes the jury to the lab results. If the court has explored only scientific acceptability and the reliability of acceptable testing procedures in camera, and then, at trial the government fails to show that the lab tests did conform to reliable procedures, the court would have to exclude the evidence for lack of foundation. In doing so, the resulting prejudice to the defendant would be obvious. Notwithstanding the fact that an objection is sustained and the evidence excluded, aside from valuable trial time wasted, the jury would be exposed to prejudicial proofs and left to speculate as to why the defendant opposed the ultimate result.

These general principles apply to the admissibility of any questionable opinion evidence, in which proper foundation as to acceptability as well as to reliability is a focal issue. This approach, whether it be under Rule 702 or *Frye*,[7] should require the court to satisfy itself that the evidence meets all three tests laid out in *Castro*. Depending on the circumstances, the court may exercise its discretion in allowing preliminary cross examination by the defendant or to allow on voir dire the defendant's counter evidence. We agree with the government that generally such counter evidence will go only to the weight and not to the admissibility. However, this is not always true. Generally, in determining the scientific acceptability and reliability of testing procedures, the court should hear both sides of the issue. Simply because one expert may verify such scientific acceptability does not make it true. For example, the court would not accept and feel bound by the testimony from one polygrapher that tests were scientifically acceptable.

Although several courts have found DNA evidence to be admissible because it is reliable and generally accepted, many cases state that DNA evidence remains subject to attack based on prejudice, relevancy, and laboratory procedures. *See Pennington,* 327 N.C. at -, 393 S.E.2d at 854; *Ford,* - S.C. at -, 392 S.E. 2d at 784. It seems only logical that if scientific evidence is questionable in terms of acceptability and reliability that the district court should hear both sides of the question before ruling. Certainly one government witness testifying that new evidence is acceptable does not necessarily make it so.

This circuit has applied this reasoning to expert evidence dealing with polygraph tests, *Alexander,* 526 F.2d at 163-64, and to opinion evidence discussing addictive gambling, *United States v. Lewellyn,* 723 F.2d 615, 619 (8th Cir.1983). In *Lewellyn,* the court stated that reliability was one of the most important factors in considering whether the scientific principle met the *Frye* test. *Id.* In *Sprynczynatyk,* the court found that hynotically enhanced testimony was admissible if its reliability was established and if it was not overly prejudicial. *Sprynczynatyk,* 771 F.2d at 1123. The court stated that the trial court should consider (1) whether procedural safeguards had been used, (2) whether hypnosis was appropriate for the type of memory loss involved, and (3) whether there was any corroborating evidence. *Id.* The court also stated that once the trial court decided the evidence was reliable then it had to determine whether the probative value of the evidence outweighed its prejudicial effect. *Id.*

We hold that it was error for the trial court to determine the admissibility of the DNA evidence without determining whether the testing procedures used by the FBI lab in this case were conducted properly. In weighing the overall admissibility of such evidence, the court should hear testimony from experts on both sides as to the scientific acceptability and reliability of any novel scientific tests. The trial judge should rule as a matter of law (1) whether the DNA evidence is scientifically acceptable, (2) whether there are certain standard procedures that should be followed in conducting these tests, and (3) whether these standards were followed in this case. *Cf. Caldwell,* 260 Ga. at 286, 393 S.E.2d at 441. If the trial court is preliminarily satisfied that these requirements have been met the evidence should be admitted and the jury should be allowed to determine the weight that should be allocated to it.

We order Two Bulls' conviction vacated and the conditional plea set aside. We remand the case to the trial court with instructions to hold an expanded pre-trial hearing on the admissibility of the DNA evidence. The trial court is to decide (1) whether DNA evidence is generally accepted by the scientific community, (2) whether the testing procedures used in this case are generally accepted as reliable if performed properly, (3) whether the test was performed properly in this case, (4) whether the evidence is more prejudicial than probative in this case, and (5) whether the statistics used to determine the probability of someone else having the same genetic characteristics is more probative than prejudicial under Rule 403. *Cf. Schwartz,* 447 N.W.2d at 428 (limiting use of population frequency statistics because "juries in criminal cases may give undue weight and deference to presented statistical evidence and we are reluctant to take that risk"); *State v. Joon Kyu Kim,* 398 N.W.2d 544, 548 (Minn.1987) (suppressing statistical population frequency evidence because it may have "'potentially exaggerated impact on the trier of fact'" (quoting *State v. Boyd,* 331 N.W.2d 480, 482 (Minn.1983).

It is so ordered.

NOTES

1. DNA "is an organic substance found in the chromosomes in the nucleus of a cell. It provides the genetic code which determines a person's characteristics." *Caldwell v. State,* 260 Ga. 278, 279, 393 S.E.2d 436, 437 n. 1 (1990).

2.   The statistical probability that the DNA prints match "is based on the probability that a random individual has the same DNA banding pattern as the sample." *State v. Schwartz,* 447 N.W.2d 422, 428 (Minn.1989). In this case the statistical probability of someone other than Two Bulls providing a match was one in 177,000, based on a Native American population data base. Suppression Hearing Tr. at 63-64.

3.   Two Bulls entered a conditional guilty plea under Federal Rule of Criminal Procedure 11(a)(2). Rule 11(a)(2) provides that:

> [w]ith the approval of the court and the consent of the government, a defendant may enter a conditional plea of guilty or nolo contendere, reserving in writing the right, on appeal from the judgment, to review of the adverse determination of any specified pretrial motion.   A defendant who prevails on appeal shall be allowed to withdraw the plea.

Fed.R.Crim.P. 11(a)(2).

4.   Rule 702 states that "[i]f scientific, technical, or other specialized knowledge will assist the trier of fact to understand the evidence or to determine a fact in issue, a witness qualified as an expert by knowledge,

skill, experience, training, or education, may testify thereto in the form of an opinion or otherwise." Fed.R.Evid.702.

5. In *Frye,* the court stated that a new scientific discovery would be admitted into evidence when it had gained general acceptance in the field in which it belonged. *Frye,* 293 F. at 1014.

6. Some of the difficulties encountered in DNA profiling include (1) having too small a sample for typing, (2) having the sample be unsuitable for testing because of environmental effects on the sample, (3) interpreting the results, and (4) having few laboratories doing DNA testing. Gordon, DNA *Identification tests–On the Way Toward Judicial Acceptance,* 6 J.Suffolk Acad.L.1, 12-18 (1989). *See also* Note, *The Dark Side of DNA Profiling: Unreliable Scientific Evidence Meets the Criminal Defendant,* 42 Stan.L.Rev. 465, 479-94 (1990).

Another observation has been made that: [w]henever novel scientific evidence is offered in court, the legal system faces competing concerns. One [sic] one hand, there a danger that excessive caution will prevent valuable evidence from being admitted in a timely manner. On the other hand, there is a danger that evidence accepted quickly and uncritically will later prove less reliable than promised.

DNA typing poses this dilemma in a striking manner. The stakes are high. It is an extraordinarily powerful and promising innovation, but the complexity of the techniques may hide some dangerous pitfalls and, in routine forensic use, it may fail to live up to the high expectations of its proponents. Until additional validation studies are done, the legal profession would be well advised to approach the new techniques with caution.

Thompson & Ford, DNA *Typing*, Trial (Sept. 1988) at 64.

Other commentators argue that "[b]efore forensic DNA testing can be generally accepted as reliable, the scientific community must reach a consensus on appropriate standards for declaring matches and calculating probabilities." Neufeld & Scheck, *DNA Testing*, A.B.A.J. (Sept. 1990) at 35. *See also* Sherman, *DNA Tests Unravel?*, Nat'l L.J., Dec. 18, 1989 at 1, col. 1.

7. Many speculate that Rule 702 does supersede *Frye*. The government requests us to so rule. For the purpose of our discussion, we view the two rules as generally compatible and not as mutually exclusive.

Chapter Eleven

PRIVILEGES AND JUDICIAL NOTICE

Privileges and Rule 501

Rule 501[1]
GENERAL RULE

Except as otherwise required by the Constitution of the United States or provided by Act of Congress or in rules prescribed by the Supreme Court pursuant to statutory authority, the privilege of a witness, person, government, State, or political subdivision thereof shall be governed by the principles of the common law as they may be interpreted by the courts of the United States in the light of reason and experience. However, in civil actions and proceedings, with respect to an element of a claim or defense as to which State law supplies the rule of decision, the privilege of a witness, person, government, State, or political subdivision thereof shall be determined in accordance with State law.

Rule 501 is the only rule dealing with privileges found in the Federal Rules of Evidence. The first sentence is applicable to federal criminal cases and civil cases based upon a federal law claim. As to such cases, the federal "common law" applies, and such common law "may be interpreted by the courts of the United States in the light of reason and experience." The second sentence of Rule 501 is applicable to so-called federal diversity actions. A diversity action is a federal civil action grounded upon diversity of citizenship (i.e., diversity of residency). In other words, in the action all of the plaintiffs and the defendants must be from different states.

Example.

> Plaintiff is a resident of Indiana. She wishes to sue the defendant, a resident of the State of Illinois, for damages she received in an automobile accident in Indiana. Diversity of citizenship exists. Where such diversity exists (and the claimed damages, the so-called "amount in controversy," are

sufficient to meet the statutory sum
required for suit, currently
$50,000), the plaintiff may bring
what would otherwise have been a
state court action in federal court.
As to these state law claims allowed
in federal court, the state law of
privilege applies.

The Nature of
Witness Privilege

As to testimony at trial, the concept of
privilege allows a particular individual to
withhold his or her testimony as a witness or
allows a particular person to prevent another
witness from presenting some testimony. The law
of privilege is founded upon the rationale that
certain relationships should be confidential and
that public policy (i.e., society's interest) is
served by protecting such confidences.

A privilege is generally considered
"personal." In other words, it is held by the
party or parties whom the law seeks to protect.
As such, a privilege may be waived by the
holder(s) of the privilege, allowing the
disclosure of information at trial.

A number of specific privileges exist
among the various jurisdictions in our country.
Some are quite old. Others are relatively new,
reflecting the changes that constantly occur in

our society (e.g., the psychotherapist-patient privilege which exists in some states). An overview of the most common (non- exclusive) categories of privilege is presented below.

The Attorney-Client Privilege

The attorney-client privilege may be the best known privilege. Brief reference has been made to this privilege previously, when discussing the competency of attorneys as witnesses (Chapter Four). The privilege is firmly grounded in our law and its purpose is to promote free and complete disclosure of facts by the client to his or her attorney.

The attorney-client privilege is held by the client, not the attorney. Only the client may waive the privilege. While the client need not actually retain the attorney to have the privilege attach, the client must have consulted the attorney in the course of seeking legal advice.

While public policy is enhanced by such a privilege, it is not enhanced if the privilege is applied to protect communications regarding the client's plans to commit a crime or fraud (or, at least, a crime which the attorney believes will result in death or serious bodily injury, see the footnote 2 commentary concerning the American Bar Association's Model Code of Professional Responsibility). Therefore, the attorney is not prevented from disclosing such communications.[2]

The client must intend his or her communications to be confidential. Therefore, communications made in front of strangers to the relationship (i.e., those unnecessary to the communication, nor attorney's agents) are not privileged.[3]

A special issue for defense attorneys involves the situation where the defendant is about to perjure himself or herself, and this fact is made known to the defense attorney by the defendant. In view of the importance of the attorney-client privilege, must the attorney remain silent and allow the perjury to occur? This issue is reviewed in detail in Focus V, which follows immediately after this chapter.

The Spousal Privilege

Two separate privilege issues are raised by the husband-wife relationship.

Protection from Disclosure of
Confidential Communications

A spousal privilege protecting confidential communications from disclosure is generally recognized among the jurisdictions.[4] Assuming the existence of a valid marriage, confidential communications between spouses are protected, and, while limited to communications occurring during the marriage period, the privilege may be effected after divorce or death.[5] The rationale for the privilege is grounded in the belief that public policy is enhanced by promoting the trust and intimacies of the spousal relationship.

As with the attorney-client privilege, the communications must be "confidential," i.e., they must not be made before third parties and must be such that the parties would likely desire confidentiality. Some states consider certain nonverbal actions by a spouse to be akin to confidential verbal communications and, therefore, fitting within the privilege.

Example.

> Spouse A sees spouse B carry home boxes of stolen goods, hiding them in the cellar. A confidential communication (by implication) may exist.[6] Other jurisdictions reject the inclusion in the privilege of such nonverbal actions.[7]

Since this privilege is held by both spouses, one spouse may claim the privilege in refusing to give testimony, or the other spouse may raise the privilege to preclude the spouse from testifying.

Protection from Spousal Testimony

The spousal privilege discussed above involves the privilege regarding protection from the disclosure of confidential communications. Another spousal "privilege" has been noted at law. It is more accurately an issue of witness incompetency than privilege and provides for the exclusion of a witness spouse's testimony against the other spouse in a criminal trial. In *Trammel v. United States*, 445 U.S. 40 (1980), the United States Supreme Court greatly restricted the use of this "privilege" in federal courts by holding that the privilege belongs to the witness spouse, only he or she (not the accused spouse) can raise it. Therefore, if the witness spouse chooses to testify, then the accused spouse could not prevent her or him from doing so.

This privilege can only be used by the witness spouse where she or he is still married to the accused spouse, although the privilege extends as to testimony concerning happenings before the marriage event.[8] The privilege should not apply where the relevant offense is one against the witness spouse, and the witness spouse now seeks to assert the privilege to protect the accused spouse.[9]

The Medical Treatment Privilege

While there is no federal physician-patient common law privilege to be applied to federal criminal cases and civil cases based upon a federal law claim (i.e., sentence #1 of Rule 501), a number of states have by statute enacted a physician-patient privilege to protect information provided to the physician by the patient.[10] Therefore, federal courts may apply such law in cases arising under federal diversity of citizenship jurisdiction where state law governs (i.e., sentence #2 of Rule 501).

The privilege generally applies where the information is such that confidentiality is likely desired. It is often not limited to oral communications by the patient to the physician, but may include the results of tests and x-rays, as well. The purpose of the privilege is to promote a free and complete disclosure of facts by the patient to his or her attending physician, to aid diagnosis and treatment.

However, many states which have adopted the privilege impose a number of limitations or exceptions on its use in court. For example, most states limit the privilege to civil cases only. Even then, states may exclude the privilege in cases where the patient is the plaintiff seeking damages for injuries received (e.g., in the automobile accident case).

The privilege belongs to the patient and, as with other privileges, may be waived by the holder, that is, the patient. Also, disclosures before strangers to the relationship will result in the privilege being unavailable. Some states include psychotherapists and other medical personnel within the privilege.[11] As with all privileges, a particular state's law should be reviewed specially.

The Priest (Clergy)-
Penitent Privilege

A so-called priest (more accurately clergy)-penitent privilege is recognized in most states and by federal common law to protect confidential communications between an individual and his or her religious advisor.[12]

In general, the privilege applies to both civil and criminal proceedings. The communications must be deemed confidential in the course of religious practice. While the limitations vary with the jurisdiction, one example of the boundaries of the privilege is shown by Indiana law where the privilege applies to "confessions or admissions made to them (clergy) in the course of discipline by their respective churches."[13] Basically, if the clergy's church does not recognize a confidentiality as to the particular communications, then the privilege will not apply.[14]

In general, while some states view the privilege as belonging to the penitent only, most jurisdictions allow the privilege to be held by both the clergy and the penitent.

The Privileges of Government

Government is often granted special privileges. For example, the federal government can raise privileges as to the following general areas:

(1) State Secrets. Military and other confidential national security information are generally privileged. However, the court will be allowed to establish the propriety of the claim in a given case.[15]

(2) Ongoing Investigatory Files. To prevent harm to the law enforcement activities of government, a privilege generally exists as to the ongoing investigatory files of such law enforcement agencies as the FBI.[16] However, this privilege is not absolute, and it requires a court balancing/weighing of the need for disclosure versus the protection necessities.[17]

(3) Governmental Informants. There is a qualified (non-absolute) privilege of government to withhold the identity of an informant. This privilege is designed to enhance the activities of law enforcement agencies by encouraging individuals to communicate information to

them.[18] Again, the court must balance the interest of society in encouraging such communication of information versus the need of the defendant to provide for his or her defense.[19]

(4) <u>Executive Privilege</u>. The principle of separation of powers and the need of the President to interact freely with advisors provides a basis for a presidential executive privilege. The landmark case *United States v. Nixon*, 418 U.S. 683 (1974), clearly establishes that such privilege is not absolute. The court will consider whether disclosure is required by the demands of due process for a fair trial.

The Privilege Against Self-Incrimination

The Fifth Amendment to the United States Constitution states in part: "No person... shall be compelled in any criminal case to be a witness against himself." It is from this source that the current privilege against self-incrimination has evolved. This privilege applies to the states, as well as to the federal government.[20]

The privilege includes the right of the defendant not to take the stand to testify in the criminal trial. It also includes the right of a witness to refuse to answer questions (in a civil or criminal case) which might incriminate him or her.[21] However, if a witness is given proper immunity, he or she may be compelled to give testimony. In *Kastigar v. United States*, 406 U.S. 441 (1972), the United States Supreme Court held that immunity "from the use of compelled testimony, as well as evidence derived directly and indirectly therefrom," afforded proper immunity to a witness such as to compel testimony (i.e., the so-called "use and derivative use" immunity).[22]

As with other privileges, the privilege against self-incrimination may be waived. However, the privilege must be knowingly and voluntarily waived.[23]

Miranda Warnings

The privilege against self-incrimination is certainly not limited to courtroom situations. In the landmark case *Miranda v. Arizona*, 384 U.S. 436 (1966), the United States Supreme Court held that, as a precondition to the admissibility of statements, certain warnings were required to be made by the police to a suspect held in police custody, so as to protect the privilege against self-incrimination:

> "...the prosecution may not use statements, whether exculpatory or inculpatory, stemming from custodial interrogation of the defendant unless it demonstrates the use of

procedural safeguards effective to secure the privilege against self-incrimination. By custodial interrogation, we mean questioning initiated by law enforcement officers after a person has been taken into custody or otherwise deprived of his freedom of action in any significant way. As for the procedural safeguards to be employed, unless other fully effective means are devised to inform accused persons of their right to silence and to assure a continuous opportunity to exercise it, the following measures are required. Prior to any questioning, the person must be warned that he has a right to remain silent, that any statement he does make may be made against him, and that he has a right to the presence of an attorney, either retained or appointed. The defendant may waive effectuation of these rights, provided the waiver is made voluntarily, knowingly and intelligently. If, however, he indicates in any manner and at any stage of the process that he wishes to consult with an attorney before speaking there can be no questioning. Likewise, if the individual is alone and indicates in any manner that he does not wish to be interrogated, the police may not question him."[24]

As noted above, statements elicited from the suspect in violation of the *Miranda* decision are inadmissible. However, more recent Supreme Court decisions have tended to limit the effect of *Miranda*. For example, in *Harris v. New York*, 401 U.S. 222 (1971), and *Oregon v. Hass*, 420 U.S. 714 (1975), the Supreme Court allowed statements received in violation of *Miranda* to be used at trial to impeach the defendant (i.e., to impeach his or her credibility as a witness, should he or she take the stand).[25] More recently, in *New York v. Quarles*, 467 U.S. 649, 52 U.S.L.W. 4790, 81 L.Ed.2d 550 (1984), the Supreme Court established a "public safety" exception to *Miranda*.

In *Quarles*, the defendant was stopped by police as a suspected rapist. In frisking the defendant, the police found an empty holster. Without the necessary giving of *Miranda* warnings, the police asked where the weapon to the holster was. The defendant nodded to a location and said, "The gun is over there." The gun was found where indicated, and the defendant was arrested. At trial for the illegal possession of a weapon, the court suppressed the weapon and the statement by the defendant as to its location. The Supreme Court found that public safety needs justified the failure to give the warnings *before* asking the question as to the location of the gun. The threat to public safety outweighed the need for the warnings to be first given, and, therefore, the suppressed evidence is admissible.

Testimonial Compulsion

The privilege against self-incrimination protects one from being required to give testimony (i.e., it protects one from testimonial compulsion). Therefore, certain tests, examinations, and identification processes do not violate the privilege, as they do not amount to testimonial compulsion.[26] For example, required fingerprints, photographs, and measurements of the accused do not violate the privilege.[27] Also, demonstrations of voice and handwriting, and the requirement of standing in a police lineup for identification do not violate the privilege.[28]

Other Privileges

Other privileges have been recognized to varying degrees among the jurisdictions.[29] The student is urged to consult state law as to the boundaries of privilege in his or her own state.

Judicial Notice and Rule 201

Rule 201[30]
JUDICIAL NOTICE OF
ADJUDICATIVE FACTS

(a) Scope of rule. This rule governs only judicial notice of adjudicative facts.

(b) Kinds of facts. A judicially noticed fact must be one not subject to reasonable dispute in that it is either (1) generally known within the territorial jurisdiction of the trial court or (2) capable of accurate and ready determination by resort to sources whose accuracy cannot reasonably be questioned.

(c) When discretionary. A court may take judicial notice, whether requested or not.

(d) When mandatory. A court shall take judicial notice if requested by a party and supplied with the necessary information.

(e) Opportunity to be heard. A party is entitled upon timely request to an opportunity to be heard as to the propriety of taking judicial notice and the tenor of the matter noticed. In the absence of prior notification, the request may be made after judicial notice has been taken.

(f) Time of taking notice. Judicial notice may be taken at any stage of the proceeding.

(g) Instructing jury. In a civil action or proceeding, the court shall instruct the jury to accept as conclusive any fact judicially noticed. In a criminal case, the court shall instruct the jury that it may, but is not required to, accept as conclusive any fact judicially noticed.

The Concept of Judicial Notice

The application of judicial notice by the court allows for facts to be established without the submission of proof. Rule 201 is the sole provision in the Federal Rules of Evidence to regulate the process of judicial notice.[31]

Adjudicative Facts

Rule 201 governs judicial notice of adjudicative facts only. Adjudicative facts are to be distinguished from legislative facts:

> The precise line of demarcation between adjudicative facts and legislative facts are not always easily identified. Adjudicative facts have been described as follows:
>
> 'When a court ... finds facts concerning the immediate parties-who did what, where, when, how, and with what motive or intent-the court ... is performing an adjudicative function and the facts are conveniently called adjudicative facts.
>
> Stated in other terms, the adjudicative facts are those to which the law is applied in the process of adjudication. They are the facts that normally go to the jury in a jury case. They relate to the parties, their activities, their properties, their businesses.'
>
> 2 K. Davis, *Administrative Law Treatise* 15.03, at 353 (1958).

Legislative facts, on the other hand, do not relate specially to the activities or characteristics of litigants .... A court generally relies upon legislative facts when it purports to develop a particular law or policy and thus considers material wholly unrelated to the activities of the parties.

Legislative facts are established truths, facts or pronouncements that do not change from case to case but apply universally, while adjudicative facts are those developed in a particular case.[32]

In general, when the court takes judicial notice of an adjudicative fact, it is taking notice of a fact, which in a jury case, would be a fact to go to the jury. Legislative facts are not facts used by a jury in its determinations. They are facts relevant to legal reasoning and decision (e.g., court precedent):

Adjudicative facts are simply the facts of the particular case. Legislative facts, on the other hand, are those which have relevance to legal reasoning and the law-making process whether in the formulation of a legal principle or ruling by a judge or court of in the enactment of a legislative body.[33]

The taking of judicial notice of legislative facts is not regulated by the Federal Rules of Evidence. This does not mean that legislative facts may not be recognized by the court. It only means that the process of recognizing such legislative facts is not regulated by the rules of evidence and lies generally within federal court discretion.[34]

Facts Not Subject
To Reasonable Dispute

The court may only take judicial notice of a fact which is "not subject to reasonable dispute." Rule 201(b) establishes that such lack of reasonable dispute may exist if the fact is "generally known within the territorial jurisdiction of the trial court" or is "capable of accurate and ready determination by resort to sources whose accuracy cannot reasonably be questioned."

"Generally known" means commonly known by informed people, that is, of common notoriety in the territorial jurisdiction of the court. It does not mean knowledge possessed by the court due to the judge's personal knowledge and not known generally to all persons.[35]

Even if a fact is not "generally known," judicial notice may be available if the fact is "capable of accurate and ready determination." Here, the judge may look to sources "whose accuracy cannot reasonably be questioned" (e.g., almanacs, dictionaries, encyclopedias, and other sources of established accuracy).

The Issue of Discretion

The judge may take judicial notice in proper situations, even if he or she is not requested to do so by one of the parties. Rule 201(c). However, under Rule 201(d) of the Federal Rules of Evidence, the judge must take judicial notice of a fact if requested by a party to do so.[36] If the fact is not one of common notoriety, the party requesting the judicial notice must supply the court "with the necessary information" for the judge to determine its propriety for notice (e.g., the almanac item, calendar, encyclopedia citation, etc.).

Under Rule 201(e) of the Federal Rules of Evidence, if the opposing party questions the propriety of the notice, then he or she may request a hearing to determine such propriety. The court will hear arguments as to whether or not the adjudicative fact is "not subject to reasonable dispute."

Time for Notice and the
Conclusiveness of Notice

The court may take judicial notice "at any stage of the proceeding." Rule 201(f). This includes appellate courts taking judicial notice on appeal.[37]

The conclusiveness of a judicially noticed fact upon a jury depends on whether the jury is hearing a civil action or a criminal action. In a civil action, the fact noticed by the judge is conclusive upon the jury. However, in a criminal action, the fact noticed may or may not be accepted by the jury as conclusive. Rule 201(g).

NOTES

1. FED. R. EVID. 501.

2. Of course, the limitation does not apply as to consultations regarding a client's past unlawful conduct. See generally Alexander v. United States, 138 U.S. 353, 34 L.Ed. 954, 11 S.Ct. 350 (1891). See also the Model Code of Professional Responsibility, Model Rule 1.6, not requiring, but allowing an attorney to disclose his or her client's plans to commit crimes likely to result in death or serious bodily injury, where such disclosure is reasonably believed necessary to stop the crime from taking place. The Model Rules are noted generally in

Chapter Four, note 11. Model Rule 1.6 has been a highly controversial provision of the new rules, as they have been considered by the various states for adoption. See Kelbley, "Lawyer Ethics on Trial," 12 Barrister 4 for a critical view of Model Rule 1.6.

3. For a view of the extent of the privilege see United States v. Schmidt, 360 F.Supp. 339 (1973); see also Code of Professional Responsibility, DR 4-101.

4. Including in the federal courts, see United States v. Lustig, 555 F.2d 737 (9th Cir. 1977).

5. See Pereira v. United States, 347 U.S. 1, 98 L.Ed. 435, 74 S.Ct. 358 (1954), as to divorce; see Hopkins v. Grimshaw, 165 U.S. 342, 41 L.Ed. 739, 17 S.Ct. 401 (1895), as to death.

6. So found the court in People v. Daghita, 229 N.Y. 194 (1949).

7. See United States v. Lustig, supra.

8. See United States v. Bolzer, 556 F.2d 948 (9th Cir. 1977); United States v. Apodaca, 522 F.2d 568 (10th Cir. 1975).

9. See Wyatt v. United States, 362 U.S. 525, 4 L.Ed.2d 931, 80 S.Ct. 901 (1960).

10.   See Re Grand Jury Subpoena, 460 F.Supp 150 (1978).

11.   As to the psychotherapist-patient privilege see United States v. Meager, 531 F.2d 752 (1976), cert. denied 429 U.S. 853. See also 44 ALR 3d 24.

12.   See Totten v. United States, 92 U.S. 105 (1876).

13.   Indiana Code (I.C.) 34-1-14-5.

14.   See Ball v. State, Ind., 419 N.E.2d 137 (1981).

15.   See United States v. Nixon, 418 U.S. 683, 41 L.Ed.2d 1039, 94 S.Ct. 3090 (1974). Other official information not amounting to the protection of national security (e.g., information concerning policy opinions or deliberations) may be the source of a qualified privilege. See Joran v. U.S. Dept. of Justice, 591 F.2d 753 (1978). The court must balance the need for confidentiality against disclosure. See Community Sav. & Loan Assoc. v. Federal Home Loan Bank Board, 68 FRD 378 (1975). While beyond the scope of this book, the student should consider the Freedom of Information Act, 5 USC 552, provisions, and the related case interpretations, as well as be aware of the existence of federal statutes affecting privileges.

16. See Kenyatta v. Kelly, 375 F.Supp. 1175 (1974).

17. See United States v. Leggett & Pratt, Inc., 542 F.2d 655 (6th Cir. 1976).

18. See Roviaro v. United States, 353 U.S. 53 (1957); United States v. Skeens, 449 F.2d 833 (D.C. Cir. 1966).

19. Roviaro v. United States, supra.

20. In Malloy v. Hogan, 376 U.S. 1, 12 L.Ed.2d 653, 84 S.Ct. 1489 (1964), the Supreme Court held that the privilege against self-incrimination of the Fifth Amendment applied (through the Fourteenth Amendment) to the states. Most states also have a similar privilege in their state constitutions.

21. The privilege for the witness applies if there is a real (not fanciful) danger of prosecution. See generally Zicarelli v. New Jersey State Com. of Investigation, 406 U.S. 472 (1972).

22. This "use" immunity prevents the prosecution from using the compelled testimony "in any respect." Note that "transactional" immunity, i.e., full and complete immunity from prosecution as to the offense to which the compelled testimony is related, is not required.

The defendant may be prosecuted based upon evidence *independent* of the testimony.

23.   See Letkowitz v. Turly, 414 U.S. 70, 38 L.Ed.2d 274, 94 S.Ct. 316 (1973). For a discussion of the factors a court should consider in determining the voluntariness of a Miranda waiver, see State of New Jersey v. Bey, 548 A.2d 887 (N.J. 1988). The Miranda aspect of the privilege against self-incrimination is discussed infra.

24.   384 U.S. at 444.

25.   The use of illegally seized evidence (inadmissible in the direct case of the government) may be admissible to impeach the defendant in the cross-examination of the defendant. United States v. Havens, 446 U.S. 620, 64 L.Ed.2d 559, 100 S.Ct. 1912 (1980).

26.   Other constitutional issues may be raised, e.g., due process of law and the protections against unreasonable searches and seizures (noted in Chapter Ten).

27.   United States v. Wade, 388 U.S. 218, 18 L.Ed.2d 1149, 87 S.Ct. 1926 (1967).

28.   Id. However, the accused has a right to counsel at the lineup. Id. Also, a DUE PROCESS RIGHT to a fair police process exists. See Foster v. California, 395 U.S. 440, 22

L.Ed.2d 402, 89 S.Ct. 1127 (1969), where the Court reiterated the rule that, "judged by the 'totality of the circumstances,' the conduct of identification procedures may be 'so unnecessarily suggestive and conducive to irreparable mistaken identification' as to be a denial of due process." 394 U.S. at 442.

29. Other privileges may include a journalist's privilege (as to the confidentiality of sources), an accountant-client privilege, or a social worker-client privilege, among others. See Yaron v.Yaron, 83 Misc.2d 276, 372 NYS2d 518 (1975) for a discussion of New York's social worker-client privilege.

30. FED. R. EVID. 201.

31. Brief reference to judicial notice has already been made in Chapter Two.

32. United States v. Gould, 536 F.2d 216, 219-20 (8th Cir. 1976). The terminology of adjudicative facts and legislative facts was developed by Professor Kenneth Davis, whom the court quotes in the Gould decision.

33. "Notes of Advisory Committee on Proposed Rules" to Federal Rule 201, Fed. Rules Evid Rule 201, 28 U.S.C.A.

34.   See   Schifieling,   "Judicial Intervention in Evidence," 10 Loyola U.L.J. 585.

35.   Government of the Virgin Islands v. Gereau, 523 F.2d 140 (3rd Cir. 1975).

36.   Again, it must be an adjudicative fact which meets the demands of Rule 201(b).

37.   See Massachusetts v. Westcoff, 431 U.S. 322, 52 L.Ed.2d 349, 97 S.Ct. 1755 (1977).

REVIEW AND DISCUSSION QUESTIONS

1.   What is a federal diversity action? As to such actions, does the federal common law apply? If not, what privilege law does apply?

2.   How is public policy served by the application of a privilege to the attorney-client relationship?

3.   Distinguish between the two separate privilege issues raised by the husband-wife relationship.

4.   Read *United States v. Nixon*, 418 U.S. 683, 41 L.Ed.2d 1039, 94 S.Ct. 3090 (1974). Note that the Court said:

Absent a claim of need to protect military, diplomatic or sensitive national security secrets, we find it difficult to accept the argument that even the very important interest in the confidentiality of presidential communications is significantly diminished by production of such material for *in camera* inspection with all the protection that a district court will be obliged to provide (emphasis added).

What is the process of in camera inspection? Explain.

5. Distinguish between use (and derivative use) immunity and transactional immunity.

6. What are the so-called Miranda warnings? What is the affect of the *Quarles* case on the *Miranda* decision?

7. The privilege against self-incrimination protects one from testimonial compulsion. What is the import of the testimonial compulsion limitation? Explain.

8. Distinguish adjudicative facts from legislative facts in judicial notice.

9. The court may only take judicial notice of a fact which is not subject to reasonable dispute. When may such lack of reasonable dispute exist? Explain. <u>Note</u>: Review Rule 201(b).

FOCUS V:

THE ATTORNEY-CLIENT PRIVILEGE AND THE CLIENT'S DESIRE TO TESTIFY UNTRUTHFULLY

Issue: One of the great ethical dilemmas a defense attorney can face is the dilemma of knowing a client will testify untruthfully. The following article discusses this dilemma.

ETHICS AND CRIMINAL DEFENSE:

A CLIENT'S DESIRE TO TESTIFY UNTRUTHFULLY

By Joseph M. Pellicciotti, J.D.

Indiana University Northwest

in Schmalleger, ed., ETHICS IN CRIMINAL JUSTICE, Wyndham Hall Press, pp. 62-77. Copyright 1990.

ABSTRACT

The overriding function of the criminal justice profession is to attempt to do justice. The criminal defense attorney advances the function through zealous and loyal representation of the client.

Ethical demands require such representation. Ethical demands also require moral firmness and good faith conduct by the defense attorney. When these demands conflict, ethical balances must be struck. Such a process is needed when the defense attorney's client desires to testify untruthfully. This article considers the propriety of remedial measures advanced for the attorney to deal with client perjury. For known perjury, it advocates an active response of rectification by disclosure.

INTRODUCTION

The criminal justice professional is often confronted with ethical issues in performing his or her duties. Professionalism requires one to conform his or her conduct to ethical demands. However, a great challenge to professionalism is to strike a balance among conflicting ethical demands. Such a challenge faces the criminal defense attorney when his or her client desires to testify untruthfully.

ETHICAL DEMANDS

Ethical demands are principles that regulate professional conduct. They represent statements as to what is considered proper conduct in a particular profession. They may, as in the attorney context, have the force of law, subjecting the violator to disciplinary action.

The determination of ethical demands should be logically based on a consideration of the primary function or functions of the profession in issue. The overriding function of the criminal justice profession is to attempt to do justice. While justice may not always be done, by attempting to do justice in every case, criminal justice professionals help to produce a system that is acceptable to and appropriate for a civilized society. The attempt to do justice is advanced by applying principles of fundamental fairness to law enforcement and adjudication procedures.

ETHICAL DEMANDS AND THE CRIMINAL DEFENSE ATTORNEY

The overriding function to attempt to do justice applies as much to the criminal defense attorney as to any other criminal justice professional. The defense attorney advances the function by advocating his or her client's cause in a sophisticated manner. The defense attorney's skills help to equalize the defendant's position vis a vis the prosecution and provide the vehicle for the defendant to take advantage of fundamentally fair procedures in the system (e.g., equal opportunities to present and argue evidence). Therefore, the defense attorney's role as an advocate is important to the attempt to do justice.

Ethical Demands for Zealous and Loyal Representation

To be most effective as an advocate, the defense attorney must provide zealous representation, which places on the attorney "the overreaching duty to advocate the defendant's cause" (**Strictland v. Washington**, 1984, p. 688). The attorney is required under pain of professional discipline to represent his or her client "zealously" (Model Code, Canon 7 (1)). Additionally, the attorney must have the confidence of the client, so as to promote full disclosure of the facts. To secure this confidence, the client must be assured of the attorney's loyal representation. This aspect of effective advocacy is enhanced by the ethical demand that the attorney maintain the confidences and secrets of the client (Model Code, Canon 4).

Ethical Demands for Moral Firmness and Good Faith Conduct

Moral corruption and dishonest intent are anathema to the attempt to do justice. Therefore, ethical demands for moral firmness and good faith conduct also exist in the law regulating attorney conduct.

Moral firmness is the clear understanding of, and a strict adherence to morally right action. It is necessary to resist the corrupting influences too often confronted by the defense attorney (or other criminal justice professionals). As Justice Frankfurter states, "(i)t is a fair characterization of the lawyer's responsibility in our society that he stands 'as a shield' ... in defense of right and to ward off wrong" (**Schware v. Bd. of Bar Examiners,** 1957, p. 806). In the law regulating attorney conduct, ethical demands for moral firmness are found in a number of rules regulating attorney conduct. For example, the attorney must not engage in conduct involving "moral turpitude" (Model Code, DR 1-102 (A)(3)) Additionally, the attorney is forbidden from engaging in conduct involving dishonesty, deceit, misrepresentation, or fraud (Model Code, DR 1-102 (A)(4)). The demand for moral firmness tempers the force of the ethical demand for zealous representation. The U.S. Supreme Court has stated that an attorney's overreaching duty to advocate the defendant's cause is "limited to legitimate, lawful conduct compatible with the very nature of a trial as a search for truth" (**Nix v. Whiteside,** 1986, p. 134). Zealous representation must be confined within the bounds of the law (Model Code, Canon 7).

Good faith conduct requires honest dealings. For the defense attorney it requires an honest intent in dealing not only with the client, but, importantly, with the court and others with whom the attorney interacts. Without good faith conduct, dishonesty of intent prevails. In the law regulating attorney conduct, an attorney has an ethical obligation not to interfere with the proper administration of justice (Model Code, EC 7-27). This is an obligation of good faith conduct. The demand for good faith conduct toward others can temper the requirement to maintain the confidences and secrets of the client. For example, an attorney may reveal the client's intention to commit a crime (Model Code, DR 4-101 (C)(1)).

Ethical Demand Conflicts

Ideally, ethical demands, such as zealous representation, maintenance of client confidences, moral firmness, and good faith conduct, do not conflict. Of course, in reality, they can. When they conflict, some adjustment is required. For example, as stated above, zealous representation must be confined within the bounds of the law. Additionally, an attorney may reveal the client's intention to commit a crime. In other words, when conflict exists, ethical balances must be struck. Such a process is needed when the defense attorney's client desires to testify untruthfully.

THE DESIRE TO TESTIFY UNTRUTHFULLY: KNOWN OR SUSPECTED PERJURY

A client's desire to testify untruthfully may be known to the attorney or merely suspected by counsel. Suspected perjury involves situations where the client's testimony is uncorroborated or is inconsistent with the testimony of other witnesses. It is represented by a doubt in the attorney's mind as to the veracity of his or her client. Both types of perjury are considered in this article.

KNOWN PERJURY

In a 1920 Missouri case decision the state court colorfully states that "(t)he law does not make a law office a nest of vipers in which to hatch out frauds and perjuries" (**Gebhardt v. United Rys. Co. of St. Louis,** 1920, p. 679). Ample laws exist to support a rule that the attorney may not present testimony he or she knows to be untruthfull.

The attorneys' codes of professional conduct[1] prohibit the attorney from assisting the client in a criminal act. Perjury, of course, is criminal. The Model Code of Professional Responsibility specifically states that an attorney shall not "(k)nowingly use perjured testimony or false testimony" (DR 7-102 (A)(4)). It also prohibits the attorney from assisting his or her client "in conduct that the lawyer knows to be illegal or fraudulent" (DR 7-102 (A)(7)). The Model Rules of Professional Conduct similarly prohibit the attorney from assisting a client in criminal and fraudulent acts (Rule 1.2 (d)). A number of criminal case decisions, including the U.S. Supreme Court case **(Nix v. Whiteside** (discussed below in detail), also prohibit the attorney from presenting perjured testimony **(Nix v. Whiteside**, 1986; **Bennett v. State**, 1977; **State v. Henderson**, 1970; **People v. Pike**, 1962, among others).

Zealous representation is confined; the attorney may not present evidence he or she knows to be untruthfull. However, while the prohibition is clear, the proper procedures in response to it are less clear.

An Attempt to Dissuade

An attorney is obliged to attempt to dissuade his or her client from perjurious conduct **(Nix v. Whiteside**, 1986, p. 136). The Model Rules of Professional Conduct state: "Upon ascertaining that material evidence is false, the lawyer should seek to persuade the client that the evidence should not be offered or, if it has been offered, that its false character should immediately be disclosed" (Rule 3.3, Comment).

This obligation is critical. If the attorney is successful in dissuading the client from perjury, then the matter is resolved, without publicly overt procedures that raise difficult questions for our justice system. However, if the client cannot be dissuaded, then publicly overt procedures are required.

A Request to Withdraw

There is authority that an attorney has a duty to seek to withdraw where his or her client insists on presenting untruthfull testimony (**State v. Trapp**, 1977; ABA Committee on Ethics, Informal Opinion No. 1318). While the value of withdrawal is doubtful (discussed below), the request to withdraw may be made to the court. However, granting the request is within the sound discretion of the judge. Particularly in criminal cases and during trial, a request to withdraw is not lightly granted. Therefore, a dilemma is imposed. If withdrawal is sought, what basis for withdrawal should be given by the attorney? To increase the likelihood of granting the request, should the attorney disclose the client's intent to offer perjury?

There is authority that disclosure is an appropriate course of action (**State v. Henderson**, 1970; Model Code, DR 4-101 (C)(3)). In **State v. Henderson**, the court stated:

> While as a general rule counsel is not allowed to disclose information imparted to him by his client or acquired during their professional relation, unless authorized to do so by the client himself..., the

announced intention of a client to commit perjury, or any other crime, is not included within the confidences which an attorney is bound to respect (p. 141).

While disclosure will more likely result in the granting of the request, problems remain. First, with disclosure, the attorney has prejudiced the judge. Even in a jury trial, if the defendant is convicted, the judge will impose sentence. Second, a successful withdrawal will only pass the dilemma on to the defendant's new counsel. Third, depending on the course of the case, granting of withdrawal will likely cause a delay in the proceedings and possible mistrial.

There is authority that disclosure is inappropriate (**People v. Schultheis**, 1981; ABA Standards, Criminal Defense SS 7.7 (c)). In **People v. Schultheis**, the court stated that "(e)ven when counsel makes a motion to withdraw, however, the defendant is always entitled to an impartial trial judge, untainted by accusations that the defendant has insisted upon presenting fabricated testimony" (p. 14). The court recommended that the attorney only give "irreconcilable conflict" with his or her client as the basis for the request to withdraw, since such basis could include, in addition to perjury, conflict of interest, personality or trial strategy (**People v. Schultheis**, p. 14).

However, the judge may be unsatisfied with such a general basis and deny the motion to withdraw.

The issue of whether or not to disclose the client's intent to offer perjury in the request to withdraw, passes over the primary issue of whether or not a withdrawal is appropriate. Withdrawal is not useful to the attempt to do justice. It serves the attorney's interest, since he or she does not become a part of a deception on the court. However, the dilemma will likely only be passed on to another attorney who must take the withdrawing attorney's place and after a delay or mistrial, which may reward the defendant's dishonest interest. This does not serve the interests of justice. However, if withdrawal is sought, on balance, the right to disclose is the better position. Its usefulness is not in the disclosure, but in the deterrent impact the right has on the client. In attempting to dissuade the client from perjurious conduct, the attorney is much better armed with a right to disclose than with only an ability to raise "irreconcilable conflict."

Nonwithdrawal Situations

If withdrawal from the case is not sought or available, then the attorney must decide how to properly effect his or her continued representation of the client. If the untruthfull testimony is to come from witnesses other than the defendant (e.g., an alibi witness testifying falsely about the existence of defendant's alibi), then the attorney should refuse to call such witnesses to testify, or, if called, refuse to inquire into the area which will result in the perjury. As a general rule, the decision of what witnesses to call and strategic decisions belong to the attorney, albeit after consultation with the client (ABA Standard, Criminal Defense Sec. 4-5.2 (b)). Therefore, authority exists that a client cannot force the attorney to call witnesses who will testify untruthfully **(People v. Schultheis,** 1981). However, where the defendant seeks to personally introduce the untruthfull statements, the proper attorney response is less clear.

The right of a defendant to testify in a criminal trial has constitutional and ethical dimensions. While there is authority that an attorney's refusal to put a defendant who intends to testify untruthfully on the witness stand is not a violation of the defendant's constitutional rights **(United States v. Curtis,** 7th Cir., 1984), there is authority to the contrary **(Whiteside v. Schurr,** 8th Cir., 1984). The law remains unclear, even though the U.S. Supreme Court has said that "(w)hatever the scope of a constitutional right to testify, it is elementary that such a right does not extend to testifying falsely" **(Nix v. Whiteside,** 1986, p. 138). In **United States v. Curtis,** the court stated expressly that the holding considered **only** the constitutional issue and not the ethical issue (p. 1076). Ethically, it is a question as to whether a rule, even if constitutional, should be devised to allow the attorney to refuse to permit his or her client to testify, since the decision to testify on one's own behalf has historically been viewed as one of the few decisions exclusively belonging to the defendant, not to the attorney (ABA Standards, Criminal Defense Sec. 4-5.2 (a)). Also, in **Nix v. Whiteside**, the Supreme Court did not indicate that its statement could be used by an attorney to refuse to put the client on the witness stand. The Court's statement was rendered in a case with a different factual setting and where the defendant did testify.

An Overview of Nix v. Whiteside

Nix v. Whiteside, decided February 26, 1986, held that an attorney's refusal to assist a defendant in presenting perjured testimony did not violate the defendant's Sixth Amendment right to effective assistance of counsel.

In this murder case, the defendant had told his attorney that he had not seen a gun in the victim's hand. No gun had been found on the premises. The defendant was, however, convinced that the victim did have a gun. Later, the defendant told his attorney that he had seen something "metallic" in the victim's hand (p.

131). The defendant then told the attorney: "If I don't say I saw a gun, I'm dead" (p. 131). The defendant insisted he would testify that he had seen something "metallic." The attorney told the defendant that, if the defendant testified falsely, he would advise the court of the defendant's perjury, he would have to impeach the defendant, and he would seek to withdraw from the case. The defendant responded to the attorney's pressure and ultimately testified without reference to the "metallic" object. The defendant was found guilty, and he raised the effective assistance of counsel issue.

The Court found that "the right to counsel includes no right to have a lawyer who will cooperate with planned perjury" (p. 139). In the case, the defendant "enjoyed continued representation within the bounds of reasonable professional conduct and did in fact exercise his right to testify; at most he was denied the right to have the assistance of counsel in the presentation of false testimony" (p. 139). The defendant's attorney had treated the planned perjury in accordance with professional standards, and his representation was acceptable under the Sixth Amendment.

A Passive v. Active Response

There are two basic approaches to the dilemma faced by the attorney when the defendant, insisting on perjury, takes the witness stand. One provides for a passive performance, and the other calls for rectification by disclosure.

The passive route calls for the attorney to stand mute as the defendant presents the false testimony in narrative form. This approach is best described in the ABA Standards regarding the defense function:

> Before the defendant takes the stand..., the lawyer should make a record of the fact that the defendant is taking the stand against the advice of counsel in some appropriate manner without revealing the fact to the court. The lawyer may identify the witness as the defendant and may ask appropriate questions of the defendant when it is believed that the defendant's answers will not be perjurious. As to matters for which it is believed the defendant will offer perjurious testimony, the lawyer should seek to avoid direct examination of the defendant in the conventional manner, instead, the lawyer should ask the defendant if he or she wishes to make any additional statement concerning the case to the trier or triers of the facts. A lawyer may not later argue

the defendant's known false version of the facts to the jury as worthy of belief, and may not recite or rely upon the false testimony in his or her closing argument (ABA Standards, Criminal Defense Sec. 7.7 (c)).

The active route, however, calls for disclosure of the perjury by the attorney to the court. This approach is described in the comment to the ABA Model Rules of Professional Conduct:

If withdrawal will not remedy the situation or is impossible, the advocate should make disclosure to the court. It is for the court then to determine what should be done-making a statement about the matter to the trier of fact, ordering a mistrial or perhaps nothing (Model Rules, Rule 3.3 Comment).

Choosing Between the Basic Approaches

Both approaches pose serious problems for the defense attorney. By taking the active route, the attorney is placed in the unhappy position of increasing his or her client's chances of conviction. The attorney discloses the client's secret to the court and raises the issue of a prosecution of the client for perjury. Also, the attorney increases the likelihood of a mistrial. On the other hand, the passive route requires the attorney, even though passively, to participate in a deception on the court. A serious crime is allowed to occur, and the attorney, in fact, assists in the crime by setting the stage for its commission.

While the choice between the two approaches is a difficult one, on balance, the active role is the better for two reasons. First, the attempt to do justice is better served by preventing perjury and deception. In **State v. Henderson** (1970), the Kansas court stated that the objective of the criminal trial is "to ascertain an accused's guilt or innocence in accordance with established rules of evidence and procedure designed to develop the facts truthfully and fairly" (p. 141). Allowing known perjury can prevent the objective from being fulfilled. Second, a professional acceptance of the active approach may provide to the attorney an important tool to dissuade a client from perjurious conduct. If the attorney is successful in dissuading the client from perjury, then the matter is resolved without the difficulty of the attorney having to choose a publicly overt procedure such as court disclosure. In other words, the ability of the attorney to tell the defendant that the defendant's perjury must be disclosed to the court is a deterrent. The necessity to disclose is perhaps the best reason for the defendant to think twice about testifying untruthfully.

SUSPECTED PERJURY

As noted previously, suspected perjury involves situations where the client's testimony is uncorroborated or inconsistent with the testimony of other witnesses. It is represented by a doubt in the attorney's mind as to the veracity of his or her client. It is not uncommon for such doubts to exist.

However, there is no prohibition on the presentation of testimony that the attorney merely suspects to be untruthfull. The attorney must have knowledge of an intended perjury. That knowledge cannot be based upon mere inconsistency in the client's story:

> A lawyer's belief that a witness intends to offer false testimony, however, must be based upon an independent investigation of the evidence or upon distinct statements by his client or the witness which supports that belief. A mere inconsistency in the client's story is insufficient in and of itself to support the conclusion that a witness will offer false testimony **(People v. Schultheis,** 1981, p. 11).

Also, the fact that the client's testimony is uncorroborated must be insufficient to establish the requisite knowledge. It is, if anything, less sufficient to show intent than inconsistent statements. There is also no requirement that the attorney independently investigate whether his client's version of the facts is truthful; that role belongs to the trier of fact, not to an advocate.

Not only is there no prohibition on the presentation of testimony that the attorney merely suspects to be untruthfull, any disclosure by the attorney based merely on unsubstantiated opinion is improper:

> It is essential to our adversary system that a client's ability to communicate freely and in confidence with his counsel be maintained inviolate. When an attorney unnecessarily discloses the confidences of his client, he creates a chilling effect which inhibits the mutual trust and independence necessary to effective representation. It is apparent that an attorney may not volunteer a mere unsubstantiated opinion that his client's protestation of innocence are perjured. To do so would undermine a cornerstone of our

system of criminal justice **(United States v. Johnson,** 1977, p. 122).

Therefore, unless the attorney is fully satisfied and convinced of the client's intent to commit perjury, it is highly unlikely that the attorney will risk breaching his or her duty to represent the client zealously and maintain the client's confidences. The attorney should submit the evidence in a suspected perjury situation.

CONCLUSIONS

It is clear that professional requirements prohibit the attorney from presenting testimony that he or she knows to be untruthfull. However, other than the attorney's duty to attempt to dissuade the client from perjurious conduct, no unanimity exists as to the proper procedures needed to abide by the prohibition.

A request to withdraw may be made. Of course, withdrawal serves the attorney's interest, since he or she does not become a part of a deception on the court. However, it is doubtful that withdrawal is useful to the attempt to do justice, since the dilemma will likely only be passed on to another member of the bar and after a delay or mistrial, which may reward the defendant.

In arguing withdrawal, there is disagreement as
to whether or not disclosure of the client's
intention to commit perjury should be made.
While neither position is without problems, the
right to disclose is the better position, on
balance, since such right is valuable to an
attorney in attempting to dissuade the client
from perjurious conduct in the first place.

As to the two basic approaches to the dilemma
faced by the attorney when the defendant,
insisting on perjury, takes the witness stand,
the active response is the better route to take
because the attempt to do justice is better
served by preventing perjury and deception.
Additionally, the right to disclose, as in the
withdrawal context, serves to have the defendant
think twice of deceiving the court. Since
dissuading the client from perjurious conduct is
the only universally acceptable remedial
measure, providing the attorney with better
tools to dissuade is logical.

Finally, the attorney will not likely volunteer
a mere suspicion that his or her client will
commit perjury. Some may feel that this will
allow deceptions to go unchecked. However, the
duties to represent a client zealously and to
maintain the client's confidences are important
to the attempt to do justice. They should not
be pushed aside without actual knowledge of the
client's intent. If there is doubt as to the
client's truthfulness, the determination of

veracity should be left to the judge or jury. The attorney should remain an advocate on behalf of the client.

FOOTNOTES

1. Currently, there are two uniform codes of professional standards for attorneys, the Model Code of Professional Responsibility (hereinafter "Model Code") and the Model Rules of Professional Conduct (hereinafter "Model Rules"). The Model Code was adopted by almost every state (48) and the District of Columbia. Adoption occurs with the acceptance by the State's high court. Attorneys are subject only to those ethical requirements in the state(s) where they practice. The Model Rules were adopted by the ABA in 1983, as a replacement for the earlier Model Code. The Model Rules have been adopted by some states. See **Nix v. Whiteside,** where the Court identifies eleven states as having adopted (in substantial form) the Model Rules (p. 135 n. 4). Also, see Franek, **Report of Special Committee on Implementation of the Model Rules of Professional Conduct,** October, 1985.

REFERENCES

ABA Committee on Ethics and Professional Responsibility, Informal Opinion No. 1318 (January 13, 1975).

ABA Model Code of Professional Responsibility, Canon 4, 7, DR 1-102 (A)(3), (A)(4), DR 4-101 (c)(1), (c)(4), DR 7-120 (a)(4), (a)(7), EC 7-27 (1969).

ABA Model Rules of Professional Conduct, Rule 1.2 (d), 3.3 & Comment (1983).

ABA Project on Standards for Criminal Justice: The Prosecution Function and the Defense Function, Proposed Defense Function Standards, 4-5.2 (a), (b) & 4-7.7 (c) (2nd ed. 1980).

Bennett v. State, 549 S.W.2d 585 (1977).

Franek, M. (1985, October). **Report of Special Committee on Implementation of the Model Rules of Professional Conduct.** (Available from America Bar Association, 750 N. Lake Shore Drive, Chicago, IL 60611).

Gebhardt v. United Rys. Co. of St. Louis, 220 S.W. 677 (1920).

Nix v. Whiteside, 475 U.S.-, 89 L.Ed.2d 123 (1986).

People v. Pike, Cal., 372 P.2d 646 (1962).

People v. Schultheis, Colo., 638 P.2d 8 (1981).

Schware v. Bd. of Bar Examiners, 247 L.Ed.2d 796 (1957) (Frankfurter, J., concurring).

State v. Henderson, Kan., 468 P.2d 136 (1970).

State v. Trapp, Ohio, 368 N.E.2d 1278 (1977).

United States v. Curtis, 742 F.2d 1070 (7th Cir. 1984).

Unites States v. Johnson, 555 F.2d 115 (3rd Cir. 1977)

Whiteside v. Schurr, 744 F.2d 1323 (8th Cir. 1984).

DISCUSSION QUESTIONS

1. The defense attorney can face other ethical dilemmas, in addition to known perjury. For example, the attorney may have knowledge that the client intends to commit some other crime. How would you react to the client telling you that he intends to abduct the prosecutor's child? What if the client tells you that he intends to defraud an elderly person of his or her life savings? Should your reaction be different?

2. Does the disclosure by the defense attorney of the client's known perjury square with your understanding of the concepts of the constitutional right to counsel and due process of law for the criminal defendant? Explain.

3. This article has focused on the defense attorney's ethical dilemma, when his or her

client intends to commit perjury. What of the concerns of the prosecutor when he or she has knowledge of intended perjury? For example, if you were the prosecutor and you gained knowledge of the complainant's intent to lie at trial, what would you do? Do you have any opportunity to rectify which is unavailable to the defense attorney?

4. As stated in this article, there is general disagreement as to the proper course or action when the defense attorney is faced with the situation of known perjury. The only area of procedural agreement is that the attorney must attempt to dissuade the client of such action. How would you attempt to dissuade? What would you tell the client?

5. In addition to the two basic approaches (i.e., the active approach and passive approach) to the dilemma when the defendant, insisting on perjury, takes the witness stand, the defense attorney could simply let the client lie, since it is the client's liberty which is at stake. How often do you think this happens in everyday practice? Would you be comfortable with a professional rule of conduct which excuses the defense attorney from any obligation to deal with known perjury? Explain.

APPENDIX A

THE FEDERAL RULES OF EVIDENCE

(AS AMENDED THROUGH JANUARY 1, 1991)

Note: Some of the less lengthy federal rules have been set forth throughout the book where relevant to serve as examples of law. Those rules are not restated here. Each such rule is omitted with a citation to the chapter where it may be found.

ARTICLE I:

GENERAL PROVISIONS

Rule 101

SCOPE

These rules govern proceedings in the courts of the United States and before United States magistrates, to the extent and with the exceptions stated in Rule 1101.

Rule 102

PURPOSE AND CONSTRUCTION

These rules shall be construed to secure fairness in administration, elimination of unjustifiable expense and delay, and promotion of growth and development of the law of evidence to the end that the truth may be ascertained and proceedings justly determined.

Rule 103

RULINGS ON EVIDENCE

(a) Effect of Erroneous Ruling. Error may not be predicated upon a ruling which admits or excludes evidence unless a substantial right of the party is affected, and

1. Objection. In case the ruling is one admitting evidence, a timely objection or motion to strike appears of record, stating the specific ground of objection, if the specific ground was not apparent from the context; or

2. Offer of Proof. In case the ruling is one excluding evidence, the substance of the evidence was made known to the court by offer or was apparent from the context within which questions were asked.

(b) Record of Offer and Ruling. The court may add any other or further statement which shows the character of the evidence, the form in which it was offered, the objection made, and the ruling thereon. It may direct the making of an offer in question and the answer form.

(c) Hearing of Jury. In jury cases, proceedings shall be conducted, to the extent practicable, so as to prevent inadmissible evidence from being suggested to the jury by any means, such as making statements or offers of proof or asking questions in the hearing of the jury.

(d) Plain Error. Nothing in this rule precludes taking notice of plain errors affecting substantial rights although they were not brought to the attention of the court.

Rule 104
PRELIMINARY QUESTIONS

(a) Questions of Admissibility Generally. Preliminary questions concerning the qualification of a person to be a witness, the existence of a privilege, or the admissibility of evidence shall be determined by the court, subject to the provisions of subdivision (b). In making its determination it is not bound by the rules of evidence except those with respect to privileges.

(b) Relevancy Conditioned on Fact. When the relevancy of evidence depends upon the fulfillment of a condition of fact, the court shall admit it upon, or subject to, the introduction of evidence sufficient to support a finding of the fulfillment of the condition.

(c) Hearing of Jury. Hearings on the admissibility of confessions shall in all cases be conducted out of the hearing of the jury. Hearings on other preliminary matters shall be so conducted when the interests of justice require, or when an accused is a witness and so requests.

(d) Testimony by Accused. The accused does not, by testifying upon a preliminary matter, become subject to cross-examination as to other issues in the case.

(e) Weight and Credibility. This rule does not limit the right of a party to introduce before the jury evidence relevant to weight or credibility.

Rule 105
LIMITED ADMISSIBILITY

When evidence which is admissible as to one party or for one purpose but not admissible as to another party or for another purpose is admitted, the court, upon request, shall restrict the evidence to its proper scope and instruct the jury accordingly.

Rule 106

REMAINDER OF OR RELATED WRITINGS

OR RECORDED STATEMENTS

(Omitted, see Chapter Nine)

ARTICLE II:

JUDICIAL NOTICE

Rule 201

JUDICIAL NOTICE OF ADJUDICATIVE FACTS

(Omitted, see Chapter Eleven)

ARTICLE III:

PRESUMPTIONS IN CIVIL ACTIONS AND PROCEEDINGS

Rule 301

PRESUMPTIONS IN GENERAL

IN CIVIL ACTIONS AND PROCEEDINGS

In all civil actions and proceedings not otherwise provided for by Act of Congress or by these rules, a presumption imposes on the party against whom it is directed the burden of going forward with evidence to rebut or meet the presumption, but does not shift to such party the burden of proof in the sense of the risk of nonpersuasion, which remains throughout the trial upon the party on whom it was originally cast.

Rule 302

APPLICABILITY OF STATE LAW

IN CIVIL ACTIONS AND PROCEEDINGS

In civil actions and proceedings, the effect of a presumption respecting a fact which is an element of a claim or defense as to which state law supplies the rule of decision is determined in accordance with state law.

ARTICLE IV:

RELEVANCY AND ITS LIMITS

Rule 401

DEFINITION OF "RELEVANT EVIDENCE"

(Omitted, see Chapter Three)

Rule 402

RELEVANT EVIDENCE GENERALLY ADMISSIBLE,

IRRELEVANT EVIDENCE INADMISSIBLE

(Omitted, see Chapter Three)

Rule 403

EXCLUSION OF RELEVANT EVIDENCE ON GROUNDS

OF PREJUDICE, CONFUSION, OR WASTE OF TIME

(Omitted, see Chapter Three)

Rule 404

CHARACTER EVIDENCE NOT ADMISSIBLE

TO PROVE CONDUCT; EXCEPTIONS; OTHER CRIMES

(Omitted, see Chapter Three)

Rule 405

METHODS OF PROVING CHARACTER

(Omitted, see Chapter Three)

Rule 406

HABIT; ROUTINE PRACTICE

(Omitted, see Chapter Three)

Rule 407

SUBSEQUENT REMEDIAL MEASURES

(Omitted, see Chapter Three)

Rule 408

COMPROMISE AND OFFERS TO COMPROMISE

Evidence of (1) furnishing or offering or promising to furnish, or (2) accepting or offering or promising to accept, a valuable consideration in compromising or attempting to compromise a claim which was disputed as to either validity or amount, is not admissible to prove liability for or invalidity of the claim or its amount. Evidence of conduct or statements made in compromise negotiations is likewise not admissible. This rule does not require the exclusion of any evidence otherwise discoverable merely because it is presented in the course of compromise negotiations. This rule also does not require exclusion when the evidence is offered for another purpose, such as proving bias or prejudice of a witness, negativing a contention of undue delay, or proving an effort to obstruct a criminal investigation or prosecution.

Rule 409

PAYMENT OF MEDICAL AND SIMILAR EXPENSES

Evidence of furnishing or offering or promising to pay medical, hospital, or similar expenses occasioned by an injury is not admissible to prove liability for the injury.

Rule 410

INADMISSIBILITY OF PLEAS, PLEA DISCUSSIONS,

ADD RELATED STATEMENTS

(Omitted, see Chapter Three)

Rule 411

LIABILITY INSURANCE

(Omitted, see Chapter Three)

Rule 412

SEX OFFENSE CASES; RELEVANCE OF

VICTIM'S PAST BEHAVIOR

(a) Notwithstanding any other provision of law, in a criminal case in which a person is accused of an offense under chapter 109A of title 18, United States Code, reputation or opinion evidence of the past sexual behavior of an alleged victim of such offense is not admissible.

(b) Notwithstanding any other provision of law, in a criminal case in which a person is accused of an offense under chapter 109A of title 18, United States Code, evidence of a victim's past sexual behavior other than reputation or opinion evidence is also not admissible, unless such evidence other than reputation or opinion evidence is-

(1) admitted in accordance with subdivisions (c)(1) and (c)(2) and is constitutionally required to be admitted; or

(2) admitted in accordance with subdivision (c) and is evidence of-

(A) past sexual behavior with persons other than the accused, offered by the accused upon the issue of whether the accused was or was not, with respect to the alleged victim, the source of semen or injury; or

(B) past sexual behavior with the accused and is offered by the accused upon the issue of whether the alleged victim consented to the sexual behavior with respect to which such offense is alleged.

(c)(1) If the person accused of committing an offense under chapter 109A of title 18, United States Code, intends to offer under subdivision (b) evidence of specific instances of the alleged victim's past sexual behavior, the accused shall make a written motion to offer such evidence not later than fifteen days before the date on which the trial in which such evidence is to be offered is scheduled to begin, except that the court may allow the motion to be made at a later date, including during trial, if the court determines either that the evidence is newly discovered and could not have been obtained earlier through the exercise of due diligence or that the issue to which such evidence relates has newly arisen in the case. Any motion made under this paragraph shall be served on all other parties and on the alleged victim.

(2) The motion described in paragraph (1) shall be accompanied by a written offer of proof. If the court determines that the offer of proof contains evidence described in subdivision (b), the court shall order a hearing in chambers to determine if such evidence is admissible. At such hearing the parties may call witnesses, including the alleged victim, and offer relevant evidence. Notwithstanding subdivision (b) of Rule 104, if the relevancy of the evidence which the accused seeks to offer in the trial depends upon the fulfillment of a condition of fact, the court, at the hearing in chambers or at a subsequent hearing in chambers scheduled for such purpose, shall accept evidence on the issue of whether such condition of facts is fulfilled and shall determine such issue.

(3) If the court determines on the basis of the hearing described in paragraph (2) that

the evidence which the accused seeks to offer is relevant and that the probative value of such evidence out weighs the danger of unfair prejudice, such evidence shall be admissible in the trial to the extent an order made by the court specifies evidence which may be offered and areas with respect to which the alleged victim may be examined or cross-examined.

(d) For purposes of this rule, the term "past sexual behavior" means sexual behavior other than the sexual behavior with respect to which an offense under chapter 109A of title 18, United States Code, is alleged.

Note: Chapter 109A of Title 18, United States Code, prohibits "Sexual Abuse," including aggravated sexual abuse, sexual abuse, sexual abuse of a minor or ward, and abusive sexual conduct. See 18 U.S.C. Sec. 2241-2245.

ARTICLE V:

PRIVILEGES

Rule 501

GENERAL RULE

(Omitted, see Chapter Eleven)

ARTICLE VI:

WITNESSES

Rule 601

GENERAL RULE OF COMPETENCY

(Omitted, see Chapter Four)

Rule 602

LACK OF PERSONAL KNOWLEDGE

(Omitted, see Chapter Four)

Rule 603

OATH OR AFFIRMATION

(Omitted, see Chapter Four)

Rule 604

INTERPRETERS

(Omitted, see Chapter Four)

Rule 605

COMPETENCY OF JUDGE AS WITNESS

The judge presiding at the trial may not testify in that trial as a witness. No objection need be made in order to preserve the point.

Rule 606

COMPETENCY OF JUROR AS WITNESS

(a)   At the Trial. A member of the jury may not testify as a witness before that jury in the trial of the case in which the juror is sitting.   If the juror is called so to testify, the opposing party shall be afforded an opportunity to object out of the presence of the jury.

(b)   Inquiry into Validity of Verdict or Indictment. Upon an inquiry into the validity of a verdict or indictment, a juror may not testify as to any matter or statement occurring during the course of the jury's deliberations or to the effect of anything upon that or any other juror's mind or emotions as influencing the juror to assent to or dissent from the verdict or indictment or concerning the juror's mental processes in connection therewith, except that a juror may testify on the question whether extraneous prejudicial information was improperly brought to the jury's attention or whether any outside influence was improperly brought to bear upon any juror.   Nor may a juror's affidavit or evidence of any statement by the juror concerning a matter about which the

juror would be precluded from testifying be
received for these purposes.

Rule 607

WHO MAY IMPEACH

(Omitted, see Chapter Five)

Rule 608

EVIDENCE OF CHARACTER

AND CONDUCT OF WITNESS

(a)   Opinion and Reputation Evidence of
Character. The credibility of a witness may be
attacked or supported by evidence in the form of
opinion or reputation, but subject to these
limitations: (1) the evidence may refer only to
character for truthfulness or untruthfulness,
and (2) evidence of truthful character is
admissible only after the character of the
witness for truthfulness has been attacked by
opinion or reputation evidence or otherwise.

(b)   Specific Instances of Conduct.
Specific instances of the conduct of a witness,
for the purpose of attacking or supporting the
witness' credibility, other than conviction of
crime as provided in rule 609, may not be proved
by extrinsic evidence. They may, however, in
the discretion of the court, if probative of
truthfulness or untruthfulness, be inquired into

on cross-examination of the witness (1) concerning the witness' character for truthfulness or untruthfulness, or (2) concerning the character for truthfulness or untruthfulness of another witness as to which character the witness being cross-examined has testified.

The giving of testimony, whether by an accused or by any other witness, does not operate as a waiver of the accused's or the witness' privilege against self-incrimination when examined with respect to matters which relate only to credibility.

Rule 609
IMPEACHMENT BY EVIDENCE
OF CONDUCTION OF CRIME

(a) General Rule. For the purpose of attacking the credibility of a witness, (1) evidence that a witness other than an accused has been convicted of a crime shall be admitted, subject to Rule 403, if the crime was punishable by death or imprisonment in excess of one year under the law under which the witness was convicted, and evidence that an accused has been convicted of such a crime shall be admitted if the court determines that the probative value of admitting the evidence outweighs its prejudicial effect to the accused; and (2) evidence that any witness has been convicted of a crime shall be admitted if it involved dishonesty or false statement, regardless of the punishment.

(b)   Time Limit. Evidence of a conviction under this rule is not admissible if a period of more than ten years has elapsed since the date of conviction or of the release of the witness from the confinement imposed for that conviction, whichever is the later date, unless the court determines, in the interests of justice, that the probative value of the conviction supported by specific facts and circumstances substantially outweighs its prejudicial effect. However, evidence of a conviction more than 10 years old as calculated herein, is not admissible unless the proponent gives to the adverse party sufficient advance written notice of intent to use such evidence to provide the adverse party with a fair opportunity to contest the use of such evidence.

(c)   Effect of Pardon, Annulment, or Certificate of Rehabilitation. Evidence of a conviction is not admissible under this rule if (1) the conviction has been the subject of a pardon, annulment, certificate of rehabilitation, or other equivalent procedure based on a finding of the rehabilitation of the person convicted, and that person has not been convicted of a subsequent crime which was punishable by death or imprisonment in excess of one year, or (2) the conviction has been the subject of a pardon, annulment, or other equivalent procedure based on a finding of innocence.

(d) Juvenile Adjudications. Evidence of juvenile adjudications is generally not admissible under this rule. The court may, however, in a criminal case allow evidence of a juvenile adjudication of a witness other than the accused if conviction of the offense would be admissible to attack the credibility of an adult and the court is satisfied that admission in evidence is necessary for a fair determination of the issue of guilt or innocence.

(e) Pendency of Appeal. The pendency of an appeal therefrom does not render evidence of a conviction inadmissible. Evidence of the pendency of an appeal is admissible.

Rule 610
RELIGIOUS BELIEFS

Evidence of the beliefs or opinions of a witness on matters of religion is not admissible for the purpose of showing that by reason of their nature the witness' credibility is impaired or enhanced.

Rule 611
MODE AND ORDER OF
INTERROGATION AND PRESENTATION

(Omitted, see Chapter Five)

Rule 612
WRITING USED TO REFRESH MEMORY

Except as otherwise provided in criminal proceedings by section 3500 of title 18, United States Code, if a witness uses a writing to refresh memory for the purpose of testifying, either-

(1)   while testifying, or

(2)   before testifying, if the court in its discretion determines it is necessary in the interests of justice, an adverse party is entitled to have the writing produced at the hearing, to inspect it, to cross-examine the witness thereon, and to introduce in evidence those portions which relate to the testimony of the witness. If it is claimed that the writing contains matters not related to the subject matter of the testimony the court shall examine the writing in camera, excise any positions not so related, and order delivery of the remainder to the party entitled thereto. Any portion withheld over objections shall be preserved and made available to the appellate court in the event of an appeal. If a writing is not

produced or delivered pursuant to order under
this rule, the court shall make any order
justice requires, except that in criminal cases
when the prosecution elects not to comply, the
order shall be one striking the testimony or, if
the court in its discretion determines that the
interests of justice so require, declaring a
mistrial.

Rule 613
PRIOR STATEMENTS OF WITNESSES

(Omitted, See Chapter Five)

Rule 614
CALLING AND INTERROGATION
OF WITNESSES BY COURT

(Omitted, see Chapter Five)

Rule 615
EXCLUSION OF WITNESSES

(Omitted, see Chapter Five)

ARTICLE VII:

OPINIONS AND EXPERT TESTIMONY

Rule 701

OPINION TESTIMONY BY A LAY WITNESS

(Omitted, see Chapter Six)

Rule 702

TESTIMONY BY EXPERTS

(Omitted, see Chapter Six)

Rule 703

BASES OF OPINION TESTIMONY BY EXPERTS

(Omitted, see Chapter Six)

Rule 704

OPINION ON ULTIMATE ISSUE

(Omitted, see Chapter Six)

Rule 705

DISCLOSURE OF FACTS OR DATA

UNDERLYING EXPERT OPINION

(Omitted, see Chapter Six)

Rule 706

COURT-APPOINTED EXPERTS

(a) Appointment. The court may on its own motion or on the motion of any party enter an order to show cause why expert witnesses should not be appointed, and may request the parties to submit nominations. The court may appoint any expert witnesses agreed upon by the parties, and may appoint expert witnesses of its own selection. An expert witness shall not be appointed by the court unless the witness consents to act. A witness so appointed shall be informed of the witness' duties by the court in writing, a copy of which shall be filed with the clerk, or at a conference in which the parties shall have opportunity to participate. A witness so appointed shall advise the parties of the witness' findings, if any; the witness' deposition may be taken by any party; and the witness may be called to testify by the court or any party. The witness shall be subject to cross-examination by each party, including a party calling the witness.

(b) Compensation. Expert witnesses so appointed are entitled to reasonable compensation in whatever sum the court may allow. The compensation thus fixed is payable from funds which may be provided by law in criminal cases and civil actions and proceedings involving just compensation under the Fifth Amendment. In other civil actions and proceedings the compensation shall be paid by the parties in such proportion and at such time as the court directs, and thereafter charged in like manner as other costs.

(c) Disclosure of Appointment. In the exercise of its discretion, the court may authorize disclosure to the jury of the fact that the court appointed the expert witness.

(d) Parties' Experts of Own Selection. Nothing in this rule limits the parties in calling expert witnesses of their own selection.

ARTICLE VIII:

HEARSAY

Rule 801

DEFINITIONS

The following definitions apply under this article:

(a) Statement. A "statement" is (1) an oral or written assertion or (2) nonverbal conduct of a person, if it is intended by the person as an assertion.

(b) Declarant. A "declarant" is a person who makes a statement.

(c)   Hearsay. "Hearsay" is a statement, other than one made by the declarant while testifying at the trial or hearing, offered in evidence to prove the truth of the matter asserted.

(d)   Statements Which Are Not Hearsay. A statement is not hearsay if-

(1)   Prior statement by witness. The declarant testifies at the trial or hearing and is subject to cross-examination concerning the statement, and the statement is (A) inconsistent with the declarant's testimony, and was given under oath subject to the penalty of perjury at a trial, hearing, or other proceeding, or in a deposition, or (B) consistent with the declarant's testimony and is offered to rebut an express or implied charge against the declarant of recent fabrication or improper influence or motive, or (C) one of identification of a person made after perceiving the person; or

(2)   Admission by party-opponent. The statement is offered against a party and is (A) the party's own statement in either the party's individual or a representative capacity or (B) a statement of which the party has manifested an adoption or belief in its truth, or (C) a statement by a person authorized by him to make a statement concerning the subject, or (D) a statement by the party's agent or servant concerning a matter within the scope of the

agency or employment, made during the existence of the relationship, or (E) a statement by a co-conspirator of a party during the course and in furtherance of the conspiracy.

Rule 802

HEARSAY RULE

Hearsay is not admissible except as provided by these rules or by other rules prescribed by the Supreme Court pursuant to statutory authority or by Act of Congress.

Rule 803

HEARSAY EXCEPTIONS;

AVAILABILITY OF DECLARANT IMMATERIAL

The following are not excluded by the hearsay rule, even though the declarant is available as a witness:

(1) Present sense impression. A statement describing or explaining an event or condition made while the declarant was perceiving the event or condition, or immediately thereafter.

(2) Excited utterance. A statement relating to a startling event or condition made while the declarant was under the stress of excitement caused by the event or condition.

(3) Then existing mental, emotional, or physical condition. A statement of the declarant's then existing state of mind, emotion, sensation, or physical condition (such as intent, plan, motive, design, mental feeling, pain, and bodily health), but not including a statement of memory or belief to prove the fact remembered or believed unless it relates to the execution, revocation, identification, or terms of declarant's will.

(4) Statements for purposes of medical diagnosis or treatment. Statements made for purposes of medical diagnosis or treatment and describing medical history, or past or present symptoms, pain, or sensations, or the inception or general character of the cause or external source thereof insofar as reasonably pertinent to diagnosis or treatment.

(5) Recorded recollection. A memorandum or record concerning a matter about which a witness once had knowledge but now has insufficient recollection to enable the witness to testify fully and accurately, shown to have been made or adopted by the witness when the matter was fresh in the witness' memory and to reflect that knowledge correctly. If admitted, the memorandum or record may be read into evidence but may not itself be received as an exhibit unless offered by an adverse party.

(6) Records of regularly conducted activity. A memorandum, report, record, or data compilation, in any form, of acts, events, conditions, opinions, or diagnoses, made at or near the time by, or from information transmitted by, a person with knowledge, if kept in the course of a regularly conducted business activity, and if it was the regular practice of that business activity to make the memorandum, report, record, or data compilation, all as shown by the testimony of the custodian or other qualified witness, unless the source of information or the method of circumstances of preparation indicate lack of trustworthiness. The term "business" as used in this paragraph includes business, institution, association, profession, occupation, and calling of every kind, whether or not conducted for profit.

(7) Absence of entry in records kept in accordance with the provisions of paragraph (6) Evidence that a matter is not included in the memoranda, reports, or data compilations, in any form, kept in accordance with the provisions of paragraph (6), to prove the nonoccurrence or nonexistence of the matter, if the matter was of a kind of which memorandum, report, record, or data compilation was regularly made and preserved, unless the sources of information or other circumstances indicate lack of trustworthiness.

(8) Public records and reports. Records, reports, statements, or data compilations, in any form, of public offices or agencies, setting forth (A) the activities of the office or agency, or (B) matters observed pursuant to duty imposed by law as to which matters there was a duty to report, excluding, however, in criminal cases matters observed by police officers and other law enforcement personnel, or (C) in civil actions and proceedings and against the government in criminal cases, factual findings resulting from an investigation made pursuant to authority granted by law, unless the sources of information or other circumstances indicate lack of trustworthiness.

(9) Records of vital statistics. Records or data compilations, in any form, of births, fetal deaths, deaths, or marriages, if the report thereof was made to a public office pursuant to requirements of law.

(10) Absence of public record or entry. To prove the absence of a record, report, statement, or data compilation, in any form or the nonoccurrence or nonexistence of a matter of which a record, report, statement, or data compilation, in any form, was regularly made and preserved by a public office or agency, evidence in the form of a certification in accordance with Rule 902, or testimony, that diligent search failed to disclose the record, report, statement, or data compilation, or entry.

(11) Records of religious organizations. Statements of births, marriages, divorces, deaths, legitimacy, ancestry, relationship by blood or marriage, or other similar facts of personal or family history, contained in a regularly kept record of a religious organization.

(12) Marriage, baptismal, and similar certificates. Statements of fact contained in a certificate that the maker performed a marriage or other ceremony or administered a sacrament, made by a clergyman, public official, or other person authorized by the rules or practices of a religious organization or by law to perform the act certified, and purporting to have been issued at the time of the act or within a reasonable time thereafter.

(13) Family records. Statements of fact concerning personal or family history contained in family Bibles, genealogies, charts, engravings on rings, inscriptions on family portraits, engraving on urns, crypts, or tombstones, or the like.

(14) Records of documents affecting an interest in property. The record of a document purporting to establish or affect an interest in property, as proof of the content of the original recorded document and its execution and delivery by each person by whom it purports to have been executed, if the record is a record of

a public office and an applicable statute authorizes the recording of documents of that kind in that office.

(15) Statements in documents affecting an interest in property. A statement contained in a document purporting to establish or affect an interest in property if the matter stated was relevant to the purpose of the document, unless dealings with the property since the document was made have been inconsistent with the truth of the statement or the purport of the document.

(16) Statements in ancient documents. Statements in a document in existence twenty years or more the authenticity of which is established.

(17) Market reports, commercial publications. Market quotations, tabulations, lists, directories, or other published compilations, generally used and relied upon by the public or by persons in particular occupations.

(18) Learned treatises. To the extent called to the attention of an expert witness upon cross-examination or relied upon by the expert witness in direct examination, statements contained in published treatises, periodicals, or pamphlets on a subject of history, medicine, or other science or art, established as a reliable authority by the testimony or admission

of the witness or by other expert testimony or by judicial notice. If admitted, the statements may be read into evidence but may not be received as exhibits.

(19) Reputation concerning personal or family history. Reputation among members of a person's family by blood, adoption, or marriage, or among a person's associates, or in the community, concerning a person's birth, adoption, marriage, divorce, death, legitimacy, relationship by blood, adoption, or marriage, ancestry, or other similar fact of personal or family history.

(20) Reputation concerning boundaries or general history. Reputation in a community, arising before the controversy, as to boundaries of or customs affecting lands in the community, and reputation as to events of general history important to the community or state or nation in which located.

(21) Reputation as to character. Reputation of a person's character among associates or in the community.

(22) Judgment of previous conviction. Evidence of a final judgment, entered after a trial or upon a plea of guilty (but not upon a plea of nolo contendere), adjudging a person guilty of a crime punishable by death or imprisonment in excess of one year, to prove any

fact essential to sustain the judgment, but not including, when offered by the government in a criminal prosecution for purposes other than impeachment, judgments against persons other than the accused. The pendency of an appeal may be shown but does not affect admissibility.

(23) Judgment as to personal, family, or general history, or boundaries. Judgments as proof of matters of personal, family or general history, or boundaries, essential to the judgment, if the same would be provable by evidence of reputation.

(24) Other exceptions. A statement not specifically covered by any of the foregoing exceptions but having equivalent circumstantial guarantees of trustworthiness, if the court determines that (A) the statement is offered as evidence of a material fact; (B) the statement is more probative on the point for which it is offered than any other evidence which the proponent can procure through reasonable efforts; and (C) the general purposes of these rules and the interests of justice will be best served by admission of the statement into evidence. However, a statement may not be admitted under this exception unless the proponent of it makes known to the adverse party sufficiently in advance of the trial or hearing to provide the adverse party with a fair opportunity to prepare to meet it, the proponent's intention to offer the statement and

the particulars of it, including the name and address of the declarant.

Rule 804

HEARSAY EXCEPTIONS; DECLARANT UNAVAILABLE

(a) Definition of Unavailability. "Unavailability as a witness" includes situations in which the declarant—

(1) Is exempted by ruling of the court on the ground of privilege from testifying concerning the subject matter of the declarant's statement; or

(2) Persists in refusing to testify concerning the subject matter of the declarant's statement despite an order of the court to do so; or

(3) Testifies to a lack of memory of the subject matter of the declarant's statement despite an order of the court to do so; or

(4) Is unable to be present or to testify at the hearing because of death or then existing physical or mental illness or infirmity; or

(5) Is absent from the hearing and the proponent of a statement has been unable to procure the declarant's attendance (or in case of a hearsay exception under subdivision (b)(2),

(3), or (4), the declarant's attendance or testimony) by process or other reasonable means.

A declarant is not unavailable as a witness if exemption, refusal, claim of lack of memory, inability, or absence is due to the procurement or wrongdoing of the proponent of a statement for the purpose of preventing the witness from attending or testifying.

(b) Hearsay Exceptions. The following are not excluded by the hearsay rule if the declarant is unavailable as a witness:

(1) Former testimony. Testimony given as a witness at another hearing of the same or a different proceeding, or in a deposition taken in compliance with law in the course of the same or another proceeding, if the party against whom the testimony is now offered, or, in a civil action or proceeding, a predecessor in interest, had an opportunity and similar motive to develop the testimony by direct, cross or redirect examination.

(2) Statement under belief of impending death. In a prosecution for homicide or in a civil action or proceeding, a statement made by a declarant while believing that the declarant's death was imminent, concerning the cause or circumstances of what the declarant believed to be impending death.

(3) Statement against interest. A statement which was at the time of its making so far contrary to the declarant's pecuniary or proprietary interest, or so far tended to subject the declarant to civil or criminal liability, or to render invalid a claim by the declarant against another, that a reasonable man in the declarant's position would not have made the statement unless believing it to be true. A statement tending to expose the declarant to criminal liability and offered to exculpate the accused is not admissible unless corroborating circumstances clearly indicate the trustworthiness of the statement.

(4) Statement of personal or family history. (A) A statement concerning the declarant's own birth, adoption, marriage, divorce, legitimacy, relationship by blood, adoption, or marriage, ancestry, or other similar fact of personal or family history, even though declarant had no means of acquiring personal knowledge of the matters stated; or (B) a statement concerning the foregoing matters, and death also, of another person, if the declarant was related to the other by blood, adoption, or marriage or was so intimately associated with the other's family as to be likely to have accurate information concerning the matter declared.

(5) Other exceptions. A statement not specifically covered by any of the foregoing

exceptions but having equivalent circumstantial guarantees of trustworthiness, if the court determines that (A) the statement is offered as evidence of a material fact; (B) the statement is more probative on the point for which it is offered than any other evidence which the proponent can procure through reasonable efforts; and (C) the general purposes of these rules and the interests of justice will best be served by admission of the statement into evidence. However, a statement may not be admitted under this exception unless the proponent of it makes known to the adverse party sufficiently in advance of the trial or hearing to provide the adverse party with a fair opportunity to prepare to meet it, the proponent's intention to offer the statement and the particulars of it, including the name and address of the declarant.

Rule 805

HEARSAY WITHIN HEARSAY

(Omitted, see Chapter Eight)

Rule 806

ATTACKING AND SUPPORTING CREDIBILITY OF DECLARANT

When a hearsay statement, or a statement defined in Rule 801(d)(2), (C), (D), or (E), has been admitted in evidence, the credibility of the declarant may be attacked, and if attacked may be supported, by any evidence which would be admissible for those purposes if declarant had testified as a witness. Evidence of a statement or conduct by the declarant at any time, inconsistent with the declarant's hearsay statement, is not subject to any requirement that the declarant may have been afforded an opportunity to deny or explain. If the party against whom a hearsay statement has been admitted calls the declarant as a witness, the party is entitled to examine the declarant on the statement as if under cross-examination.

ARTICLE IX:

AUTHENTICATION AND IDENTIFICATION

Rule 901

REQUIREMENT OF AUTHENTICATION OR IDENTIFICATION

(a) General Provision. The requirement of authentication or identification as a condition precedent to admissibility is satisfied by evidence sufficient to support a finding that the matter in question is what its proponent claims.

(b) Illustrations. By way of illustration only, and not by way of limitation, the following are examples of authentication or identification conforming with the requirements of this rule:

(1) Testimony of witness with knowledge. Testimony that a matter is what it is claimed to be.

(2) Nonexpert opinion on handwriting. Nonexpert opinion as to the genuineness of handwriting, based upon familiarity not acquired for purposes of the litigation.

(3) Comparison by trier or expert witness. Comparison by the trier of fact or by expert witnesses with specimens which have been authenticated.

(4) Distinctive characteristics and the like. Appearance, contents, substance, internal patterns, or other distinctive characteristics, taken in conjunction with circumstances.

(5) Voice identification. Identification of a voice, whether heard firsthand or through mechanical or electronic transmission or recording, by opinion based upon hearing the voice at any time under circumstances connecting it with the alleged speaker.

(6) Telephone conversations. Telephone conversations, by evidence that a call was made to the number assigned at the time by the

telephone company to a particular person or business, if (A) in the case of a person, circumstances, including self-identification, show the person answering to be the one called, or (B) in the case of a business, the call was made to a place of business and the conversation related to business reasonably transacted over the telephone.

(7) Public records or reports. Evidence that a writing authorized by law to be recorded or filed and in fact recorded or filed in a public office, or purported public record, report, statement, or data compilation, in any form, is from the public office where items of this nature are kept.

(8) Ancient documents or data compilation. Evidence that a document or data compilation, in any form, (A) is in such condition as to create no suspicion concerning its authenticity, (B) was in a place where it, if authentic, would likely be, and (C) has been in existence 20 years or more at the time it is offered.

(9) Process or system. Evidence describing a process or system used to produce a result and showing that the process or system produces an accurate result.

(10) Methods provided by statute or rule. Any method of authentication or

identification provided by Act of Congress or by other rules prescribed by the Supreme Court pursuant to statutory authority.

Rule 902

SELF-AUTHENTICATION

Extrinsic evidence of authenticity as a condition precedent to admissibility is not required with respect to the following:

(1) Domestic public documents under seal. A document bearing a seal purporting to be that of the United States, or of any state, district commonwealth, territory, or insular possession thereof, or the Panama Canal Zone, or the Trust Territory of the Pacific Islands, or of a political subdivision, department, officer, or agency thereof, and a signature purporting to be an attestation or execution.

(2) Domestic public documents not under seal. A document purporting to bear the signature in the official capacity of an officer or employee of any entity included in paragraph (1) hereof, having no seal, if a public officer having a seal and having official duties in the district or political subdivision of the officer or employee certifies under seal that the signer has the official capacity and that the signature is genuine.

(3)   Foreign public documents. A document purporting to be executed or attested in an official capacity by a person authorized by the laws of a foreign country to make the execution or attestation, and accompanied by a final certification as to the genuineness of the signature and official position (A) of the executing or attesting person, or (B) of any foreign official whose certificate of genuineness of signature and official position relates to the execution or attestation or is in a chain of certificates of genuineness of signature and official position relating to the execution or attestation. A final certification may be made by a secretary of embassy or legation, consul general, consul, vice consul, or consular agent of the United States, or a diplomatic or consular official of the foreign country assigned or accredited to the United States. If reasonable opportunity has been given to all parties to investigate the authenticity and accuracy of official documents, the court may, for good cause shown, order that they be treated as presumptively authentic without final certification or permit them to be evidenced by an attested summary with or without final certification.

(4)   Certified copies of public records. A copy of an official record or report or entry therein, or of a document authorized by law to be recorded or filed and actually recorded or

filed in a public office, including data compilations in any form, certified as correct by the custodian or other person authorized to make the certification, by certificate complying with paragraph (1), (2), or (3) of this rule or complying with any Act of Congress or rule prescribed by the Supreme Court pursuant to statutory authority.

(5) Official publications. Books, pamphlets, or other publications purporting to be issued by public authority.

(6) Newspapers and periodicals. Printed materials purporting to be newspapers or periodicals.

(7) Trade inscriptions and the like. Inscriptions, signs, tags, or labels purporting to have been affixed in the course of business and indicating ownership, control, or origin.

(8) Acknowledged documents. Documents accompanied by a certificate of acknowledgment executed in the manner provided by law by a notary public or other officer authorized by law to take acknowledgments.

(9) Commercial paper and related documents. Commercial paper, signatures thereon, and documents relating thereto to the extent provided by general commercial law.

(10) Presumptions under Acts of Congress. Any signature, document, or other matter declared by Act of Congress to be presumptively or prima facie genuine or authentic.

Rule 903

SUBSCRIBING WITNESS' TESTIMONY UNNECESSARY

(Omitted, see Chapter Nine)

ARTICLE X:

CONTENTS OF WRITINGS, RECORDINGS, AND PHOTOGRAPHS

Rule 1001

DEFINITIONS

For purposes of this article the following definitions are applicable:

(1) Writings and recordings. "Writings" and "recordings" consist of letters, words, or numbers, or their equivalent, set down by handwriting, typewriting, printing, photostating, photographing, magnetic impulse, mechanical or electronic recording, or other form of data compilation.

(2) Photographs. "Photographs" include still photographs, X-ray films, video tapes and motion pictures.

(3) Original. An "original" of a writing or recording is the writing or recording itself or any counterpart intended to have the same effect by a person executing or issuing it. An "original" of a photograph includes the negative or any print therefrom. If data are stored in a computer or similar device, any printout or other output readable by sight, shown to reflect the data accurately, is an "original."

(4) Duplicate. A "duplicate" is a counterpart produced by the same impression as the original, or from the same matrix, or by means of photography, including enlargements and miniatures, or by mechanical or electronic re-recording, or by chemical reproduction, or by other equivalent techniques which accurately reproduces the original.

Rule 1002

REQUIREMENT OF ORIGINAL

(Omitted, see Chapter Nine)

Rule 1003

ADMISSIBILITY OF DUPLICATES

(Omitted, see Chapter Nine)

Rule 1004

ADMISSIBILITY OF OTHER EVIDENCE OF CONTENTS

(Omitted, see Chapter Nine)

Rule 1005

PUBLIC RECORDS

The contents of an official record, or of a document authorized to be recorded or filed and actually recorded or filed, including data compilations in any form, if otherwise admissible, may be proved by copy, certified as correct in accordance with Rule 902 or testified to be correct by a witness who has compared it with the original. If a copy which complies with the foregoing cannot be obtained by the exercise of reasonable diligence, then other evidence of the contents may be given.

Rule 1006

SUMMARIES

(Omitted, see Chapter Nine)

Rule 1007

TESTIMONY OR WRITTEN ADMISSION OF PARTY

Contents of writings, recordings, or photographs may be proved by the testimony or deposition of the party against whom offered or by that party's written admission, without accounting for the nonproduction of the original.

Rule 1008

FUNCTIONS OF COURT AND JURY

When the admissibility of other evidence of contents of writings, recordings, or photographs under these rules depends upon the fulfillment of a condition of fact, the question whether the condition has been fulfilled is ordinarily for the court to determine in accordance with the provisions of Rule 104. However, when an issue is raised (a) whether the asserted writing ever existed, or (b) whether another writing, recording, or photograph produced at the trial is the original, or (c) whether other evidence of contents correctly reflects the contents, the issue is for the trier of fact to determine as in the case of other issues of fact.

ARTICLE XI:

MISCELLANEOUS RULES

Rule 1101

APPLICABILITY OF RULES

(a)   Courts and Magistrates. These rules apply to the United States district courts, the District Court of Guam, the District Court of the Virgin Islands, the District Court for the Northern Mariana Islands, the United States courts of appeals, the United States Claims Court, and to United States bankruptcy judges and United States magistrates, in the actions, cases, and proceedings and to the extent hereinafter set forth. The terms "judge" and "court" in these rules include United States bankruptcy judges and United States magistrates.

(b)   Proceedings Generally. These rules apply generally to civil actions and proceedings, including admiralty and maritime cases, to criminal cases and proceedings, to contempt proceedings except those in which the court may act summarily, and to proceedings and cases under Title 11, United States Code.

(c)   Rule of Privilege. The rule with respect to privileges applies at all stages of all actions, cases, and proceedings.

(d)   Rules Inapplicable. The rules (other than with respect to privileges) do not apply in the following situations:

(1)   Preliminary questions of fact. The determination of questions of fact preliminary to admissibility of evidence when the issue is to be determined by the court under Rule 104.

(2) Grand jury. Proceedings before grand juries.

(3) Miscellaneous proceedings. Proceedings for extradition or rendition; preliminary examinations in criminal cases; sentencing, or granting or revoking probation; issuance of warrants for arrest, criminal summonses, and search warrants; and proceedings with respect to release on bail or otherwise.

(e) Rules Applicable in Part. In the following proceedings these rules apply to the extent that matters of evidence are not provided for in the statutes which govern procedure therein or in other rules prescribed by the Supreme Court pursuant to statutory authority: the trial of minor and petty offenses by United States magistrates; review of agency actions when the facts are subject to trial de novo under section 706(2)(F) of Title 5, United States Code; review of orders of the Secretary of Agriculture under section 2 of the Act entitled "An Act to authorize association of producers of agricultural products" approved February 18, 1922 (7 U.S.C. 292), and under sections 6 and 7(c) of the Perishable Agricultural Commodities Act, 1930 (7 U.S.C. 499f, 499g(c)); naturalization and revocation of naturalization under sections 310-318 of the Immigration and Nationality Act (8 U.S.C. 1421-1429); prize proceedings in admiralty under sections 1765-7681, of Title 10, United States

Code; review of orders of the Secretary of the Interior under section 2 of the Act entitled "An Act authorizing associations of producers of aquatic products" approved June 25, 1934 (15 U.S.C. 522); review of orders of petroleum control boards under section 5 of the Act entitled "An Act to regulate interstate and foreign commerce in petroleum and its products by prohibiting the shipment in such commerce of petroleum and its products produced in violation of State law, and for other purposes," approved February 22, 1935 (15 U.S.C. 715d); actions for fines, penalties, or forfeitures under part V of title IV of the Tariff Act of 1930 (19 U.S.C. 1581-1624), or under the Anti-Smuggling Act (19 U.S.C. 1701-1711); criminal libel for condemnation, exclusion of imports, or other proceedings under the Federal Food, Drug, and Cosmetic Act (21 U.S.C. 301-392); disputes between seamen under sections 4079, 4080, and 4081 of the Revised Statutes (22 U.S.C. 256-258); habeas corpus under sections 2241-2254 of Title 28, United States Code; motions to vacate, set aside or correct sentence under section 2255 of Title 28, United States Code; actions for penalties for refusal to transport destitute seamen under section 4578 of the Revised Statutes (46 U.S.C. 679); actions against the United States under the Act entitled "An Act authorizing suits against the United States in admiralty for damage caused by and salvage service rendered to public vessels belonging to

the United States, and for other purposes,"
approved March 3, 1925 (46 U.S.C. 781-790), as
implemented by section 7730 of Title 10, United
States Code.

Rule 1102

AMENDMENTS*

Amendments to the Federal Rules of
Evidence may be made as provided in section 2076
of Title 28 of the United States Code.

Rule 1103

TITLE

These rules may be known and cited as the
Federal Rules of Evidence.

*Note: 28 U.S.C. Sec. 2076 was repealed by
Title IV of the Judicial Improvement and Access
to Justice Act of 1988, Pub. L. 100-702.
Amendment procedure for the Federal Rules of
Evidence is now governed by 28 U.S.C. 2072-2074.
The procedure for amendment involves the Supreme
Court, as well as Congress. The Supreme Court
promulgates proposed amendments, and the
proposals are submitted to Congress. Congress
has, under the current law, 7 months to
scrutinize the proposed rule changes. The
approval process allows for a passive approval

by Congress. In other words, if Congress does nothing within the review period, the proposal of the Supreme Court is approved. The only exception is as to Supreme Court amendments regarding evidence privileges (see Chapter 11). As to privileges, they do not take effect unless they are expressly approved by Congress (i.e., affirmative action by Congress is required; if Congress does nothing in such a case, the proposal does not become law).

At this writing, the Supreme Court has submitted 2 proposed changes to Congress for its review. On April 30, 1991, the Supreme Court ordered changes to Rule 404(d) and Rule 1102. Effective December 1, 1991, Rule 404(d) will read as follows:

(b) Other Crimes, Wrongs, or Acts. Evidence of other crimes, wrongs, or acts is not admissible to prove the character of a person in order to show action in conformity therewith. It may, however, be admissible for other purposes, such as proof of motive, opportunity, intent, preparation, plan, knowledge, identity, or absence of mistake or accident, *provided that upon request by the accused, the prosecution in a criminal case shall provide reasonable notice in advance of trial, or during trial if the*

*court excuses pretrial notice on
good cause shown, of the general
nature of any such evidence it
intends to introduce at trial*
(emphasis added; for the full text
of Rule 404, see Chapter Three).

Rule 1102 will read:

Amendments to the Federal
Rules of Evidence may be made as
provided in section 2072 of Title 28
of the United States Code.

The Rule 1102 amendment will recognize the
repeal of section 2076 by Title IV of the
Judicial Improvement and Access to Justice Act
of 1988 and the current application of section
2072.

THE CONSTITUTION OF THE UNITED STATES:

SELECTED PASSAGES

ARTICLE III AND

AMENDMENTS CRITICAL TO THE TRIAL PROCESS

ARTICLE III

Section 1. The judicial power of the United States, shall be vested in one supreme Court, and in such inferior Courts as the Congress may from time to time ordain and establish. The judges, both of the supreme and inferior Courts, shall hold their Offices during good behaviour, and shall, at stated Times, receive for their Services a Compensation, which shall not be diminished during their Continuance in Office.

Section 2. (1) The judicial Power shall extend to all Cases, in Law and Equity, arising under this Constitution, the Laws of the United States, and Treaties made, or which shall be made, under their Authority;-to all Cases affecting Ambassadors, other public Ministers and Consuls;-to all Cases of admiralty and maritime Jurisdiction;-to Controversies to which the United States shall be a Party;-to Controversies between two or more States;-between a State and Citizens of another State;-between Citizens of different States;-between Citizens of the same State claiming Lands under the Grants of different States, and between a State, or the Citizens thereof, and foreign States, Citizens or Subjects.

(2) In all Cases affecting Ambassadors, other public Ministers and Consuls, and those in which a State shall be a Party, the supreme Court shall have original Jurisdiction. In all other Cases before mentioned, the supreme Court shall have appellate Jurisdiction, both as to Law and Fact, with such Exceptions, and under such Regulations as the Congress shall make.

(3) The trial of all Crimes, except in Cases of Impeachment, shall be by Jury; and such Trial shall be held in the State where the said Crimes shall have been committed; but when not committed within any State, the Trial shall be at such Place or Places as the Congress may by Law have directed.

Section 3. (1) Treason against the United States, shall consist only in levying War against them, or, in adhering to their Enemies, giving them Aid and Comfort. No Person shall be convicted of Treason unless on the Testimony of two Witnesses to the same overt Act, or on Confession in open Court.

(2) The Congress shall have Power to declare the Punishment of Treason, but no Attainder of Treason shall work Corruption of Blood, or Forfeiture except during the Life of the Person attainted.

AMENDMENT IV

The right of the people to be secure in their persons, houses, papers, and effects, against unreasonable searches and seizures, shall not be violated, and no Warrants shall issue, but upon probable cause, supported by Oath or affirmation, and particularly describing the place to be searched, and the persons or things to be seized.

AMENDMENT V

No person shall be held to answer for a capital, or other infamous crime, unless on a presentment or indictment of a Grand Jury, except in cases arising in the land or naval forces, or in the Militia, when in actual service in time of War or public danger; nor shall any person be subject for the same offence to be twice put in jeopardy of life or limb; nor shall be compelled in any criminal case to be a witness against himself, nor be deprived of life, liberty, or property, without due process of law; nor shall private property be taken for public use, without just compensation.

AMENDMENT VI

In all criminal prosecutions, the accused shall enjoy the right to a speedy and public trial, by an impartial jury of the State and district wherein the crime shall have been committed, which district shall have been previously ascertained by law, and to be informed of the nature and cause of the accusation; to be confronted with the witnesses against him; to have compulsory process for obtaining witnesses in his favor, and to have the Assistance of Counsel for his defense.

AMENDMENT VII

In Suits at common law, where the value in controversy shall exceed twenty dollars, the right of trial by jury shall be preserved, and no fact tried by a jury, shall be otherwise re-examined in any Court of the United States, than according to the rules of the common law.

AMENDMENT VIII

Excessive bail shall not be required, nor excessive fines imposed, nor cruel and unusual punishments inflicted.

AMENDMENT XIV

Section 1. All persons born or naturalized in the United States, and subject to the jurisdiction thereof, are citizens of the United States and of the State wherein they reside. No State shall make or enforce any law which shall abridge the privileges or immunities of citizens of the United States; nor shall any State deprive any person of life, liberty, and property, without due process of law; nor deny to any person within its jurisdiction the equal protection of the laws.

. . . .

Section 5. The Congress shall have power to enforce, by appropriate legislation, the provisions of this article.

APPENDIX C

SAMPLE FINAL EXAMINATION

While each instructor uses his or her own examination format, examinations in undergraduate Evidence classes typically include a mix of objective, short essay, and "hypothetical" or "fact pattern" questions. For many undergraduate students, the fact pattern section of an Evidence examination offers a new experience. Therefore, this section of the examination is often the most challenging. The fact pattern question is more than an essay question. It demands an ability to sift through facts and zero-in on relevant legal issues. It involves problem analysis. The more fact patterns a student tackles, the better he or she gets. As you review the sample questions below, spend extra time with the fact patterns. Work them through and ask your instructor to review your analyses. The sample examination is designed to be completed within two hours.

SAMPLE OBJECTIVE QUESTIONS (25 POINTS):

1. Fill in the missing activities of the trial process:

JURY SELECTION;

PRELIMINARY JURY INSTRUCTION

_____ (1 pt.);

PRESENTATION OF PLAINTIFF'S (CIVIL)

OR STATE'S (CRIMINAL) CASE;

MOTION FOR NON-SUIT/DIRECTED VERDICT;

_____ (1 pt.);

PLAINTIFF'S (CIVIL) OR STATE'S (CRIMINAL)
REBUTTAL;

_____ (1 pt.);

CLOSING STATEMENTS;

_____ (1 pt.);

DELIBERATION;

RETURN OF VERDICT;

JUDGMENT (CIVIL).

2. Upon being sued, the defendant may assert a claim he/she has against the plaintiff. The filing of such claim is called a _____. (1 pt.)

3. In a criminal case, the defendant is not required to prove his innocence, the state must prove the defendant's guilt by a preponderance of the evidence. True or False? (1 pt.)

4. Relevant evidence is always admissible. True or False? (1 pt.)

5. Under Federal Rule 605, a judge is competent to testify at a trial over which he or she presides. True or False? (1 pt.)

6. Several means to authentication of writings exist under the federal rules. One such means is to have a lay witness who is familiar with a subject's handwriting take an admittedly authentic specimen of the subject's handwriting and compare it with the contested writing (i.e., the comparison technique). True or False? (1 pt.)

7. Under the federal rules, acknowledged documents are self-authenticating. True or False? (1 pt.)

8. Unavailability is required under the federal rules for use of the hearsay exception for "market reports, commercial publications." True or False? (1 pt.)

9. The requirement of making a(n) _____ is not a burden on the party making an objection-it is a burden on the party to whose

proposed evidence an objection has been made. It applies where the court has sustained an objection. (1 pt.)

10. The privilege against self-incrimination is limited to courtroom situations only. True or False? (1 pt.)

11. Under the federal rules, the court may only take judicial notice of a fact that is not subject to reasonable dispute. True or False? (1 pt.)

12. There is an ancient document exception to the hearsay rule that provides an exception for statements in documents at least _____ years old. (1 pt.)

13. An "Excited Utterance" is one of the listed exceptions to the best evidence rule. True or False? (1 pt.)

14. The President's executive privilege is absolute? True or False? (1 pt.)

15. Under the Federal Rules of Evidence, an admission by a party is a Rule 803 exception to the hearsay rule. True or False? (1 pt.)

16. Ordinarily, leading questions are permitted on cross-examination. True or False? (1 pt.)

17. _____ evidence involves the submission of some physical object which was a direct part of the situation/incident. (1 pt.)

18. Unavailability is required under the federal rules for use of the hearsay exception for "records of vital statistics." True or False? (1 pt.)

19. The expert witness may base his or her opinion upon facts personally observed? True or False? (1 pt.)

20. Direct evidence must be contrasted with _____ evidence. (1 pt.)

21. Under the federal rules, character evidence is generally admissible to prove conduct, i.e., to prove that an individual "acted in conformity therewith on a particular occasion." True or False? (1 pt.)

22. Statements elicited from the suspect in violation of the *Miranda* decision are not admissible for any purpose. True or False? (1 pt.)

SAMPLE ESSAY QUESTIONS (75 pts.)

23. Distinguish the witness subpoena from the subpoena ducus tecum. (5 pts.)

24. Is there a difference between the admissibility of character evidence in criminal cases and civil cases? Explain. (5 pts.)

25. Rule 604 of the Federal Rules of Evidence regulate the use of interpreters at trial. In what way(s) does the rule affect interpreters? (5 pts.)

26. Distinguish between the restrictive view and the "wide-open" view as to the proper scope of cross-examination. What view is found within the Federal Rules of Evidence? (5 pts.)

27. Distinguish "present recollection revived" from "past recollection recorded." (5 pts.)

28. What is the purpose of witness impeachment? Give two (2) examples of ways to impeach a witness. Additionally, explain the process of witness "rehabilitation." (5 pts.)

29. A large volume of cases exist on the subject of proper lay witness opinion testimony. Some non-exclusive, common categories of allowable lay witness opinions were discussed in the text. List two (2) such categories and provide one example of testimony that would fit within each such category listed. (5 pts.)

30. List the three (3) sources ("bases") mentioned in class from which facts for an expert witness opinion may come. How are these

bases broader than in the lay witness opinion situation? (5 pts.)

31. Distinguish between the two separate privilege issues raised by the husband-wife relationship. (5 pts.)

32. Federal judges may appoint their own court experts. How might such an appointment (or the power of appointment) help the process of litigation in a case? (5 pts.)

33. Define: a) The Rule of Completeness, and

   b) The Parole Evidence Rule.

(5 pts.)

34. How is public policy served by the use of a privilege in the attorney-client relationship? Explain. (5 pts.)

35. List and describe three (3) of the Rule 901 means to authentication of writings. (5 pts.)

36. What is the exclusionary rule? Is the "good faith" exception to the exclusionary rule good policy? Explain. (5 pts.)

37. What is the general rationale for the chain of custody foundation? Must every moment of possession be accounted for? Explain. (5 pts.)

SAMPLE FACT PATTERNS (100 pts.)

38. Plaintiff was severely injured when a sign fell on his head in front of a business place. Plaintiff sues the defendant, and the defendant denies he owned or otherwise controlled the sign. After the accident, the defendant purchased and installed heavy chain on the sign, and he re-hung the sign with the chain rather than wire (as it had been hung before the accident). Is evidence of the defendant purchasing the chain and re-hanging the sign with the chain admissible? Why/why not? Explain. (10 pts.)

39. Defendant D is charged with the crime of battery, for striking V in the face with his fist. In addition to the state prosecuting D for the crime of battery, V sues D in civil court for damages for the battery (also a civil wrong). Is it possible for V, the plaintiff, to prevail against D in civil court, and yet, D win in the criminal court action? Why/why not? Explain. (10 pts.)

40. Defendant D is claiming self-defense as the defense in his murder trial. The defendant has a witness who can testify as to the victim's reputation for violence (victim's violent tendencies). May such evidence of the victim's violent tendencies be introduced at trial? Why/why not? Explain. (10 pts.)

41. A and B are partners in a real estate management business. The plaintiff is suing the

partnership for money owed. C tells the plaintiff before suit, "The partnership does owe you $1,000." Is such a statement hearsay under the Federal Rules of Evidence? Explain. <u>Please note</u>: C is the partnership's security guard. (10 pts.)

42. Defendant D drove his car through a red light, striking Doe and Smith as they were crossing the street. Doe sued D and, after trial, was awarded a judgement. Doe lives on the other side of town. Smith also sued D. He has obtained a copy of a transcript of Doe's testimony against D. May he use the testimony in his trial against D? Explain. (10 pts.)

43. Plaintiff sues the defendant in civil court for damages resulting from a wrong by the defendant (i.e., a battery). The defendant has already been convicted of the crime in criminal court. Plaintiff now seeks to use evidence of the prior conviction to help sustain her claim in the civil action. The question becomes whether or not she can use such evidence? May she? Explain. (10 pts.)

44. Salesperson of X,Y,Z, Inc. reports her weekly sales to A, the X,Y,Z, Inc. bookkeeper, who enters the data in the company books. May the books be entered into evidence at trial. Why/why not? Explain. (10 pts.)

45. The declarant, after his automobile accident, goes to his doctor and tells the doctor: "I have terrible pain in my right arm and shoulder." Is this statement hearsay? If so, is the statement admissible nevertheless under one of the exceptions to the hearsay rule found in the federal rules? Explain. (10 pts.)

46. The attorney for the defendant in a federal civil case rises at trial and, invoking Federal Rule 615, asks the court to exclude the plaintiff from the courtroom, since the plaintiff will be a witness in the case. May the plaintiff be excluded? Explain. (10 pts.)

47. John Smith is suing Jane Doe for breach of contract and faulty workmanship. John brought his automobile into Jane's auto repair shop. He asked Jane to repair the automobile's transmission. Jane did so, but the transmission soon failed. John did not pay Jane, but sued for the extra costs he incurred in getting the transmission repaired again at another repair shop. You are Jane's attorney. Other than denying liability for the breach of contract and faulty workmanship, what will you do to enhance Jane's position? Explain. (10 pts.)

INDEX

- A -

ACKNOWLEDGED DOCUMENTS:
    Self-authentication, 262
ADJUDICATIVE FACTS, see JUDICIAL NOTICE
ADMISSIBLE EVIDENCE:
    Constitutional dimensions, 292-302
    Defined, 89
    Objections, 288-290
ADMISSIONS BY PARTY:
    Non-hearsay, 213-217
    Written admissions, 271
AFFIRMATION (OR OATH): 124-126
ANCIENT DOCUMENTS:
    As hearsay exception, 228
    Authentication of, 261
ANSWER, 27-30
APPEARANCE, SEE INITIAL APPEARANCE
ARRAIGNMENT, 21
ATTORNEYS:
    As witnesses, 131-132, 133, n.11
    Attorney-client privilege, 323-324, 349-373
    Code of Professional Responsibility, 131-
    132, 370, n.1
    Model Rules of Professional Conduct, 133,
    n.11, 370, n. 1

- X, Y, Z -